LOSING CHUCK, FINDING SALLIE

The Thirty-Six Year Odyssey of a Wife
Whose Husband Was MIA in Vietnam

A Memoir by Sallie Stratton

This book is a memoir, and the author assumes all responsibility for the accuracy of the content within, as well as liability for permissions.

Cover design: Jennifer Leigh Selig

MANDORLA BOOKS
WWW.MANDORLABOOKS.COM

DEDICATION

This memoir is dedicated to Chuck Stratton, love of my life, who expanded my world beyond anything I ever dreamed possible; and to our sons, Charles Jr. who joined him in death just last year, Scott and Stephen, in whom he was and is always present.

TABLE OF CONTENTS

BOOK III
EXCAVATION OF SITE AND SOUL

BOOK IV
ALOHA

FOREWORD

Sallie Stratton and I seemed to connect purely by chance.

Sallie contacted me in September of 2017 when a friend told her about a poster he had seen in Lawrence, Kansas, advertising a museum exhibition I curated entitled *The League of Wives: Vietnam's POW/MIA Allies & Advocates*, that had recently premiered the Robert J. Dole Institute of Politics at the University of Kansas. The poster featured a black and white photo circa 1971 of a group of wives of American prisoners and the missing, who met with United States National Security Advisor Dr. Henry Kissinger at the White House. Emblazoned on the poster was a quote from Louise Mulligan, a Virginia Beach Navy wife whose husband, Navy Captain Jim Mulligan, was shot down in 1966. The quote from late 1968 read: "We were tired of being quiet. We weren't military. We didn't have to follow orders."

The quote refers to the United States government's "Keep Quiet" policy for POW and MIA wives. These women were not allowed to tell anyone (aside from immediate family) about the whereabouts of their missing husbands. For years, these women carried this heavy burden while trying to go on about their daily lives, raising their children, working, and volunteering.

When Air Force pilot Captain Charles W. "Chuck" Stratton was shot down in January of 1971 over Laos and declared Missing in Action, his wife Sallie automatically became part of a national community of grieving military wives. She was now part of a "reluctant sorority"—one no one wanted to belong to. However, once a woman entered this group, she became part of a larger society

i

of women whose bonds with each other were even stronger at times than those with blood relatives. Sallie told me that one of the biggest coping tools she found during this trying time was "the support of women friends and women's circles."

Sallie became more and more involved in the POW/MIA cause. The wives finally came out in the national press with their stories beginning in 1968. Sallie became deeply involved in Dallas Cares, local POW/MIA group, working with other area POW/MIA wives like Bonnie Singleton, and Dallas entrepreneur Ross Perot, to bring awareness to the cause. Under the leadership of Coronado Navy POW wife Sybil Stockdale, The National League of Families of American Prisoners and Missing in Southeast Asia was founded in 1970, bringing all local and regional POW/MIA groups under one umbrella organization.

In September of 1971, Sallie was elected to the National League of Families board, serving a one year term until the following fall of 1972. While on the board, Sallie worked on the Identifications and Discrepancies Committee and was the chairman of the Nomination Committee. At this point in the war, many members of POW/MIA families had begun to lose hope, fearing that the war might never end. Sallie recalled that at this point, "the families were just as split" as the country was on the war. Sallie helped me establish this very fact thanks to her meticulous note-taking and her personal archive of National League board documents which she graciously shared with me. Sallie was able to help me reconstruct missing threads of the early history of the National League of Families that had been lost.

In her memoir, Sallie writes eloquently of the importance of the Greek goddess Athena who "is the protector of cities, patron of military forces, and the goddess of weavers. She led me out of my small insular world as wife and mother into the larger polis and the realm of the warrior women who had organized the National League of Families of American Prisoners and Missing in Southeast Asia."

Despite her own involvement in the POW/MIA movement on a national level, the major focus of *Loosing Chuck, Finding Sallie* is not Sallie's activism. While she participated in that effort whole-heartedly, the primary focus of her memoir is about her spiritual journey as an MIA wife and the many facets of her often distressing situation. I know of *no other* MIA wife memoir like this one. It is unique, heartbreaking, and written with unflinching honesty. Sallie displays a courageous willingness to address the pain of the MIA experience head-on, without hiding her grief within the day-to-day business of life.

As it turned out, I don't think Sallie and I met by chance. I don't believe in chance anymore. When you study and write about women's history, overlapping webs of stories show us that nothing is coincidental. Sallie's recurring theme in her memoir of women as the weavers—those who maintain the fabric of family and memory—is an appropriate one. She has woven a vivid tapestry of her life story, while at the same time helped to reconstruct the national tapestry of other POW/MIA wives and their collective journey to bring their husbands home.

Heath Hardage Lee

Heath Hardage Lee's narrative nonfiction book entitled The League of Wives: The Untold Story of the Women Who Took on the U.S. Government to Bring Their Husbands Home from Vietnam, *about the courageous wives of aviators who were Prisoners of War or Missing in Action during the Vietnam War, was published by St. Martin's Press in 2019. Heath was the 2017 Robert J. Dole Curatorial Fellow, and her exhibition entitled "The League of Wives: Vietnam POW MIA Advocates & Allies" about Vietnam POW MIA wives premiered at the Dole Institute of Politics in May of 2017. The exhibit is currently traveling through 2020 to museum venues all over the country.*

PREFACE

People experience someone going missing from their lives other than just in wartime. Just read the news every day to learn of someone who's gone missing—a child, a teenager, an elder—and a search is being conducted. In stories that don't make the news, mothers and fathers go missing from their children's lives, and partners and spouses may literally leave or just "check out" from the relationship, and go missing emotionally. Friends whom we were once close to disappear when life circumstances change, and death itself insures that everyone will eventually go missing from the lives of those who love them.

Perhaps we're all missing someone all the time. We all need healing from those experiences, and perhaps the sharing of my own healing story about my husband can help someone else learn to navigate the terrain of the missing. I have certainly learned lots about myself from all the psychological work and the reading I have done, particularly when I learned to recognize the myth I was living.

Penelope is the archetype constellated during Vietnam with the POW/MIA situation that went on for years. Penelope, you may remember from your study of mythology, was the wife of Odysseus, the great warrior hero of the Trojan War. Odysseus fought that war for ten years, and then took another ten years to return home to his long-suffering wife, Penelope. Some of us didn't have to wait twenty years for our hero husbands to return; others of us have waited much longer. And we've had to weave new lives despite the uncertainty. Penelope's name in Greek means weaver. We all weave the tapestry of our lives, and all of us experienced some necessary unraveling and reweaving throughout the years after someone we love goes missing.

Ithaca was willing to write Odysseus off after some 17 years and many suitors began pursuing Penelope, wanting her property, and she fought them all off. The strong Penelope wives during Vietnam used their own wiles to try to gain their husband's return, refusing to let the government write them off. And they did this while raising their children alone and running a household. Some remained long-suffering wives; others eventually moved on.

I reverted to a life more like Odysseus when I grew tired of fighting—I took on a life of adventure. I was called to return to college, then a career (albeit in another warzone), and then to Ireland for the overseas adventure I was never able to have with Chuck.

Vietnam left the whole country wounded and in need of healing from this divisive, unpopular conflict. Those who served in this very contested conflict were spat upon or jeered upon their return home—if they were so lucky to return—rather than thanked for their service. Times have changed. The crowds who currently stand in lines along the roads to welcome home the recovered remains of soldiers, making the news weekly, indicate we're ready now for a proper homecoming. It's time all warriors, then and now, are honored for their service.

Chuck's awesome homecoming in 2007 definitely reawakened my passion to write this memoir. The news media coverage was fantastic. I am particularly thankful for Dave Tarrant's and Chris Salcedo's coverage. The *Dallas Morning News* must have spent a fortune on developing the story they ran in December 2007 entitled "Losing Chuck, Finding Sallie." Virtually every network was present at the funeral and group burial.

I have Dave to thank for the title that captures my journey in only four words, as well as his encouragement for me to write this memoir. And Chris' question off-camera that gave me pause was incredibly clarifying. "Would you change anything if you could?" When I wrote to Jane Fonda, after reading her autobiography, I told her I would never have volunteered to become an MIA wife and I wouldn't have wished it upon my worst enemy, but neither would I take for granted where it brought me.

So my answer to Chris's question is a simple but emphatic "no." When I told that to my oldest son, Charles Jr., he argued with me. "Of course we would, we'd have Dad come home." I asked him then, "So would you have had Haley, Briana, or Dustin [his children] if that had happened?" And he got the drift of my statement. I would not choose to give up all I've learned or done since Chuck became missing. They are the threads I've woven that make me who I am today.

I'm one of the lucky ones. I got Chuck's remains back. I know for sure what happened to him. I even have the picture of where he spent those thirty years before his body was recovered in Laos. And I have a long list of groups and individuals I need to acknowledge for making that happen.

The National League of Families of American POW/MIAs is first on my list because had it not been for their tireless efforts to demand an accounting for all our servicemen lost in Vietnam, I'm afraid the government would have been content to dismiss them all with any further effort. They took over and nationalized The League of Wives, started by Sybil Stockdale on the West Coast; Jane Denton, Louise Mulligan, and Phyllis Galanti on the East Coast; and later Helene Knapp in the Interior West. I had the good fortune to join their "reluctant sorority" later and have them as mentors and heroines who gave me courage to become active too, even when I sometimes disagreed with their political positions.

Without the dedication of the Joint POW/MIA Accounting Command and Central Identification Laboratory at Hickam Air Force Base in Hawaii, established in April 30, 1975, some 993 Americans were recovered from Vietnam War-related losses, plus more now from WWI, WWII, and Korea, would never have been accounted for. Kudos to all those teams still hard at work for further accountings, and to Jonnie Webb who was there to greet me in Hawaii and prepare me for meeting with and bringing home Chuck's remains.

Personally I have to acknowledge the many men from the USAF Casualty Office and Life Science Lab technicians, for their assistance over all these years. You will find them mentioned throughout the chapters. I always knew I had a number to call if I needed help with anything and they were always extremely accommodating.

Without the support of my family and dear friends, I could never have completed this memoir. So many women and men I'd always thought "taller" than me gave me encouragement to be all I could be. I'm sure you'll probably recognize them throughout the chapters—

pastors, bosses, professors, therapists, and more. I have been blessed beyond measure.

I owe a special thanks to Heath Hardage Lee for all her encouragement and support to publish this memoir, and to Jennifer Leigh Selig, my editor and publisher who has been nothing but encouraging, always offering very constructive criticism, and helpful suggestions as well as weeding out the parts that did not forward the story. Without them, you would not be reading this memoir now.

Finally, I want to thank you, the reader, for your interest in this story. In some ways, it is very particular, one woman's odyssey through a long period of loss and then, eventually, through gain. In other ways, it is a universal story, the underworld journey we all go through when we suffer from a loss we think we cannot survive, and what happens on the other side of that loss, when we, hopefully, eventually thrive.

Sallie Stratton
20 August 2019

BOOK I

NEWS OF HOMECOMING

"We had one last night together...
Made love with a fierce intensity...
We both knew he did know when this would be over...
He just asked me to keep his love and presence alive
until he returned...
In the morning I acted the role of a seemly queen,
one I did not feel."

Penelope's Story: The Shroud Weaver's Tale[1]

CHAPTER 1

THE CALL

Thursday 5 July 2007 0521 hours
Happy "B" Olin!

Love waking to the sound of light rain on the tree branches outside my patio. Amazing that it's cool enough to sleep with the door open in July.

My little brother Olin, the delayed firecracker, is 64 today. I must call him when he gets home from work. Lots to do today since I was such a slug yesterday. I need to call the woman at Old City Park about the deposit for Haley's wedding. Get to Curves and go by the office before I head for the dentist to be fit for my crown. Want to catch the jeweler this afternoon too for a new watch battery.

I drew the Gratitude Angel Card after turning the kettle on for my second cup of tea. Sure feeling grateful that I don't have to work this afternoon; and that my tooth is no longer sore from the root canal started a couple weeks ago. Finishing it up today and preparing for the crown should be a piece of cake.

So read my journal entry for the day. By two o'clock, with my to-do list completed, I was sitting in front of my computer checking emails, waiting for the numbness to wear off from my jaw, when the phone rang.

"May I speak to Sallie Stratton?"

"This is she."

"Ms. Stratton, Trevor Dean with the Mortuary Office at Randolph. I'm calling to tell you that we have just received positive DNA identification of your husband's remains."

Speechless, I just sat silently for a minute.

"Mrs. Stratton, are you still there?"

"What did you say your name was again?"

"Trevor Dean, ma'am, with Mortuary here at Randolph."

"Trevor, I don't understand. I was told in 2005 the bone fragments from the crash site were too small for DNA testing. I've been waiting for those remains to be turned over so we could have a group burial, since the physical evidence from all the excavations clearly showed both men were in the plane at the time of the crash."

"I hear this is a shock for you, ma'am. I know that technology's made rapid strides over the past couple years with their testing techniques. Apparently enough so that both your husband and Col. Ayres have been positively identified from samples sent. They probably didn't tell you at the time they were sent off so as not to get your hopes up in case they couldn't get any DNA."

"So you're sure about this?"

"Yes ma'am. I have the report right here in front of me ready to mail to you and Mrs. Ayres."

The rest of our conversation was a blur as I tried to take in this stunning information. My emotions vacillated from teary to giggly, and left me at a loss for any coherent questions about what to expect next. Those short bursts of crying culminated in euphoria by the time I hung up the phone.

I looked up above my computer at Chuck's picture from Korat AFB taken that Christmas before he became missing in action (MIA) on January 3rd, 1971. My handsome, confidant, then thirty-year-old captain would soon be coming home to a much older wife, three adult sons, five grandchildren and a brand new great-granddaughter.

With that thought, I stood up, walked a few paces to the living room and suddenly this manic high erupted volcanically into a loud wailing that startled me and possibly my neighbors as well. I had never bellowed like that before. It felt as if those sounds had come from the very soles of my feet. That loud outburst was spontaneous and relatively short-lived, but the grief was from somewhere in my very depths. After regaining my composure, I felt addled, not knowing what I should do at that moment—who to call? It was the middle of the afternoon, and everyone was at work.

I paced around my apartment trying to gather my wits about me. I thought about racing down to the office to tell our apartment manager. Part of me wanted to shout the news from the rooftop, while another part of me wanted to contain the information until I received the written report. I finally realized I didn't want to tell anyone before my sons and my immediate family.

I tried to call my brother, Olin, but he wasn't home yet; then I called Wanda, Chuck's sister—no answer. I called Haley, my oldest grand-daughter, up in Minnesota. No answer, so I emailed her. At some point Brenda Ayres called me. She was as surprised as I was about the news. We rejoiced together at the prospects of our "guys" coming home at long last, missing since 1971, when their F-4 crashed during the Vietnam War somewhere in Laos.

By 1977, with no definitive word from the military, I had accepted that I'd never know what happened to my husband beyond that his plane had crashed. I requested a status review that June, after the school terms ended, not because I believed he was dead, but because I knew he was dead to me for all practical purposes. I'd done everything in my power to get an answer, but to no avail. And I felt a need to get on with my life based on something more solid than his MIA status, where every decision I made had to be considered in light of whether he might come home or not.

A presumptive finding of death was made official on July 8th, 1977. Now, almost exactly 30 years later to the day, I finally had a definitive answer to the lingering question: *Am I a widow or a wife?*

It was after five before I finally reached Wanda on her cell phone and then my brother, Olin. Scott was my first son to get the news about his dad. He was only five years old when Chuck became MIA. By six o'clock Charles Jr. got home from work and learned the good news. *You're the man of the house until I return,* his dad told him as he said goodbye that summer of 1970. What a big responsibility for an eight-year-old.

Stephen, our three-year-old baby at the time, was currently in Washington D.C. for his job doing some research at the Library of

Congress. All I could do was leave a message at his hotel and hope he would come in soon and call me back. I propped up in my bed and pulled out my journal again as I waited. It helped calm me down to write about the flood of emotions I was feeling.

A recent dream I'd had about Chuck popped into my mind. When was that exactly? I poured through the back pages of my journal to find that dream.

Sunday 10 June 0600 hours

Hmmmm—I was in a car with Chuck as I woke. A crazy man was following us...Chuck whipped off at Priestly to lose him.

The sign was so clear. "Priestly" in such large bold letters; the image piqued my curiosity. I googled it to see if there was such a street in Dallas, but found none.

Chuck was certainly an important *animus* figure in my psyche, my inner masculine in Jungian terms. As a navigator, Chuck was the one who directed the course of his aircraft. My inner navigator seemed to be taking me in a new direction. So who was the crazy man following us in the dream?

Dreams have been really important to me since my undergraduate studies at Southern Methodist University in the mid 70s. I record them faithfully for any wisdom they might offer with regard to any internal process that needs attention. However, the month of June had been quite busy with writing a presentation for the Juneteenth Annual Celebration for the Center for the Healing of Racism in Houston; wedding plans for my oldest granddaughter, Haley; the upcoming birth of a great-granddaughter; plus my paid job as an office manager for a chiropractor. With everything going on, I had yet to revisit that dream for further reflection.

Nor did I continue to ponder it long now. My mind jumped quickly back to feelings of incredible gratitude for this positive DNA identification, especially for Brenda's sake. She would finally be able to have a funeral for Jim. She had him declared dead within a couple of years after he went missing, in order to remarry, and she never had any sort of ritual to commemorate that status change. I felt like this was going to make an enormous difference for her and her children. I'd had a memorial service for Chuck in August of 1977, a month after he was officially presumed dead, because I felt it would help bring closure to that MIA chapter of my life.

The primary difference this step made for me was that I felt free to date again. As long as Chuck was missing, I was still a wife. And by the next fall I did begin to date and began to have sex again after some seven years of celibacy. I was quite content to keep it casual though and had no desire to remarry.

After a few years I began to ask myself why I always picked on men who were unwilling to commit in a relationship. Then I realized, it was me who was unwilling to commit to a relationship. My heart still belonged to Chuck. The presumptive finding of death did not change that. I don't think Brenda's conservative religious views allowed her the same freedom.

I assumed I would not be allowed another individual funeral now, but wondered about the group burial process for Chuck and Jim's remains not identifiable. Would that take place here in Dallas or in Arlington National Cemetery? I was clearly leaning toward Dallas, but yet unaware of my options. So many unasked questions were now racing through my mind. I needed to talk to Mortuary again.

Stephen called me shortly after eight, my time. While I had tried to relay there was nothing wrong in my message, he had picked up something in my voice and felt that it was about his dad. He was really happy that he could go back to the Vietnam Memorial Wall before he left D.C. the next day. It had been the special place where he'd visited his dad since September, 1994.

The Vietnam Veteran's Memorial Wall was completed and dedicated in November 1982. Maya Lin, an American of Chinese ancestry, had won the contest for her design in 1981. There were many protests over her design because it was not like other more familiar war memorials. Yet it has become one of the most visited and most healing places of all times for vets and families.

My experience of the wall had been starkly different each time I'd gone. My first visit to the wall was on March 9th, 1986. I'd flown into D.C. with the staff of Routh Street Women's Clinic to participate in the National March for Women's Lives. I will never forget that afternoon. Exhilarated after hours of marching with an estimated crowd of 125,000 men, women and children, the largest such demonstration for women's rights in the history of the US at that point, I walked to the Lincoln Memorial, and then down the hill into the gash in the earth that holds the staggered panels of this incredible black granite wall shaped like a V, the other end pointing to the Washington Monument.

Chuck's name is on panel 5W, the fifth panel before you get to the point of the V. Row 24 is close to the top of that panel and impossible to touch from the ground. Stephen went to the ground above that panel and lay in the wet grass to reach down and touch his dad's name that September. I saw it only from the ground, but that was close enough for me that Sunday.

I was quite surprised at my own reaction. My eyes filled with tears all right, but not of grief; rather they were tears of rage. Seeing Chuck's name evoked only anger—*all this to get your name on a shiny black wall!!!* I muttered under my breath as I stormed off, walking very briskly back to the hotel. My buoyant enthusiasm from the morning march went south after the wall. Thank goodness I had my ACA (Adult Children of Alcoholics) meetings back in Dallas for expressing my feelings.

By December I was back in D.C. for a conference titled "Ethical Issues in Reproductive Health: Religious Perspectives" sponsored by Catholics for a Free Choice. I went back to the Memorial Wall again before I left.

Walking from the hotel, I entered the memorial from the west at the hill where the three bronze grunts look down toward all the names of their fallen comrades in their stoic "doing my duty" pose.[2] I paused before them for a moment before entering the sidewalk that would lead me toward panel 5W where Chuck's name was located. As I walked downward, the tears began to flow, but this time they were tears of grief. There was no anger defending my heart against the pain as I looked up to that 24th line from the top and saw "Charles W. Stratton +," the cross symbolizing that he remained missing and unaccounted for. Frozen tears melted that evening as if it were 1971 again and not fifteen years later. I just let them flow, feeling no need to rush off and stop them short as I had done in the spring at my first visit there.

When the tears receded, I walked back up to the Lincoln Memorial, a beautiful monument designed after the temples of ancient Greece. Within that temple there's a huge marble statue of our 16th president regally sitting looking out across the reflecting pool toward the Washington Monument and the Capitol. Lincoln's mammoth presence is an enduring symbol of freedom whose space there invokes peace and hope.

From the top of the stairs I looked back off to the left at the tree line that obscures the path to where the Memorial Wall emerges from a gash into the earth, making it invisible from the road above. I stood in awesome wonder at the power of this place, grateful for the release I had experienced with this visit.

My third visit to the wall was after the March for Women's Lives again in 1989, this time with a record crowd of some 500,000 supporters from across the U.S. Numbers like that had not been seen since the Vietnam protests in 1969 and 1971. It was a phenomenal experience. Our group gathered for dinner that evening at a Japanese restaurant where we literally removed our shoes and sat on the floor. What a relief that was after being on our feet marching from early morning. It was a perfect end to an exhilarating, energizing day.

The next morning I went to the wall at daybreak. Fog hung thick in the air as I walked past the Washington Monument and entered the end of the East Wall. The mist muted the blackness of the wall and cast a mystical ambiance over the place that put to rest the anger and the grief I had felt so intensely during previous visits.

All I felt that morning was a tremendous sense of peace and quiet. I walked slowly down the path, the names almost invisible unless you got up very close. With no sunlight, there was no reflection mirrored back. There was just me, and line after line of faceless heroes' names, the list ever growing until they towered above me as I neared the center of the elongated V.

Chuck's name is high up, only twenty-six lines from the top on past that center apex point, leading back up toward the Lincoln Memorial. It always took a few minutes to locate his name, but especially so that morning, through the wispy cloud cover that was lifting, but not yet gone. Then, I saw it. I lingered a while until the blackness and etchings became gradually more visible, enjoying the tranquil state evoked this time.

Maya Lin's design for the Vietnam Veteran's Memorial Wall turned out to be as controversial as the war itself until it finally was built and veterans felt the cathartic nature of its black granite reflections.

Ms. Lin wrote that she remembered a reporter asking her at the very first press conference if she didn't find it ironic that the memorial was for the Vietnam War and she was of Asian descent. The *Washington Post* article was entitled "An Asia Memorial for an Asian War." I would assert that only someone coming from a background such as hers could have envisioned this minimalist, simple structure that indeed works with the land itself.

In an essay about her own experience when she saw the site of this memorial, she wrote, "I imagined taking a knife and cutting into the earth, opening it up, an initial violence and pain that in time would heal. The grass would grow back, but the initial cut would remain a pure flat surface in the earth with a polished, mirrored surface, much like the surface of a geode when you cut it and polish the edge. The need for the names to be on the memorial would become the memorial; there was no need to embellish the design further. The people and their names would allow everyone to respond and remember.

"It would be an interface, between our world and the quieter, more peaceful world beyond. I never looked at the memorial as a wall, an object, but as an edge to the earth itself, an opened side. The mirrored effect would double the size of the park, creating two worlds, one we are a part of and one we cannot enter. The two walls were positioned so that one pointed to the Lincoln Memorial and the other to the Washington Monument. By linking these two strong symbols for the country, I wanted to create a unity between the nation's past and present."[3]

Time and experience, mine and that of countless others affected by the Vietnam War, can attest to the power of her vision.

Unable to concentrate on reading a book or even sitting in front of the tv, I picked up my journal again. The angel card I'd drawn that morning was certainly indicative of the predominate energy of this day: GRATITUDE. I looked at that card again. The angel, clad in a purple robe with yellow wings outlined in red, was facing the rising sun between the distant hills, her arms outstretched, open to receive its warmth and light. I wrote:

> *I feel such gratitude for the whole experience of Chuck being MIA,—because it was conducive to my own growth and development probably far greater than had he been declared KIA then—This is absolutely awe inspiring to think of. It was a blessing financially _and_ in terms of spiritual growth. All the*

remarkable experiences I'd never have had were it not for him being listed as MIA.

With that thought, I turned out the light and fell asleep.

CHAPTER 2

REMEMBERING OUR COURTSHIP

It turned out to be a very short and restless night. I kept waking and looking at the clock. I finally decided to get up a little after four a.m. and began journaling again as I sipped my morning tea.

I am aware of the pull to __do__ something—I should walk—I need to run errands. I have a lifelong pattern of going into action and not giving myself time to be with feelings. Part of me wants to do absolutely NOTHING—Go NOWHERE.

I marveled at how the call from Mortuary had come this particular weekend, my first long period of down time in ages, with no pressing agenda to be handled. While there were other family and friends to inform, the need to contain my good news, let it sink down into my soul before doing so, was paramount.

I did get a few needed tasks done in the early part of the day— contacted my closest friends, picked up more candles, dropped off my recyclables, went to Curves, my gym. I couldn't bring myself to tell the women there about my news though. I just wasn't ready to share it that publicly yet. Tears welled up at the very thought. I just went around the circuit silently, not wanting to engage in conversation with anyone. They all respected my need for personal space. I spent the rest of that Friday at home alone, looking back at old journals and scrapbooks, our wedding album, remembering, crying, and writing in my journal, reliving the past. Memory carried me back to the beginning of my life with Chuck—New Year's Eve, 1959.

It was my junior year in high school and I worked a part-time job at Buck's TV and Record Shop for extra spending money. I was at the register that evening and with closing time rapidly approaching, I was so focused on balancing the sales to make sure I could leave soon after we locked the doors, so I didn't see Chuck and his buddy come into the store. I was oblivious to being "scoped out" as he would tell me later.

While he was trying to get my attention, my friend Pat was actively flirting as she assisted him in finding a record. She recognized him as our W.W. Samuell High School National Merit Scholarship winner the spring before and was vying for the attention of this intelligent, good-looking graduate. My first awareness of him was when he plopped a record down on the counter before me, next to the hot pink Marty Robbins' *Gunfighter Ballads* promotional album cover. "El Paso" had just reached number one on the charts, so it was a big seller that December.

When I looked up, his boyishly handsome face sparked a note of recognition with me, too. Before he could say anything, I blurted out, "Haven't I seen you somewhere before?"

He appeared momentarily taken aback, as if I had just stolen his come-on line, but he quickly regained his cool and said with a grin, "I'm sure I'd have remembered YOU if we'd met before. Chuck Stratton. Why don't we get acquainted after you finish up here?"

"Sorry, but I already have plans for tonight," I replied.

He spent the next few minutes trying to convince me to break my date and go out with him instead. I refused to do that, but I did give him my telephone number. I thought about him all the way home and couldn't wait to tell my mother about our encounter.

"He looks like Roger Smith," I gushed. I'd fallen in love with Roger after seeing him in *Auntie Mame,* my personal favorite top box office hit movie of the year.

"He's not only a doll to look at but really smart too," I continued, as I changed clothes for my date. "Oh Mama, I do so hope he really calls me!"

For me to be that excited over a boy was completely out of character. I was never a "boy crazy" teenager. I remember having a crush on our paperboy when I was maybe thirteen or fourteen. Even with my first "love" Ronnie, the appeal was more about his pursuit of me. I certainly kept my feelings guarded after we broke up. My school studies were always more important to me than boys. No, this attraction to Chuck was a new experience for me. There was a chemistry present I'd never felt before, and a mesmerizing lure in his twinkling eyes. In the midst of my raving about him to Mother, the phone rang. I nearly broke my neck racing to the hallway to answer it.

"Would you like to go out on a double date Saturday night with Bill, the guy with me earlier tonight, and his fiancé Shirley? We can catch a movie and grab a bite to eat after."

I was bouncing off the walls with excitement, but managed to calmly utter, "I'd love to." My cheeks were red hot when I hung up the phone. Every time I got really nervous when public speaking before a group, not only would my cheeks flush, but I would also get red splotches down to my waist. Such was the case that night after talking with Chuck. Could he possibly be as taken with me as I was with him, I wondered?

I had two days to decide what to wear for our first date. I chose a form-fitting, royal blue knit princess-line dress with a mink collar. I loved it because I thought it made me look slender. Of course, the long line bra I wore cinched my waist in another inch, giving me a more hourglass figure. I wore a size 9 then, but mentally inhabited the fatter body that had worn a size 16 1/2 only a couple of years before. I always thought that I was too heavy. Having integrated the message that I was fat as a child, that belief dominated my consciousness. My best friend, Risa, was always slender. She ate anything she wanted and never gained a pound. I used to joke that I gained weight just watching her pig out. I'd had to diet and really work at losing all those unwanted pounds as an adolescent.

Chuck arrived shortly after 7 p.m. Bill drove that night and had already picked up Shirley who was sitting close by his side. Their coziness was like an invitation for us in the back seat as well, though I don't think either of us needed any additional encouragement. I loved feeling the closeness of his body, holding his hand as we drove

15

away. I learned we were going to the Esquire Theater over on Oak Lawn Avenue to see *Porgy and Bess,* which had opened with much fanfare there at Christmas.

One reviewer called it "your best operatic boast at movie house prices." For Chuck that was $2 a ticket for the plush maroon reserved seats of the lower level. I was impressed. Later I would wonder how much the tickets were at the Forest Theater for the black audiences. Their version was not in TODD-AO with stereo Hi-Fi sound.

I thoroughly enjoyed the whole production and couldn't wait to purchase the soundtrack. Afterwards, we went to Brownie's, a popular hangout for teenagers back then for late-night pizza or burgers. We talked about the movie and spent some time just getting to know each other a bit. Chuck had entered Southern Methodist University that fall semester, planning to major in aeronautical engineering. He was currently more interested in joining the Air Force and becoming a pilot, however, than continuing with that degree plan.

We had both lived in Oak Cliff before moving to Pleasant Grove. Both of his parents and my mother all hailed from neighboring counties east of Dallas. Monty Stratton, the famous baseball player, was a double first cousin. I had seen and loved *The Stratton Story* as a kid. Chuck had one younger sister, Wanda, who was also at Samuell. We were both the oldest in our family and had only one sibling. The more I learned about him, the more I liked him.

Since Bill was driving that night, we necked in the back seat all the way home that evening. He was as good a kisser as a conversationalist. We walked slowly to my house holding hands, not really wanting to part yet. On the porch he asked me out again the following weekend. I quickly replied, "It's a date!" We kissed goodnight, and I forced myself to turn, open the door and go inside. I ambled to my bedroom, still on cloud nine, quite the smitten seventeen year old!

But alas, my bubble burst the next weekend when he failed to show up for our second date. Those stars in my eyes turned to daggers. I told a friend of his sister's that I was furious with Chuck for standing me up. Word got back to him of course, and he called me, denying my allegation. Seems he thought I'd said "I have a date" that night on the porch. He was convincing enough that I decided to give him another chance.

We saw each other both nights the following weekend. He told me that he loved me on our third date. When I told Mother that, she asked me how I responded. "I told him I loved him too. I really think I do." I knew I wasn't willing to risk losing him like I did Ronnie by refusing to tell him that I loved him. Mother just smiled and shook her head. She liked Chuck. They'd hit it off from the beginning.

Chuck gave me his senior ring to declare to all that we were now "going steady."

My father was pleased about this. He liked Chuck, but more than anything, he wanted me to marry and give him grandkids rather than be a doctor. He was old school enough to think it would be more fulfilling than a career. I met Chuck's parents then, and they accepted me as readily as my parents had accepted him. He did not return to SMU for the spring semester. His test scores for the Air Force had been so high that they were very actively courting him, though they were not taking on more pilots at the time. They convinced him to join up and go into the aviation cadet's program at Harlingen Air Force Base down in the Rio Grande Valley to earn his commission and navigator wings in their 10-month training program, and apply later for pilot training.

He was thrilled to get on with a flying career rather than sit in a classroom for four years. He'd done nothing but party that one semester in college and flunked his courses. His heart was not there. It was in the sky. He would be inducted into the United States Air Force on April 1, 1960.

We had barely three months together before Chuck left. We made the most of them, spending hours on the telephone during the week. I had my studies to maintain, so we went out only on weekends. By March the weather was warm enough for outings on Lake Lavon in Daddy's boat. We went flying on some weekends. Chuck didn't have his private pilot's license, but had a good friend who did willing to take us up in a little Cessna. I shared his love affair with airplanes. Whatever we did, we always had fun just being together. Then April was upon us all too quickly.

His induction was on a Friday, but he didn't have to report to Harlingen until Monday. As luck would have it, the Midway at Fair Park opened for the spring and summer season on Saturdays. Chuck thought it might provide a special setting for a memorable last time together Sunday night. We didn't go until after dinner that evening and, to my surprise, he parked his 1957 red Chevy in front of the Hall of State instead of the parking area at the end of the Midway.

We got out of the car, and he boosted me up onto one of the big pedestals at the base of the stairs. In one agile leap, he joined me. We sat there under the street light, in the peaceful quiet, holding hands and talking. Our conversation led to confessions of love.

"Wait for me. Marry me when I graduate," he entreated. "Wait for me."

I'd already surrendered myself totally to him by then—body, heart and soul. I felt like ours was a match made in heaven. We belonged together. I was ecstatic knowing he felt the same way too.

"YES! Oh YES!" The words flew out of my mouth without any hesitation. "Of course I will wait for you!"

I shook my head as I remembered our courtship. I really had no idea the breadth and depth of that eagerly made promise for my future as a military wife. I prepared for bed, knowing I still had the weekend to reminisce

CHAPTER 3

LUNCH WITH LINDA

By Saturday I felt ready to share this unfolding process with my best friend, Linda Sprague. I met Linda in 1982 when she and I served on a pro-choice panel discussion. I was a relatively new counselor at Routh Street Women's Clinic and she was the director of another abortion clinic in Dallas. We hit it off right away. Not only were we of like minds in our feminist views, but she was also an astrologer and advocate of study of the ancient goddesses, both avid interests of mine as well. We'd been there for each other throughout the war zone of abortion protestors, bomb threats, break-ins, Operation Rescue, etc. throughout the '80s and early '90s.

After I told her on the phone, she invited me to lunch at Pei Wei's that afternoon. I had asked her to do Chuck's natal chart back in May. I was curious to know what astrological aspects were present the night his plane crashed. That reading kept being postponed for various reasons. Now we both understood why it hadn't happened yet.

After we had finished our delicious spring rolls, she presented me with the sweetest note. "Your Penelope days are finally complete," it began. My Penelope days—only this amazing soul sister of some twenty-five years could have zeroed in on the core mythic significance of my DNA news so succinctly.

I first made the connection between myself and Penelope back in

LOSING CHUCK, FINDING SALLIE

1981 in a class on Greek Epic in my graduate school program at the University of Dallas. We were studying the Trojan War epic *The Odyssey*, and I could relate to Penelope, who had to wait twenty years before her warrior husband Odysseus returned home. With Linda's words, I realized I had waited over thirty-six years for this definitive DNA news about my husband. *My Penelope days are complete.* I knew those words would provide hours of reflection later.

Linda's note continued: "Your experience touches something deep and wordless in me and in others." She talked about how we, as human beings, have this deep longing "to know." That touched a familiar chord in me. "Under God, we are obligated to know what we can know." Those were the words that ignited a fire within me to return to school.

It was July of 1975, four years after Chuck went missing, and I was attending my second Educational Assistant seminar at Perkins School of Theology, at Southern Methodist University (SMU). Rev. Fred Gealy uttered that response to a question about the ethics of spending so much money for the space program when there were so many other social ills that could use those funds to help people right here on earth. *Under God, we are obligated to know what we can know.* These powerful words penetrated the very core of my being at the time. Instantly, I knew it was a calling to complete the college education I had set aside to marry Chuck.

That deep longing to know had been suppressed in 1977 when I requested the status review for Chuck because knowing for sure what happened to him seemed out of the realm of possibility. Viewing the artifacts from the excavations had given me a sense of certainty, but still did not release the buried grief. This positive DNA identification has opened a valve I shut down long ago, and I wondered why. What's the difference between these two kinds of knowing?

Upon returning home from lunch with Linda, I continued my reverie about Penelope. As with all myths, the gods and goddesses are active in the story. They give us images of archetypal energies present in the human psyche. Athene is considered the heroine of *The Odyssey*, a warrior Goddess who was patron and ally of Greek heroes, especially Odysseus who was her favorite. She helped him achieve victory over the Trojans and later intervened in a divine council with her father Zeus on his behalf to bring him home after his ten years of wandering post-war and being thwarted by Poseidon.

Athena is the protector of cities, patron of military forces, and the goddess of weavers. She led me out of my small insular world as wife and mother into the larger polis and the realm of the warrior women who had organized The National League of Families of American Prisoners and Missing in Southeast Asia. However, for all my speaking out and soliciting of support for our cause during the '70s, I remained a father's daughter, careful not to trample on the authority of my government and military, continuing to back my President and my country.

As goddess of the art of weaving, it was Athene who provided Penelope with the skills and the ploy of weaving and unraveling that shroud to keep her suitors appeased until her husband could return. I too wove and unraveled Chuck's shroud over the years. Having a memorial service in 1977 was my first attempt. I symbolically buried him and erected a tombstone, and began a new tapestry in preparation for my own future employment.

That shroud unraveled nine years later, the day before Chuck's birthday in 1986. I received a call from the military regarding a report from Laotian resistance forces indicating at least one man did not eject from an F-4 that might correlate with Chuck's crash. That meant one man may have survived, and I felt those frustrating twinges of limbo all over again. What if Chuck had ejected before the crash after all? Once again I had to acknowledge my powerlessness to achieve a definitive answer to that question.

Poseidon was the other god active in *The Odyssey*. He was clearly responsible for Odysseus' delayed return as he churned the seas and threw his ship off course numerous times. While best known as a Greek god of the seas, Poseidon was also god of earthquakes. For Penelope whose life was in Ithaca running a household, his effect on her life was that of shaking her world to the core by the prolonged absence and uncertainty regarding her husband's fate.

I related quite well to Poseidon's role as Earth-Shaker during those years before Chuck was presumed dead. Of the three Greek father gods, Poseidon psychologically represents the realm of emotion and instinct, the undersea repressed or buried feelings.[4] In the early '70s my feelings were held at bay, in limbo by virtue of the prolonged ambiguous grief of the MIA scenario, like Penelope.

Remembering what it took to finally tap into feelings that had been repressed for years made it very clear to me that I did not want to stuff my feelings this time around; no excess activity or weaving ploys of avoidance. I was being given the opportunity to finally really feel what I stifled years before. I wanted to be in the moment this time, with whatever would come up emotionally. I had been given another chance to actually achieve the ever-elusive "closure" after the loss of a loved one—no more denial or numb resignation as in my past.

The projector of my mind rolled further back to July of 1970 at George Air Force Base in the high desert area in California. Chuck was finishing up his combat training in the F-4 and awaiting orders for Southeast Asia. As a Radar Intercept Officer (RIO), he'd been spared a Vietnam tour until now because he was among the few RIOs available for the dwindling F-101 Fighter Squadrons stateside. Until recently, the F-4 had required two pilots. Now they were training former RIO's to fill the back seat Weapons Systems Operator position. Chuck was thrilled his combat tour would be done in jets as opposed to navigating another type of aircraft as so many of his friends had done.

In his ten year career, every other duty station had been in California. He had gone from Waco, Texas where he trained as a RIO in 1961, to Sacramento as a navigator in the RC-121; to the F-101 in Rome, New York; Oxnard, California; Cape Cod Massachusetts; and then in November 1969 to training in the F-4 in Tucson and Victorville. He'd never made it to pilot training, but had been quite content flying jets since 1963. In fact, it was because he was one of a dwindling number of Radar Intercept Offices for the backseat of the F-101 Voodoo that had kept him stateside for that long.

When we were at Oxnard in 1968, Chuck received orders for Vietnam. Immediately I felt terrified and had this awful gut feeling that the tour would not end well. My dear friend, Wendy, was the only one I told about my fears. She tried to assure me it would all be okay, not to worry. I couldn't bring myself to tell Chuck how I felt, just like I could never send him off angry. Always in the back of my mind I knew there was a possibility I might never see him again. His was a dangerous job, but rarely had I experienced much fear when he was flying. I was always supportive of his vocation, and flying was definitely that. I had signed up to be a military wife from the beginning.

In fact, my biggest fears regarding his flying came back in 1962 at McClellan when he suffered some sort of inner ear trouble that hospitalized him for a few days and grounded him for a short while before he was finally granted a waiver to put him back on flying status. My fears were about him *not* being able to fly, knowing it was his passion.

By May of 1963, Chuck had been transferred to the 49th Fighter Interceptor Squadron at Griffiss AFB in Rome, New York. Big change! Fighter pilots live to fly and play with that same kind of passion. If you've seen *Top Gun* you get the picture. Those guys are really like that! Chuck was in "heaven" with that assignment.

Our entry into jets was not without some tension, however. We arrived to learn the squadron had just lost a plane in Lake Michigan. The pilot's body had been recovered, but not the RIO. Three months to the day after that, another plane pitched up on take-off and both the pilot and his RIO were killed. That's when I learned that the Voodoo had a flaw—if a certain critical angle of attack was reached, the plane would pitch up and stall out. Recovery was simple, *if* you had enough altitude. But on take-off, that was not the case. Both the crew did eject, but for all practical purposes, were virtually slammed into the runway.

That morning Chuck was able to get to a phone to let me know he was okay before the news broke and the phone lines were jammed. While relieved that he was not flying, my heart broke for the young wife receiving a visit from the base commander to tell her she was now a widow. For the following three months I lived in fear of receiving such a visit, as accidents tend to come in threes, do they not?

When that time frame lapsed with no further incident, my more normal, non-worrying self regained control again. I felt that Chuck was safe and would always come home to me. But when he got those first orders for Southeast Asia, the fear returned with great intensity, probably exacerbated because I was afraid to talk about it.

Those orders were cancelled, however, and he was sent to Otis AFB instead. I breathed a huge sigh of relief and put that fear out of my mind, determined to enjoy Cape Cod. And we did. We took in all the sights whenever Chuck was off for the next fifteen months. When orders for F-4 training came in, I knew they would lead to a Southeast Asia tour, no more reprieves. Again, I vowed to make the most of every moment we would have together between now and then.

The nine-month training schedule was my ideal assignment because Chuck was home every evening and weekend with me and our three sons we had by then, a luxury we had never enjoyed before. We spent the Thanksgiving and Christmas holidays in Tucson, Arizona while Chuck completed the classroom instruction before heading for California to complete the flying portion.

The wide-open spaces and year-round sunshine made Victorville a choice area for pilot training. The runways there were perfect for viewing the class graduation air show. We were privileged to watch Chuck and his pilot demonstrate a typical mission they would be flying overseas, a sight none of us would ever forget.

Chuck's F-4 came screaming in at high speed and low on the deck before our very eyes, dropping ordinance and firing the nose Gatling gun (which he told the boys sounded like a rhino fart), cutting the target in half. That gun was integrated in the newer F-4s after combat experience in Vietnam showed it could be more effective than guided missiles in many combat situations. It was quite impressive, all happening in a matter of seconds, an awesome sight guaranteed to instill fear in the enemy. It was a sight I would never forget.

Before packing up to leave the base, there were briefings for the wives to apprise us of all we needed to know before our husbands left the country; the many papers we needed to make sure were in order; who we could contact if we had questions or needs while our guys were 10,000 miles away. These two events brought home to me the reality that soon, Chuck would really be leaving for this war I had hoped would end before he ever had to go.

We had decided that I should go back to Dallas and live with my mother for the year he would be at Korat AFB in Thailand. It would give the grandparents a chance to get better acquainted with their grandsons. My father had died in 1967 when I was seven months pregnant with Stephen, so Mother had this large three bedroom house with a den all to herself. There was plenty of room for us there. Chuck's parents, Jean and Eurcil, lived about three miles down the road from her. His sister Wanda, and her two children, Norman and Lori, had moved in with them after she and Tommy had separated.

We had the boys' furniture and toys shipped to Mother's house, and the rest put in storage until Chuck's return. Then we loaded up our nine-passenger Chevy station wagon for a little sightseeing vacation trip between California and Texas, eager to show our sons the attractions we had first enjoyed back in 1961 en route to Sacramento where Charles Jr. was born.

Driving for hours at a time could be pretty boring for three very active little boys, and what better places to get out of the car and stretch their legs and collect more rocks than Arizona's Grand Canyon, its Meteorite Crater, the Painted Desert and Petrified Forest? We had to skip Carlsbad Caverns, one of our favorite memories, because children under four were not permitted on any of the guided tours.

It was probably just as well time-wise. There were lots of family to see when we got back to Texas, all wanting to spend a little time with Chuck before he left the country. We also wanted to take a long weekend excursion to the coast to introduce the boys to Galveston at some point. They had been in both the Pacific and Atlantic Oceans, but never experienced the warm waters of the Gulf of Mexico. We intended to pack a lot of fond memories into only thirty days, enough to last us for the coming year.

It was a long day, full of memories. Ending with that pleasant thought, I put my journal aside, feeling grateful for the stroll down memory lane. Tomorrow was another day.

CHAPTER 4

ANNIVERSARY OF THE PRESUMPTIVE FINDING OF DEATH

Sunday 8 July 0549 hours

I was dreaming this same dream all night—waiting for someone to come so I could do something. Is that residue for my waiting now for that DNA report? Or for a funeral?

So began my journal entry after some much needed, very sound sleep.

Chuck is really coming home—I want him buried *here*—in Texas—not in Arlington. I pray Brenda will want this too.

As I drank my tea and continued to journal, I realized that it was exactly thirty years ago, on July 8th, 1977, that Chuck was officially presumed dead, KIA, BNR—killed in action, body not recovered. I had requested that status review after school was out in June of that year because I knew I needed some sort of closure to move forward with my life. I was back in college full time on Chuck's VA benefits and looking toward a future where I needed to find a way to support myself. It was just a matter of time before the military declared all the remaining MIAs dead. It felt important to me to have a say in that process.

The timing of this DNA identification was amazing, I thought. Thirty years ago to the day, and we finally had an identifiable fragment of his body recovered for reburial stateside instead of the jungles of Laos. During the four-year excavation process, both my son Stephen and I had felt an uneasiness that we associated with Chuck's and Jim's remains being uprooted from their long time resting place. Now they had rested at Hickam AFB in Hawaii for another three years awaiting identification. I wondered when they'll be able to come home to Texas?

When I had the memorial service at Carswell AFB on August 20th, 1977, the only moving aspect of the service was the missing man fly-over afterward. For me the service had been a pretty traditional one officiated by my pastor, a formality to mark an ending and new beginning. I knew I wanted more this time, though I wasn't sure what that would look like. I just knew it would be more real now with actually having some remains.

That first memorial service was literally seven years after Chuck's departure in 1970. We drove him to the airport the morning of August 19th. I had never made that connection before until I started creating a timeline in my journal as I continued my weekend reverie. And that took me right back to memories of that D-Day.

Chuck's leave had flown by all too quickly and we felt anything but ready for his departure. That morning, my husband was packing his one duffle bag for his solo journey. The mood of everyone was quite somber, and the boys were unusually quiet. The feeling of reluctance hung heavy in the air. Each of us, the boys, me, my mother, Chuck's parents, had all dreaded this day for some time now, dreaded driving him to Love Field for the flight that would take him 9,000 miles away from us.

When the man of the hour came out of the bedroom in his dress blues rather than his more familiar flight suit attire, ready to put his bag into the car, our youngest son Stephen, only three years old at the time, raced before him to lock the back door. He'd been locking all the exterior doors in the house so his daddy couldn't leave.

Chuck just picked him up and carried him into the den where he sat in a chair there with Stephen on his lap and Charles and Scott gathered around him. He spoke with such love and compassion, first to Stephen, but then inclusively to each of them.

"Stephen, you remember watching Daddy fly over the desert in California and shoot at the target there?" All the boys nodded. "I need to go and do that for real now," he continued, "and help the people of Vietnam run the bad guys out of their land. It's what I have trained to do this past year. I don't like having to leave you or your brothers and your mommy, but it's not forever. I'll be back before you know it. We'll all go camping then like we've talked about. But before then, Daddy has to go and do his job. Do you understand?"

The look on Stephen's face reflected the cogs of his little mind weighing those words, searching for the perfect response that would please both him and his daddy. Finally, with a satisfied grin, he nodded that he understood.

"Yes, you have to go, Daddy—so I'll go with you. I'm little. I can fit in your bag. I'll help you."

Scott's big brown eyes shifted briefly from the sadness that had been there to a moment of delight. Clearly he thought his little brother had a great idea. Maybe we could all go and keep him company there, Scott thought. Charles, the older brother at age eight, understood that, as much as we all wished we could go with his dad as we had with other base changes, it was not possible this time. Chuck took a deep breath and began to gently deflate Stephen's magical bubble.

"No, Stephen. The Air Force can't do that. Only I have been trained for this job and I am very good at what I do. *Your* job is to stay home and keep mommy company, go to school and write to me about all your new friends and good times here to help me not be sad over there. Can you do that for me?"

After careful consideration, Stephen nodded yes, as did his brothers. I was fighting back the tears myself at that point, wishing I'd had a recorder to capture those most precious few minutes. I so loved this man and the father he was to our sons.

"So can I go now?" Chuck asked, waiting for his son's permission.

Stephen hugged his daddy's neck, hopped off his lap, and ran to unlock the back door that led to the driveway, his gesture of approval. Within minutes the front doorbell rang and he ran to the living room to unlock that door as well for his grandparents, Jean and Eurcil. Chuck would be driving us all to the airport in our station wagon.

We arrived at Love Field with lots of time to spare, but we could certainly visit with Chuck there as well as at home, and with no worries about traffic delays or anything. He was booked on a flight to Honolulu. From there he would fly to Clark AFB in the Philippines for jungle survival training before departing for Cam Ranh Bay, Vietnam, and then finally Korat AFB, Thailand. He had many hours of travel ahead of him.

When it came time for him to board his plane, he hugged our four parents, then our two younger sons. He shook Charles' hand. "You're the man of the house now until I get back. Take care of your mom and little brothers."

He saved me for last and we shared a lingering embrace and one last kiss, whispering I love you to one another. He finally let me go, and turned and walked away with confidence and purpose.

For a fleeting moment, as I watched the distance grow between us, I felt a twinge of fear that I would never see him again. I shoved it back down deep inside along with the tears that were stinging my eyes.

The boys followed my lead, but both moms were crying openly, my mother a bit more reserved than Chuck's. Eurcil remained stoic as he consoled Jean. We stayed there at the window until Chuck's plane actually pulled away from the gate, unable to tear ourselves away.

Walking back to the car, Mother suggested we stop for lunch at Vincent's Seafood Restaurant on Northwest Highway on the way back home. That sounded good to everyone, so off we went to Vincent's. The waitress pulled a table together for the seven of us and took our drink orders as she left the menus. About the time she returned for our order, Charles burst into tears, unable to hold them back any longer. Mother was closest to him and quickly put her arms around him, gave him a tissue and assured him, "It's okay. Real men do cry. Don't let anyone ever tell you they don't. When you are sad or even sometimes when you are happy, tears come naturally and it's better to let them out and not feel like you have to hold them in."

Papa affirmed what Charles' grandmother had just told him. We were all glad he was able to let loose, even if he did feel embarrassed there at the restaurant. He'd been the brave older brother long enough. I was certainly not the best role model when it came to crying in public, but his emotional outburst changed that and we all had a bit of a cry for a moment, acknowledging how much we would miss Chuck, praying the coming year would pass quickly.

That evening after the house had settled down and everyone had retired to their respective bedrooms, I lay awake remembering how just the night before Chuck and I had made love in this same bed. As we engaged in our usual pillow talk afterward, he spoke of his upcoming tour.

"Honey, you know I may be different when I come back. While I'll be flying into a target area, dropping bombs in a matter of minutes, and heading back to my air-conditioned hooch and a drink at the Officer's Club, I know the devastation and death left behind in the wake of my missions. Even knowing it has to be done, I can't help but think I'll be affected, changed by that experience."

I knew what he said was probably true. But then I would probably change somewhat too after being apart for a year. I wanted so badly then to confess to him how worried I was about this Vietnam tour. But once again, as in 1968, I couldn't acknowledge my fear. It felt as though giving voice to it might somehow make it come true. So I stuffed my fear, hoping it would eventually go away. But it didn't.

My long weekend stroll down memory lane wound down on that note. I felt incredibly grateful for the weekend to process all that had come up for me. But tomorrow was a work day and I knew I must shift gears and come back into the present.

For the past six years I had been the office manager for a chiropractor. It was an ideal part-time position that brought in extra income to supplement my VA pension. I knew from my first interview with Dr. Blumer that ours would be a perfect match. She'd become a great friend as well as my "boss."

CHAPTER 5

BACK TO WORK

Monday 9 July 0440 hours

Another a.m. when my mind engaged early. But that's okay—
Should I write folks today & tell them about Chuck? The news is
like the delayed firecracker—I've had 3 full days to process that
information. It's time to talk about it now—to resurrect if you
will—come back into life—

Though I wrote these words in my journal, I felt somewhat
reluctant to do that, however. I wished I could stay home and
continue the reverie initiated by that call from Mortuary. But with a
full schedule of patients today and tomorrow, trying to get all our
regular patients in for an adjustment before Dr. Blumer's vacation, I
definitely needed to be in the office. I also wanted to share my news
with her before she left. Maybe the final DNA report Trevor said was
in the mail would arrive Tuesday, so I could use my time off while
Mel was on vacation to continue processing this event. In the
meantime, keeping busy would be good for me, I was sure. I finished
writing in my journal.

These past few days have been surreal—Stephen said he still felt
numb. He spent time at The Wall yesterday. It was the perfect
time for him to be in D.C. this particular weekend, so he could

do that. And his research had been quite successful as well. I did manage to email a few friends who lived far away but Dr. Blumer will be the first person besides Linda that I've told face to face about Chuck —Yes, good to be up early so I can have my journaling time to prepare for the day.

As luck would have it, Mel got to the office early for a change. We were able to sit down and chat before patients arrived. She hugged me after I told her which made me cry, but it also broke the ice, so to speak, making the rest of the day easier for me to function and carry out my duties. I even made it to Curves after work.

Tuesday 10 July 0500 hours

Yesterday was very busy—didn't leave the office until almost 6.—It's warm out—we've only been getting into the 90's but with the humidity, the heat index is 100—
Stephen took some incredible photos @ the Wall—indeed of D.C. What am I feeling now? Calm I think—yesterday was teary at times. I feel gratitude more than anything. Funny how I went to that place of "Was this Trevor guy legit? But he called Brenda too."

The next morning, I stopped by the office at my apartment before leaving for work to ask them if I'd gotten a FedEx package yesterday. No, none was there, they said. I told the manager about the DNA identification and asked her to please call me if the package was delivered today, since I would not make it back home in time to retrieve it before they closed. My office was only ten minutes away, and I was most eager to get my hands on that report.

Listening to my favorite radio station, Legends 770, on the way to work, I heard an oldie I'd never heard before that that really hit me emotionally, something about how "some of God's greatest gifts are unanswered prayers." I burst into tears at that chorus. I wondered who was singing it, but that information wasn't announced before I reached the office. Sure enough, one of our clients knew the song and told me it was Garth Brooks. Hearing that song felt like no coincidence that morning. I knew I would revisit it later and listen more carefully to the words.

My prayer for the DNA report to come that day was answered. I got a call just before noon and raced back to my apartment to get it. I was surprised at the size of the box. I was expecting an envelope. It was not only the DNA report per se. It was a one-inch bound book detailing the entire excavation process from beginning to end, with great color photographs. The table of contents was quite impressive, and about all I would have time to peruse at work. I was even more eager now for time to scrutinize every page of that remarkable document.

The day was even longer and busier than the day before had been. By the time I got home, I had barely enough energy left just to check my emails. I had a lovely one from my dear friend, Una, in Northern Ireland. It made me cry. I missed her and my Irish family. I'd met them during the first year I lived in Ireland and spent lots of time with them throughout the three years I was there. I had gone back a year before in September for their youngest daughter Sarah's wedding.

I scanned the Final Search and Recovery Report after heating some leftovers in the refrigerator for dinner. There was an amazing photograph of the crash site itself on page 5. It was a small pond of brownish water amidst some skinny trees, a rather peaceful looking setting one might expect to find in East Texas somewhere. That pond, however, was created by the F-4 that crashed there.

Part 1 of the report covered the excavation process itself for the first 42 pages. Then there were pages of summary conclusions, all of Chuck's medical and dental records, along with a recap of the facts and circumstances surrounding the crash of his plane. Part 2 detailed the actual Forensic Anthropology process of how the DNA identification was made. Part 3 covered all the material evidence, including the myriad of reports I was sent after each excavation of what had been recovered during that particular field activity. June 5th, 2007 was the completion date fixed on this phenomenal document from the Central Identification Laboratory at Hickam AFB, Hawaii—one full month before we were notified.

Page 3 of the Forensic report grabbed my attention with a photograph of nine pieces of skeletal remains. One "long bone" (that was approximately 2 cm long and 1 cm wide, probably a radius or ulna) was the one that had provided the needed DNA to identify Chuck, if I was reading the report correctly. It had shown eleven exact matches to his sister's DNA sample. Two "long bones" (the other, probably a tibia) had been sent out for mitochondrial DNA testing on September 11th, 2006. The "other" had shown a positive match to Jim's mother and sister. I thought back to where I was during that testing, and recalled I was in Northern Ireland that very day preparing for Sarah's wedding.

Amazed at the depth of this final report, I called Brenda to see if she'd gotten hers as well. She had and told me she wanted to bury Jim in Pampa where he was born. She was of the understanding that we could have separate individual funerals for each, plus a group burial for those remaining unidentifiable fragments. This was a possibility I had never considered. I definitely preferred to have Chuck's service in Dallas. It seemed I had a lot of re-thinking to do with regards to Chuck's homecoming. I planned to make Mortuary my first call the next morning.

Feeling pretty wired again after our conversation, I turned on the TV to wind down enough to go to sleep. I chose a recorded episode of Army Wives, which just premiered last month, and was already my latest favorite series. Though far removed from military life for many years, I continued to be drawn toward television shows or movies about that world. The military wives I bonded with during my life with Chuck were like sisters I never had. And during the years Chuck was MIA, the wives active with the National League of POW/MIA Families were a godsend.

Wednesday 11 July 0448 hours

I was dreaming about this little animal in a small cage—going to a zoo? a giraffe?—Can't believe I'm up so early—guess it's due to my eagerness to get back into that final report from JPAC.

Wednesday morning, I woke up thinking again about Chuck's homecoming. If Brenda was right about two separate services for the individual remains, did I want Chuck's remains in an urn? Did I want them placed in the ground or to keep them? Have a funeral or memorial service? Best not get too carried away until after I talked to Mortuary again, I thought.

I was thrilled that Jim would finally get the full military honors he deserved. At some point, I thought, I wanted the Dallas Morning News to help me get the word out of Chuck's identification to anyone who wore his bracelet. Dallas Cares, our local POW/MIA non-profit group established to coordinate letter writing campaigns and activities seeking answers about our POW/MIAs, had sold many during the '70s.

I was feeling a little more grounded in a way, yet also scattered with so many questions racing through my head. Thank goodness I had the rest of the week off, I thought.

My mind continued to race. In the final report, Chuck's medical records noted he had diabetes mellitus and was granted a waiver to fly because it was controllable by diet. I always thought the waiver was about the inner ear thing he had back in 1962. I never knew he had been diagnosed with diabetes mellitus. I needed to look into that—maybe the boys should be tested?

Next my mind darted to that Garth Brooks' song about God's greatest gift being unanswered prayers. I wanted to find a CD with song, and that desire got me out of bed and to the computer. I was surprised to learn that song had come out on an album in 1990 and become a number one hit in 1991. How was it I'd never heard it before? While the story told in the lyrics was written about an unanswered prayer for an old high school flame, the chorus applied to any prayer denied, and we've all had those for sure. For me, it was my prayer for an answer regarding Chuck's fate. I had come to see and appreciate some gifts of that unanswered prayer, but it had taken a long time to recognize them.

When I reached Mortuary later that morning, they confirmed that two separate services were indeed in order. "Each of those individual remains will be placed in separate urns. And the group remains can be buried anywhere and anytime you and Mrs. Ayres mutually agree upon," Trevor told me.

"Can I keep Chuck's remains if I want? Do I have to bury that bone fragment? He has a stone already in place next to his parents' plot from 1977. There would probably be enough space for an urn, even though it's not a full burial plot."

"The 'urn' used by the military is actually an 8 x 8 inch square wooden box with the USAF insignia and a plate engraved with Lt. Col. Stratton's name, birth and death dates. You have two years to decide whether to bury that urn or not. The remaining bone fragments will be placed in a casket for burial wherever you and Brenda decide you want them."

"So, I can have a service with full military honors without burying his individual remains at the same time?" I asked again.

"Yes ma'am, you certainly can."

I *had* thought about the group burial option and was leaning toward the Dallas-Ft. Worth National Cemetery over Arlington since both our guys were native Texans and all the family lived in the area. I called Brenda and she was amenable to that and suggested we visit the cemetery and check it out. I agreed to call them for an appointment to learn more about their services.

Now I had lots to consider with regards to another service for Chuck as well. I needed to confer with my sons about a good time and place. Maybe we could have his individual service and the group burial on the same day, I thought. Finding a time that Stephen could make it into Dallas for a few days would be the biggest challenge. He was running the costume shop for the Radio City Rockettes in Manhattan, and they were already geared up with fittings and costumes for the Christmas show that year.

After speaking with Mortuary, I felt like telling more friends and acquaintances about Chuck's positive DNA finding. However, I did not yet feel ready to share it with the world at large. The military hadn't yet released the information to the public, so I didn't feel pressure to do so either.

I continued to peruse that detailed report and all the artifacts retrieved from the crash site and examined by the Life Sciences Equipment (LSEL) Lab in San Antonio. The entire process of the site excavation had taken almost seven years, the same time frame of Chuck's MIA years prior to being presumed dead. It felt like I'd been given another opportunity to tap into feelings not resolved in the '70s. This new millennium was ushering back the familiar pattern of hope and waiting and disappointment I had experienced in those early MIA years, and with a surprising intensity.

By the end the week I was astonished at the realization that a penny found in the crash site measured about 2 cm wide, which meant the bone fragment that provided Chuck's DNA was not much bigger than a penny. Could that possibly be right? Seeing how widespread the osseous remains and life support items were found within that crater was also a bit startling, hard to really wrap my mind around.

These facts made it even more impressive that those teams could have been so thorough and observant to uncover all that they did, despite the restrictions they often encountered. Each Joint Field Activity (JFA) at a particular site could only be there for 30 days at a time. The first such team went to Chuck's crash site in November/December of 2001 to begin excavation. Their second visit in August/September of 2002 was during the rainy season and severely hampered by the site being inundated with water. The team moved on to another site after a few days where their efforts could be more productive. However, that meant they could not return to Chuck's site until they met with the Laotian government the following May to get permission to go back. Hence there were no more excavations until 2004 when they actually made four consecutive trips every three months into the site. I was very frustrated when I learned about those stipulations and realized this process was going to take much longer than I had initially anticipated.

On Friday the 13th, Brenda called to say that she was setting Jim's funeral for August 10th. I couldn't believe she was moving so quickly. I was still processing the DNA identification and the idea of actually having a real funeral. That particular date was not good for me. I was scheduled for a colonoscopy that day. Maybe I should cancel it so I could drive to Pampa, I thought. I told her the boys and I had not set a date yet for Chuck's service.

By the following Tuesday evening she called again with yet another surprise.

"Do you want to go to come with me to Hawaii to escort Jim's remains home? I'm thinking around August 5th. Maybe we can bring both Chuck and Jim back together."

"What?" I was speechless. I had no idea this was a possibility.

When words came back to me, I told her, "But that's only two weeks away and I still have no idea when I want to have Chuck's funeral. Let me think about it, Brenda and I'll get back to you."

Brenda was way ahead of me with Jim's funeral plans. Obviously, I needed more processing time than she did. Since she never had a funeral for Jim, I could see why she was eager to do so. But I wanted so much more for Chuck's homecoming than the memorial service I had back in 1977.

Early the next morning I was back on the phone with Mortuary. No, they assured me, I didn't have to go at the same time as Brenda. Whew! What a relief. The more I had thought about it the night before, the more I thought I would prefer to go by myself to Hawaii. Chuck and I had never been able to fulfill our plans to meet there for R&R as we had planned for our anniversary in '71. It seemed somehow very fitting that we would meet there for his return home. The gifts of this positive identification just kept on coming.

I called Brenda later that afternoon to decline her invitation to fly with her to Hawaii. "Sorry," I told her, "but I need to set a funeral date and make arrangements before retrieving Chuck. I am eager to hear all about your experience though. You can tell me what I can expect when I do go."

Several ideas popped up in my head. Within the past year I had become acquainted with a woman minister who had been an MIA wife herself. I wanted to ask her if she would officiate for Chuck's service. I envisioned a large photograph of the crash site at the funeral, the one that was pictured in that final report.

I really wanted to acknowledge JPAC and all those who had made such a service possible in the first place. And I wanted a limousine to transport the family together from his service to the Dallas-Ft. Worth National Cemetery.

I thought Pleasant Mound United Methodist Church might be the perfect location for his service since we were married there. That church had been so supportive during those early years he was missing, and Rev. Neville had put me on the track for a vocation as educational director. Would the autumnal equinox, September 23rd, be an auspicious day for the service, I wondered?

I had turned all planning for that memorial service in 1977 to my minister. This time, I wanted to handle the planning myself. I envisioned more of a wake than a funeral. I wanted people to share stories about Chuck, let his grandkids know what kind of man he was.

I couldn't wait for my weekly Sunday chat with Stephen to fill him in on all the latest news. Brenda had told me the Air Force would pay for his flight home. Charles and Scott, who both lived in Texas, were open to whatever date Stephen could manage to travel to Dallas. They were really happy that the group burial could be in Dallas instead of D.C. Charles hated the idea of flying. It would certainly be a lot cheaper for the government too.

Stephen suggested that if we had the funeral on Chuck's birthday, he would be able to attend the State Fair when he came which he would very much enjoy. The more we talked, the more we liked that idea, as did his brothers. We all agreed that October 9th, Chuck's 67th birthday, would be a perfect day to celebrate his life. Brenda had said the military funeral had to be on a weekday, and the 9th was a Tuesday. Things were finally taking shape in a way that felt really right.

Dr. Blumer had scheduled the first couple of weeks of August off for another vacation, giving me more time to get the ball rolling for Chuck's service. I asked my friend Linda if she would do the reading of Chuck's natal chart soon. I was most curious to see what his planetary influences would say about his personality, his life, and death, given how accurately my chart described me. August first was good for her.

Chuck's intelligence, occasional stubbornness, love of flying, and life of the party persona showed clearly in his reading, as did the indication his early death was dealt by destiny. Given the configuration of the planets when his F-4 crashed, it would have been a miracle if he'd survived. He'd have been severely injured. But he was spared by a sudden, instant death with no suffering.

Linda saw him harmonically connected to the times, wounded by and sacrificed for the collective. Mystery surrounded the event with his moon in Neptune. And that same configuration was present now in his progressed chart, indicating that mystery finally coming to light. She didn't think he had any intuition of the potential crash that night. It was an exciting time for him. He was living his dream.

Everything in both our charts pointed to his loss that January, as did our very happy marriage. She went on to say his was a phenomenally creative chart. He could have been a teacher of aviation. I knew she was right about that.

I felt such gratitude for the enormous amount of work Linda had done with Chuck's birth chart, the progressions, and our marriage chart, all of which supported my belief that our marriage, his loss and missing-in-action status were destined, part of our sacred contract. What a gift it was to see it there in the stars as well.

I decided to drive to Arkansas that first weekend in August while Brenda was in Hawaii. My dear friends, Ron and Bette, had graciously invited me for a visit and I chose that particular weekend so I could visit Riddles Elephant Sanctuary to see how Amy, the little elephant that had led me to Riddles, was faring with her pregnancy. I had learned about the sanctuary after reading Malcolm MacPherson's book *The Cowboy and His Elephant*. I was so taken with Amy's story that I went online to search for her whereabouts and discovered she was at Riddles. I enrolled in one of their elephant weekend retreats in October of the previous year.

More importantly, I wanted to fill Ron in on my plans for Chuck's service and ask him if he would be willing to say a few words as one of our oldest military friends. He and Chuck were inducted into the Air Force in Dallas on April 1st, 1960 and went through Aviation Cadets together down in Harlingen.

I was at their house drinking a glass of wine while Bette was preparing dinner when I received a call from my granddaughter, Briana. The Associated Press had broken the news that Chuck had been positively identified and the media were trying to get in touch with me. Charles had agreed to an interview with local reporter with CBS, a very surprising turn of events, as the boys were never ones who wanted to talk to the press. He made them promise not to put him on camera, however.

I was extremely glad I was out of town and they had been unable to reach me—I really wanted time to collect my own thoughts before speaking to the press. I had not realized DOD was releasing their monthly report that weekend and would not have liked having to respond so unexpectedly. I felt much more comfortable bouncing my thoughts off my friends before doing so to the general public. I really needed the support of the media to get the word out to all who might have worn Chuck's bracelet, but was quite content to let Charles be in the limelight that weekend.

I thoroughly enjoyed Riddles and my alone time with the elephants that next morning. It was a grounding experience. Amy had grown taller and was heavier, though still did not look very pregnant to me. I was disappointed that I did not get to see the magnificent bull, Solomon. He was out in his own field, away from the main area where visitors could go. He and Amy were two of the dozen African elephants at the sanctuary then, along with the Asian girls, Peggy and Booper.

I remembered Solomon so well from my elephant weekend in October last year. On that Sunday morning, our last day at the sanctuary, I was up at my usual 5:30 and had gone to the chow hall to enjoy my tea and journal in the quiet darkness while everyone else still slept. After my first cup I needed to go out back to the toilet behind the building. Walking back I looked over to my left and saw Solomon, his great tusks glistening in the moonlight, not fifty feet away from me. I stood there a few moments in awe of the sight, filled with gratitude to the point of tears, blessed with an image indelibly imprinted in my mind.

Ron and Bette took me into Hot Springs on Sunday for the day and showed me all the sights there. I actually recognized the place where I had come back in the '80s to do my last paper for my master's degree. That little old motel, the Vagabond, was still there. I took Monday to drive leisurely back to Dallas via Hope, Arkansas and Bill Clinton's home place. Those quiet hours in the car driving home helped me gather my thoughts for the press. I felt grateful to have had an entire month to process Chuck's identification before the news was made public.

I stopped off at Charles' around 5 p.m. to see how the interview had gone and let him know I'd made it back safely. He'd been so impressed with Chris Salcedo, the reporter from KTXA TXA-21 who'd interviewed him when I was in Arkansas. He appreciated the way Chris had honored his requests to not be on camera during the interview, and as a result, he had promised Chris that I would give him the first exclusive upon my return to Dallas. Chris called not long after I arrived and set up Wednesday afternoon, August 8th, after both Charles and Scott got off work, so they could appear with me for the story, this time with everyone on camera.

CHAPTER 6

GOING PUBLIC AGAIN

I returned home to a dozen messages from various newsmen, family and friends wanting speak to me. One message was from Paul Meyer, the reporter who had written the story for the *Dallas Morning News* (DMN). He and the others who'd left messages on my machine would have to wait until I had a good night's sleep before I would return their calls.

I did telephone Brenda, eager to learn about her Hawaii trip. She told me it was much harder than she had imagined it would be. She too needed to rest up from her emotional weekend before meeting me to discuss her experience in more detail.

Tuesday I was on the phone most of the morning. Much to my delight Chuck's best friend growing up, Charles Frank had called the DMN and given Mr. Meyer the telephone number where I could reach him. We had lost touch over the years and I had no idea until then how to reach him. I wanted to ask him to speak at the service.

His was the first of several such contacts that would come through that first DMN article and subsequent interviews. And so began a fast paced, sometimes hectic and frustrating, two-month long process of actually creating the final homecoming celebration for my long lost husband.

Topping my "to do" list was to contact Joy, that former MIA wife, now ordained minister, with whom I shared this particular experience of Vietnam, and ask if she would officiate. And to my delight, she readily agreed to do so.

Next I had to establish the place and the program I wanted for this service. The minister at Pleasant Mound United Methodist Church was out of town at a conference, so I was unable to discuss the possibility of the funeral there just yet. In the meantime, I received a call from Dave Tarrant, a journalist with the DMN. He wanted to do an in-depth story about Chuck and me. I was thrilled. This was how I had imagined getting the word out to Dallas bracelet wearers. He set up Wednesday morning for that interview. So I began pulling together information for him and Chris. All my reflections over the past month before the news broke were very helpful for this meeting.

I was very impressed with Dave Tarrant. I found that telling him my story stimulated the equivalent of a natural high without the ill effects of such an induced state via alcohol. Dave was easy to talk with too. He recorded our conversation, so he was very present to me as I responded to his questions.

When he had mentioned doing an in-depth article, I had no idea he meant that quite literally. His questions and my relating pivotal points during those early years was revealing an order to my evolution in ways just journaling about them had not. I suppose it was like what happens in therapy when you articulate out loud your dream or an event. That's when you really hear it for yourself.

I began by telling Dave how ours was almost a fairytale love story that began on New Year's Eve, 1959. I was hopelessly enamored of Chuck from our very first date a couple days later.

After a whirlwind courtship of only three months he departed for Aviation Cadets in Harlingen, Texas, almost 500 miles away. When he proposed to me at Fair Park his last weekend in Dallas, he suggested that we not tell our parents yet. They might think it was too soon or that we were too young. It would be our secret until he could afford to buy me an engagement ring.

I reminded Chuck that I had my Auntie Zona's diamond engagement ring I could wear, but he wanted to buy me one on his own. I could have cared less. All I wanted was a wide gold wedding band. It was funny though to remember Auntie Zona's ring as I sat perched on that pedestal in front of the Hall of State, wearing my favorite Neiman's dress of hers, a black and white, full-skirted frock with an off the shoulder neckline that accented my broader shoulders.

Glowing and with stars in our eyes, we departed our pedestal and strolled hand in hand toward the lights and sounds of the Midway. We walked the entire length to ride the Comet, the old 60-foot tall wooden roller coaster that had provided many a thrill with its double-out and backups and downs since 1947. It was a landmark for our state fair as well-known as Big Tex. The thrill I got on that particular night was, however, far more than I had bargained for.

The long slow chug up the first steep hill got my adrenaline pumping in anticipation of that first big drop that would leave my stomach in the air while my body plunged to the next level for a hair pin curve before climbing again. I hooked my legs back under the seat to keep myself from flying out of the car when we dropped and gripped the safety bar with both hands. Chuck's posture was far more relaxed with one arm around me and the other resting casually on the side of the car.

After the second plummeting descent I felt a sharp pain in my left leg. By the time we exited the fast but short ride my lower leg was quite swollen and hurt like hell. Our Midway fun was nipped in the bud. We slowly headed back to the car with me limping and holding onto Chuck for balance. At the time I had no idea what I had done. I could feel a knot about halfway between my knee and ankle, but didn't think I had broken any bones. It was a memorable evening in a way that neither Chuck nor I could ever have imagined.

He left for Harlingen the next morning and I went on to school. My preoccupation with how much I was going to miss him took my mind off my leg. It no longer throbbed but the swelling was uncomfortable. By mid-week, after a teacher prodded me with her taunt—*I guess you're going to wait until it falls off*—I decided maybe I should have it checked out. Mother made the appointment with a doctor that my father knew. His office was in downtown Dallas. With Daddy working, it was up to me to drive myself there.

It turned out that I had broken a blood vessel in that leg and a huge clot had formed, hence the swelling. He gave me a shot into that clot to dissolve it, the pain from which was ten times worse than when I had initially broken the blood vessel. With every pump of the clutch in that stick shift '55 Dodge, I was so wishing that Mother could drive. I cried all the way back to Pleasant Grove. The pain did subside finally as did the swelling. However, the clot drained down my leg and into my foot. It looked as though I hadn't washed my ankle and foot for weeks afterward.

Chuck wrote me within a couple of days, detailing his new routine as an aviation cadet. But it was his vivid and explicit expressions of love that I read and re-read, over and over again. Letters carry a power it seems that a phone call doesn't. I could not only hear his voice in the words, but feel his touch through them as well. His handwriting was so neat and legible, far better than mine. While I missed seeing him that next weekend, I felt comforted with that letter under my pillow, and knowing there would be more coming.

Perhaps our being apart until summer would be tolerable, I decided. I had more time now to concentrate on my studies. Soon there would be rehearsals for the senior play. I would certainly miss not having Chuck here for my senior activities and graduation. But it was a small price to pay for him to get his commission and navigator wings. Imagine my shock when he called me Friday afternoon, only two weeks into his training, to say he'd gotten a pass to go off base for the Easter weekend. "Can you come down?" he queried excitedly.

I hurriedly called Mother into the hallway, with him holding the line to plead for this whirlwind trip to the Valley. Much to both our delights she said yes. Harlingen is some 467 miles from Dallas. We'd have to drive all night. What a terrific mother I was blessed with! She never ceased to surprise me with her support. Mother was not a very spontaneous person. She was a planner, not one to do such rash things on the spur of the moment. Her consent to this crazy last minute whim really showed how much she loved Chuck too, and approved of our relationship.

Within a couple of hours we were packed and ready to roll. We reached the base before 6:00 the next morning. I was feeling pretty sleepy at that point and looking forward to a little catnap before Chuck would be free to leave the base. Seeing the cadets doing PT on the field was just the rejuvenating moment I needed. I felt wide-awake again. We looked for a motel close by before getting some breakfast. I called the barracks and left a message for Chuck to call me with instructions about when and where to meet him.

When we returned to our room Mother napped while I showered and did my hair. Before long Chuck called to say I could pick him up at the Cadet Club around noon. What an experience that was! When I arrived at the club, Chuck was nowhere in sight. But very quickly a young cadet came up and introduced himself as Dick Strine. He already knew who I was. He escorted me to a booth and asked someone to let Chuck know I was there.

Another cadet joined us as we waited. Dick was easy to remember because of his beautiful light blue Paul Newman eyes that seemed to devour me as we sat and talked. In fact, I felt as though every eye in the club was trained on me ready to pounce at the slightest provocation. While I was flattered, I did find it a bit unnerving. Never had I found myself the center of attention like that, being ogled by a room full of future flyboys.

I didn't have to wait long thank goodness. I know my cheeks were glowing red when he did appear. And as I was so prone to do when I was nervous, I could feel burning red splotches all the way down to my waist. Chuck seemed delighted that his classmates found me as attractive as he did and a little amused by my embarrassment. They were all probably imagining I were their girl back home come to see them. Dick was, no doubt, seeing his fiancé, Aris, with an intensity that made me blush.

It was grand to meet many of Chuck's classmates that weekend and see what the base was like. It was also refreshing to soak in the tropical vegetation I so loved that grew in the valley—the hibiscus, bougainvillea, and birds of paradise along with huge oleanders and palm trees. My family had come down to Mercedes in the fifties, only ten miles from Harlingen. My Auntie Merle knew the Colemans who had a motel there. Auntie Merle was Daddy's youngest sister who had treated my brother and me to many a spontaneous adventure.

The Senior Prom was on my 18th birthday. A dear friend and neighbor escorted me. I felt a little like Scarlet O'Hara trying to maneuver the yards and yards of tulle ruffles billowing over a huge hoop into the front seat of his car. My strapless gown was all white, the bodice smooth gathered tulle to a couple of inches below the waistline before the ruffles began. Then in the center back of all that ruffled skirt was a floating tulle cascade gathered with three rows of red roses to give it a unique flare.

Ken brought me a beautiful corsage of red roses to complement the detail. I felt like royalty in that gown with my tiara and long white gloves. Only my chosen king was missing, but his presence was visible in the tiny pair of sweetheart wings pinned over my heart. My old flame Ronnie and the girlfriend that had introduced us, shared our table that evening, along with Pat from Buck's TV and Record Shop and her date. I couldn't help but wonder how Chuck would have reacted to Ronnie.

The month of June was spent checking out admission to the University of Texas in Austin. I also pursued staying the rest of the summer with my Auntie Merle so I could spend the weekends with Chuck. Aransas Pass was only 125 miles from Harlingen, so an easy drive. Chuck's parents wanted to visit him down in Harlingen too, so we made plans to drive down for the 4th of July weekend. I would drive Chuck's Chevy, and Jean and Eurcil would follow me. When they came back to Dallas, I would head to Auntie Merle's, keeping his car for the summer. I was one happy camper knowing I would have transportation to see him on those precious weekends he could leave the base.

After the fall semester began, I'd not see Chuck again until Christmas. The dividends I drew from Auntie Zona's inheritance paid for my tuition and clothes for college and Chuck covered our expenses when I was with him.

On Saturday, July 16th he took me to Zale's to pick out an engagement ring. I chose a plain diamond solitaire to formalize our commitment to one another. He had written to his dad before then, and I had shared the news with Mother before coming to spend the summer with Auntie Merle, so both our families were now aware of our plans. I think Chuck wanted to make sure there was a ring on my finger before I went off to college to show I was definitely not there to find a husband. We set our wedding date for February 18th, the Saturday after his graduation on the 14th. That gave us time to get back to Dallas for our marriage license and have the necessary three-day waiting period before the ceremony.

Mother had a great surprise for me when I returned to Dallas. She'd spent that summer learning to drive again so she could take me to Austin. She had driven before the war, but with gasoline rationing and two babies to care for at home had let her license lapse and not driven a car since then. I certainly felt special to have provided that impetus for her, but was even more delighted that she would not have to depend on Daddy to take her everywhere after I was gone. Mother was such an independent woman in so many ways and always reluctant to ask for favors from any one.

Before I met Chuck, I was a very studious young woman set on a career in medicine. All I had ever wanted was to be a doctor. Marriage was not a part of that equation. I had thought it would be too difficult to have both a career and a family. My father had planted that idea into my head many times. His goal, however, was to deter me from medical school. He wanted grandchildren. My falling in love with Chuck was very much to his liking. I decided that I would be a nurse instead. That seemed do-able.

I would attend the University Of Texas for one semester before we married. I wanted to experience living "on my own" for a bit, before moving from my father's roof to Chuck's and mine. I could always finish my education later from wherever we were stationed. Had I known his first assignment would be in Waco, I could have finished that first year at UT. But I didn't. All career plans I had entertained were put on hold so I could follow him wherever duty called. Needless to say, one of the songs I had chosen for our wedding was "Wither Thou Goest."

I flew down to Harlingen for his graduation on Valentine's Day, which, of course was forever after associated with wings and bars rather than hearts and flowers. We drove back to Dallas to get our marriage license. At 18, I was of legal age to wed but Chuck was only 20, so his father had to accompany us and give written permission for him. I found it ironic that here he was, an officer in the USAF, but still too young to marry without parental consent! But the humor doesn't end there. For whatever reason, we went downtown on the bus where we ran into an old girlfriend of his from high school. He sat with her on that ride; I sat with my future father-in-law.

We had a lovely wedding at Pleasant Mound Methodist Church where I had been baptized. My brother was the only close family member missing. He was on a Navy ship somewhere in the Pacific Ocean. Our friends got together and decorated and shoe-polished our beautiful old red '57 Chevy. They proceeded to try and follow us to our honeymoon motel, knowing full well we would give them a merry chase. The soap they had put on the manifold emitted the odor of Proctor & Gamble far into the next week!

We did lose them, however, and spent our first evening together as man and wife at the Sands Motel across from the Old Circle Grill that is still there on Buckner Blvd. The next morning we picked up wedding presents from my parents' house and left for his first assignment at James Connolly AFB to train as a Radar Observer in the back seat of a jet fighter plane.

During the summer before we married we talked about buying a trailer that we could move from base to base. Well, our first apartment there in Waco was a one-room efficiency. Talk about cozy! I certainly didn't have much to clean. I enjoyed the challenge of cooking in our tiny quarters. The first time I made mashed potatoes you'd have thought I'd cooked for the whole class. I had been used to cooking at home for a dad and brother who could really put away the food. Well, we ate potato leftovers in every form possible for at least a week. In my home, wasting food was not tolerated, having been raised by a mother who'd grown up on a farm during the Depression.

But probably the biggest cooking blunder was my first attempt at gravy. Chuck put lots of it on his chicken fried steak and potatoes, then took a bite and asked, "Honey, did you put sugar in the gravy?" Defensive young bride that I was, I bristled and said, "Of course not! You don't put sugar in gravy...." But then I tasted it and was horrified. It *was* sweet. Chuck went to the trashcan and there discovered the can of Eagle Brand Milk, the sweetened condensed milk that bakers used. I had never baked much, and I hadn't a clue this was any different than other canned milks. Don't think I've ever bought Eagle Brand since, either.

After a month in that small space, our dreams of owning a trailer home vanished forever. We couldn't wait to move a bigger apartment. We found a lovely old furnished one with large rooms, high ceilings, and a grand old bathtub on claw feet. How I loved that tub! But alas, we were evicted from there because we got a puppy, which was against our lease agreement.

Ginger was a brindle mongrel whose mother, a registered English Bull dog, had escaped for a weekend fling, thereby presenting her horrified owners with thirteen mutts. Ginger was the runt of that litter. Chuck had a fondness for bulldogs, having been in Dog

Squadron in Cadets with a bulldog mascot. Thanks to Ginger, we then moved to our first house complete with fenced yard. We were off to a grand start having moved three times already during this one seven-month tour.

My first experience with base medical facilities came when I had a really bad vaginal infection. I discovered that it was from my pregnancy—surprise! We had hoped to wait a couple years before starting a family. So much for the efficacy of the rhythm method. Suddenly I found myself fearful about having a baby. When the local drive-in had a special educational film series on childbirth, Chuck insisted we go to see them. And he was right. Watching many different kinds of deliveries, including a C-section, alleviated my fears. In fact, I decided I wanted to go the natural childbirth route.

We celebrated Chuck's 21st birthday in Dallas with family before heading for our next duty station, McClellan AFC in Sacramento, California. We decided to see the sights between Dallas and the west coast, make the trip that "honeymoon" we'd never had. Carlsbad Caverns was our first stop. Ginger had to remain in the car, of course, while we went into the cave. While we were gone she ate my sunglasses and a tube of Vaseline for my raw nose from the cold I had acquired. I was not at all amused. At the Grand Canyon she could go out with us, thank God. We hit the Mojave Desert during a sand storm that completely pitted our car and nearly choked me to death. My "honeymoon" was not the ideal I had imagined.

We rented a furnished duplex in Sacramento from a young couple also expecting their first baby. It had a fireplace that I dearly loved. Chuck was back to navigating with this assignment. He flew 14-16 hour reconnaissance missions in the RC-121 patrolling the Pacific coast twenty-four seven, a very different work schedule from the basic 9-5 school at Waco.

One of my first tasks in Sacramento was to find an obstetrician. There were no maternal facilities at the military hospital. The doctor I chose was "modern" in his thinking and talked me out of going the natural childbirth route. "It's not necessary for a woman to suffer these days," he told me. I was naïve enough to think he must know best about these things. However, I did stand my ground about nursing. He discouraged that too, saying it was so inconvenient for women. I asked him if I could stop if I didn't like it. He said I could, so that was that. He was also a stickler about weight gain.

I weighed 135 pounds at my first visit with him, and was around three months into the pregnancy. He looked up at me and asked, "How tall are you?"

"Five foot two and a half inches," I replied.

"You should *never* weigh over 110," he told me and handed me a 1000-calorie diet sheet and a prescription for diet pills. My friend, Lynn, from Waco, whose husband had also been assigned to our same squadron, was a month behind me in her pregnancy and chose to come to my doctor as well. He did the same thing to her.

So, together we smoked, drank iced tea with Sweet & Low, and ate lots of carrots and celery sticks between doctor's check-ups. Then after our monthly visit weigh-in showing a couple pounds lost, we made a beeline for the soda shop where I ate a banana split and she drank a chocolate pistachio shake.

Mother came to be with me during my first delivery. She and Chuck took turns rubbing my back during labor. Having either present during the actual birth was not done back then. So they kept each other company in the waiting room when I went into delivery. Chuck had always insisted that this baby was a boy and would be a junior.

As they waited they saw a new mother coming out of delivery apologizing for having a girl. Then the grandmother went to the phone and told whoever answered, "Well, she goofed again; it's another girl." Chuck was especially upset upon hearing her very critical conversation, and asked Mother, "You don't think Sallie would do that, do you? She knows I'll be happy with a little girl too, doesn't she?"

Now he was worried about my reaction if I didn't have a boy—so much so that when the nurse told him it was a boy, he asked, "Are you sure? Have you looked?" She had to open the blanket to convince him.

Thank goodness Mother was there to show me the ropes after we brought this little bundle of joy home. I would have been lost without her! I learned to make formula so we could give him a substitute bottle. I wanted to make sure he would take either the bottle or the breast should anything happen that I couldn't nurse him successfully. I think Mother was in seventh heaven herself when she got to feed her first grandson that first time.

Unfortunately for me, she left Sacramento the same day that

Chuck went back to work, leaving me alone for the first time with my new son. Charles Jr. and I both cried throughout his entire bath. Before long I got over my fears that I'd break him, and thus began a wonderful new relationship.

We were in Sacramento only 18 months, but they were memorable. We bought our first house, first new car (a white Studebaker Lark with red interior), and had our first son during that time. And we'd had the big scare about Chuck never flying again after his bout with vertigo. After a few weeks he was granted flying status again with a waiver, which would be reevaluated at his annual physical around his birthday, October 9th, every year thereafter. The only ear damage he seemed to have suffered from that infection was the hearing loss of certain decibels like the ticking of a watch, and that would not interfere with him doing his job.

Chuck had his first temporary duty assignment (TDY), Operation Gold Digger, to fly patrolling missions over the waters between Cuba and Florida for an entire month, mid-October to mid-November of 1962. It was the only time, in all the years we were married, that I was afraid when he was gone. I received numerous lewd phone calls during that month from a man who obviously knew I was alone. And during that time period a woman in Nevada was found murdered and dismembered in her apartment. I slept with a loaded gun in the headboard of my bed. Charles Jr. could not yet climb out of his crib, so I felt safe as far as he was concerned. The gun was then locked away during the day.

In May of 1963, Chuck was transferred to Griffiss AFB in Rome, New York as a Radar Observer in the F101 Voodoo. I turned 21 the day we arrived in New York. I couldn't wait to go to a bar and order a drink, daring them to card me. In California, we always got carded because Chuck had such a baby face. They were always surprised that he was 21 and I was not. It didn't matter that I was married and a mother. Not only could I not drink, but also no one at my table could drink in public then. Well, the drinking age in New York was 18—so I missed out on getting carded and being able to thumb my nose at them, which was a big disappointment.

By fall the Officer's Wives Club had a "Show Train" going into New York City—Broadway plays, television shows—four days in the Big Apple to shop and sightsee and have fun. My good friend from Waco, Lynn, who'd been transferred with us again, agreed to keep

Charles Jr. so that I could go. He and her daughter Kim got along fabulously. I decided I could risk being away from Chuck now, feeling that he would be okay. And because I was already trying for another baby, I figured I needed to take advantage of this particular opportunity.

What an experience! All I packed in the way of shoes were 3" heels. By the third evening, my feet were so swollen I made the mistake of taking them off during the play that evening and couldn't get them back on. I thought I'd have to walk back to the hotel barefoot. Embarrassed? Understatement! I did, after what seemed a lifetime, manage to squeeze my feet back into the shoes. I came away feeling like one of the ugly sisters in the Cinderella story trying to get her big foot into the glass slipper. Thank God mine were Peau de Soie and more flexible!

My introduction to live theater was *Who's Afraid of Virginia Wolf?* Half our group left during the intermission because of the adult themes and language. I wasn't about to leave and miss whatever else I had yet to learn. I was amazed at what you could get away with on stage. After that I thought I'd heard it all. Not true!

A cab ride back from massive Christmas shopping spree, which almost made me late for our next television show, provided yet more vulgar possibilities for expressing one's anger. Seems the cabbie was in even more of a hurry than I. At the very first signal light we approached, there was a black man still in the crosswalk when the light changed. As he lay on his horn, the most foul name-calling words spewed from the cabbie's mouth; at the next intersection, he just lay on the horn and barreled through without slowing down. By the time we reached the hotel, I was on the floorboard promising to never ride in a cab again if I, along with any other pedestrians along the way, could just survive this ride. And they say we Southerners are racist!

This cab driver was not at all indicative of my experience of New Yorkers. I had been told before we came north that I would not like it because the people were rude and unfriendly. Quite the opposite was more the norm for me. I rarely could do anything quickly, be it shopping, or dealing with repairpersons, whatever. The minute I spoke people talked to me just to hear my Texas accent. I was teased, but always in a very kind and friendly manner.

We also saw *A Funny Thing Happened on the Way to the Forum,*

Tovarich, and *Oliver,* which was my favorite. I loved the music—even bought the album as I had done for *Porgy and Bess.* It was a packed few days. I took a city tour, which included the Bowery, Chinatown and the Statue of Liberty. I bought a sweater for my mother-in-law from Saks Fifth Avenue, a tiny ladybug charm for my mother from Tiffany's, and numerous other Christmas gifts from Macy's. I managed to see all the special places I'd set my heart on seeing and then some. It was a fabulous vacation for me.

Then in November, President Kennedy was assassinated and along with the rest of the shocked world, we mourned via all the television coverage of the historic events that followed. I remember feeling very reluctant to open my mouth to speak to anyone, fearing they would know I was from Dallas. I was not at all sure I would be treated with the same good-natured acceptance, as had been my previous experiences.

How I admired Jacqueline Kennedy that week. I had been the only person in my boarding house in Austin who had *not* been a Kennedy supporter. But my heart felt broken for her and her children. And so, like the rest of the nation, did I enter my "last innocent year."[5]

Fighter Squadrons were a whole different ball game from what we had thus far experienced. There were many more parties, much more drinking. I had not had much experience with alcohol myself. My father was an alcoholic (though not by his own admission) as were his brothers and one sister who had been a "friend of Bills" for years. I grew up with the memory of many a holiday ruined because of my dad and Auntie Merle having gotten into some hellacious fights due to drinking. She usually wound up in a sanatorium to dry out afterward. Pretty amazing that I would ever consider touching the stuff really!

Once in college, my roommates sent a friend out for a bottle of scotch so we could drink safely, albeit very illegally, in our room. That was the first time I'd ever been tipsy. I decided that I wanted to call Chuck because I was lonesome for him and feeling quite amorous at the moment. As it was about 2:00 a.m., my roomies convinced me that it was not a good idea. However, I refused to be talked out of sending him a telegram instead.

My message? Simply, *I want you, I need you, I love you. Sallie.* Well, some poor sergeant relayed those words to Chuck about 4:30 that morning, before revile. (Cadets were on the PT field at five.) My passion was somewhat lost in the translation, I am sure.

That was certainly my first clue about how alcohol loosened any sexual inhibitions or sense of appropriateness. Chuck and I were never prone to keeping alcohol around the house. He was raised Southern Baptist, which meant he'd been taught about the sin of the stuff. His experience with alcohol had come at SMU.

He had not expected to go to college at all. He'd just figured he'd join the Air Force after high school. Winning a scholarship to the school of his choice threw him. It's a real shame it didn't occur to him to go for the Air Force Academy. He chose SMU because it was in Dallas and he could live at home. Well, he became a party animal there and I think may have been flunking out that semester because of it.

Together, we were what you would call social drinkers only. I don't recall any parties where we drank at James Connolly AFB in Waco until graduation. Neither do I remember any particular parties at McClellan. But the 49th Fighter Interceptor Squadron was a lively crew, and we seemed to hook up with the real party animals. I remember lots of parties during those four years and lots of drinking!

The very first squadron party left me feeling pretty ashamed of myself. I was not very familiar with a bar "menu" and every time Chuck or anyone else went to get me a drink I would sample something new. No one ever told me that I was asking for trouble. I felt fine when we left, until, that is, I hit the fresh air. Then it was back into to Officer's Club ladies' room where I threw up everything but my toenails. I learned *not* to mix alcohol that evening, but I didn't learn when to quit drinking period.

I was really not very comfortable with myself at a party and I drank to get over my "nerdy" feelings. I'd never really learned to dance, but after a couple of drinks, I became more willing to let my body respond to the music. I'd never been comfortable in my body either, or with my sexuality. Chuck had always considered me a sexy, beautiful woman, but my own body image was always one of being too fat.

I was a bit hefty as an adolescent. I can remember wearing a size 16 1/2 at one time, and weighing some 165 pounds. But I consciously dieted and lost 25-30 of those pounds by high school. When I met Chuck I was wearing a longline bra to cinch my waist in and give me the curves I thought I "should have."

I was thinner than I had ever been after Charles was born. And I exercised and dieted to maintain no more than 120 pounds, so I really wasn't "fat" externally. I just never got over those internal messages. Well, the message I got from all the men of the 49th Fighter Interceptor Squadron matched Chuck's perception, and after a few drinks, I could enjoy being flirtatious and sexy.

I made my debut in the first of several memorable performances for a big Squadron Gala in the early spring of '64. One of the wives who had professional dance training choreographed a modified strip routine to the tune "Take Back Your Mink." Since the three of us who performed the number were *not* professional dancers, we used bar stools as props for our kicks, etc.

We were outfitted in opera hose, heels, and little satin bunny-like outfits (mine was red). Our fluffy boas (in lieu of minks), long gloves and strands of pearls were teasingly thrown into the audience at the appropriate times. My waistline was made smaller with the aid of a longline bra once again, for I was almost three months pregnant by then. The added breast fullness just made me appear even sexier. Our next big theme party was a luau, and a Hawaiian muumuu was definitely more my style by then!

We decided to buy a house before Scott was born. We found a lovely ranch-style one about 11 miles from the base. It was in the country, nestled in some pine trees and across the road from a small lake. We had two young couples about our age as neighbors. Their children were also the same age as Charles. It was all so perfect!

Scott was born in mid-September in the base hospital. I finally had the experience of natural childbirth without any lessons about breathing, etc. With this labor, Chuck dropped me off at the hospital and was told he'd be called when the baby was born. I was placed in a barren room with a bed and a clock on the wall to stare at for the rest of the day. After almost 12 hours with not so much as an aspirin, and one pain after another in rapid succession, the nurse couldn't hear the baby's heartbeat. The doctor was called in and I was rushed out for a caesarian because they feared the cord was wrapped around his neck.

The next hour was like a Keystone Cop cartoon caper. I was placed on my side, given oxygen and wheeled into a freezing cold operation room. The doctor couldn't find the lights—then the stirrups. Everyone (and I do mean that very literally—seemed like half of the hospital staff had joined us by this time) was racing around frantically trying to get everything in place for the surgery. I remember the doctor saying, "Roll her over and prep her stomach"—at which point I felt my first bearing down pain and the urge to push. Of course, I was told not to do that. Any woman who has experienced this pushing urge knows how absurd a command that was! I was not in control at that point. Apparently the cord had loosened and this baby was coming down the canal quite properly at this point. Then I was asked to sit up while they gave me a spinal. I kept saying no, I can't, because I could feel his head right there. I have yet to figure out why they even bothered at that point. I felt his birth, even with that spinal, but I suppose it may have taken the edge off. At that point, my only concern was for the baby.

I had watched Charles Jr. being born via mirrors and thought it was the most beautiful sight I had ever witnessed. But let me tell you, the sound of Scott's cry was even more beautiful. I had never worried that anything would go wrong that first time like I had with this delivery. Knowing he was alive was more than music to my ears. The pediatrician was right there to examine him immediately. He brought him over to me, assured me that he seemed okay, and whisked him off to the nursery to get him warm. I was exhausted, but oh so relieved.

My parents came up to visit, arriving just before they released me from the hospital. Military hospitals keep you for five days. (I was home in three with the first!) And once again, Mother had to show me how to fold the diapers. How was it that after only 2 1/2 years I had forgotten what she still remembered from *my* birth? We really enjoyed showing them the incredible autumn fall in the mountains just north of us. You just don't see color like that in Texas!

It was that same fall that Butch (Charles Jr.'s nickname given to him at birth by Papa Stratton), in his new red western shirt and cowboy hat Grandma and Grandpa Hodges had brought him from Texas, and our dog Ginger took off in search of an adventure while I was out shopping and Chuck was babysitting. Around a curve, across and down the road from us was a dairy farm. Outfitted for a round up, they herded all the cows into a corner of the pastures.

Chuck became aware of the situation when he answered a knock at the door and a farmer asked if he had a boy about this size (holding his hand about three feet off the ground) and a big brown dog. It seemed that Ginger wouldn't let anyone near Charles—not cows, not farmer, and the poor man was afraid the boy would get hurt.

Chuck was not a happy camper, needless to say, having to pack up the baby and race to rescue his oldest son. By the grace of God, no one was hurt, though I doubt those cows gave decent milk for a few days after their ordeal. My neighbor, Mary, said she couldn't help but chuckle watching them returning home, Ginger with her head hung low, Butch too—and Chuck swatting at his behind every few paces.

Ginger had protected Butch. In fact, she was quite protective of all the neighborhood kids. She wouldn't let anyone hit a child. At the slightest threat she would grab that person's arm, preventing any spanking from occurring, no matter whether deserved or not. I was called out on more than one occasion to call her in when a parent needed to reprimand his or her child and Ginger was guarding the said child who had run behind her. She was part bulldog and had the broad hulky chest and stubbornness of that breed. She would not give in and was formidable enough in appearance that one would not be inclined to argue with her.

One day we decided to see what she would do if Chuck threatened to hit one of the boys. Sure enough, she grabbed his arm and prevented any strike. You could see the anguish in her eyes. It was as though she was saying, *I love you too, but I can't let you hurt him— please don't make me hurt you.*

Ginger was a great dog and traveled with us from base to base. At one point we even had this trailer made for her to ride in that had its own little evaporative window cooler. When Chuck got orders for Southeast Asia and I'd decided to return to Dallas for that year, we flew her back to my mother's—yet another funny Ginger tale. By that time, Ginger was quite a hefty animal and she needed to be sedated to fly. Chuck gave her the pills before leaving for the airport. Big mistake! They'd begun to take effect before he could get her to the gate and she would walk a few paces, stop and shit, walk a few paces, stop and shit—all the way to the crate for boarding.

Living in the country in Rome, in upstate New York, was quite different than anything we'd ever known weather-wise. There were definite seasons. Summers were cooler than those of Texas. And we loved picnics by the lake with our neighbors across the road. The autumn colors were a glory to behold.

And the winters produced snow like we had never seen, giving us hours of tobogganing and sledding fun. With small children, it was quite the ordeal, however. Just getting them dressed appropriately for an hour of play left me with tons of clothes to be dried. Then they were ready to go outside again. The snow in New York was dry and powdery. If you wanted a snowball you had to take water out with you. We didn't build many snowmen! Spring brought warmth to thaw the six months of accumulation, allowing us to see grass again.

The winter of 1965 brought a blizzard that dropped 54" of snow in 24 hours. My neighbor Jerry across the road was out in it all night keeping his driveway shoveled so we'd have access to supplies when the roads were open. Chuck was not home and our neighbor next door couldn't get home from town due to the snow. His wife and children came over to my house. She was a native of Rome and was far more frightened than I was.

The next morning when it had stopped and the plows made it up the main road, Jerry called and asked if I'd like to go down to the store for milk and bread. I donned my boots, coat, gloves etc. and proceeded to try and maneuver through the drifts in my driveway that peaked at about eight feet. I wiggle my way through the shallowest parts—got stuck chest-high at one point and thought that was my end, right there. However, I managed to keep wriggling and pushing and shoving with all my might and broke through. But it was quite scary there for a few minutes.

I had to pay a bulldozer to clear my driveway—our regular snowplow guy couldn't manage it. We had a 4' high decorative ranch-style fence with a light post next to the driveway. The snow was level across the top of that fence. It was beautiful! Watertown north of us had 108" of snow with that storm. I was very fortunate to have close and friendly neighbors, being so far from the base and our military family. We all looked after one another.

The following summer Chuck was sent to Alabama for Squadron Officer's School. I went back to Texas for a long visit with the grandparents while he was there. My parents had plenty of room for us and they loved having the boys to spoil for three months. I flew into Montgomery when Chuck graduated—and we had a mini-honeymoon driving back through New Orleans.

Traveling back to New York, we had one very long night of driving. The World's Fair was in New York at that time. We started trying to find motel accommodations in Ohio, but had to drive all the way to Erie, Pennsylvania before we got the last room in a big hotel downtown. It was several floors up overlooking the lake, a dormitory-like room with some six beds in it.

I was driving that last leg of the trip, having to pinch myself to stay awake. The boys were sleeping soundly, of course. So early the next morning, they were raring to go again. I had to get up with them because I was afraid they could fall out the windows. Needless to say, I was one tired mother by the time we arrived home.

It was shortly after Scott's first birthday that the Northeast Blackout occurred (November 9th, 1965, 5:27 p.m. to be exact). Chuck was home and we waited anxiously for a bit, listening for planes departing. If they scrambled, we'd have known there was some military threat and Chuck would have taken off for the base. But all remained quiet, so our neighbors came over to our house and we listened to the radio by the fire as the kids played up and down the hall by candlelight. It was great fun actually.

We moved onto the base before Stephen was born. We had figured it would be easier to sell the house in the summer should we receive orders for a new assignment in the winter. After four years in a cold climate, Chuck was eligible for what they referred to as a "banana belt" transfer. Then in January of 1967 my father died and we all flew back to Dallas. I remember that the trunk lock froze and we had to finally remove the back seat of the car at the airport to get to our luggage.

I stayed in Dallas to be with Mother for a month or so after the funeral. I was reluctant to stay longer, since I was due in April. It seemed like I was sick from the time I returned to New York. I had pink eye the day of Butch's birthday party. I'd planned this lovely outer space theme complete with blue moon milk with lunch. Not one of the kids would drink it, even though it was only food coloring that did not affect the taste. And I thought I was being so clever!

The week before I was due to deliver, the Air Force sent Chuck to Florida for Water Survival School. I was furious. His parting words to me as I took him to the squadron were: "Don't have the baby until I get back," to which I screeched, "I will too!" Well, I didn't. He returned the following Sunday and I went into labor that afternoon.

I finished my laundry and all my household chores, showered and washed my hair before going to the hospital, which was just down the street. I was *not* going to spend 12 hours alone staring at a white wall and clock again. Much to Chuck's surprise, he was called within only a couple of hours to say the baby had been born. "Are you sure it's *my* wife? She doesn't work that fast," he said.

Mother sent me the most beautiful yellow roses this time. Always before I had gotten red ones. They were the envy of the entire ward. And the day before I was to be released from the hospital, I woke with a terrible headache. They were doing some sort of construction down the hall, hammering and making all kinds of racket. I had strep throat.

Chuck had come back with it from Florida, and he and the boys at home were all on antibiotics. They started me on a regimen too and had me nurse the baby with a mask on. If this was not enough to deal with, the woman from the state of New York kept coming in to see if I'd named the baby yet. Finally she told me he would go on the books as a junior if I didn't give her something different within x number of hours. Well, feeling pretty bitchy at that point, I simply said, fine—but there's already a junior.

I did finally have a conversation with Chuck about a name. We had girl names picked out, but not another boy name. I had really wanted to name the baby Shawn whether it was a boy or a girl, but for some reason Chuck hated that idea and was quite adamant about it. "You can name him anything *but* Shawn!" he told me. So I decided to give him my initials and named him Stephen Michael.

Poor little tyke—well, actually *not* so little. Chuck almost won the bet that he'd finally get an 8 pounder. Stephen weighed in at 7 pounds, 15 ounces. He had quite the chubby face. The first time I saw him though, I thought he was so ugly and dreaded taking him home and having to show him to anyone.

Of course, he was anything but ugly. It was my state of mind that was ugly. I must have cried for the first two weeks I was home from the hospital. Then I started seeing my father everywhere—once very clearly at my kitchen window. I had not yet grieved his death. I was focused on taking care of Mother and I think, afraid to grieve because of my pregnancy. It had taken the form of illness and then anger at Chuck and the military. Well, I was grieving now, but probably more appropriately now that I understood the root of all those feelings.

We all recovered from the strep. Stephen remained healthy the whole time. But I know he inherited a lot of grief in his little soul due to the trauma of his last months in utero and his first few challenging weeks with me. I made the mistake of telling him this story as an adult and within a week I received this adorable picture of him standing in his crib when he was several months old—hair all spiked in umpteen directions, chocolate all over his face from something one of his brothers had given him to eat, eyes still looking a tad sleepy—above which he'd written, *Who you callin' ugly?*

It's on my refrigerator now and I can't help but smile every time I see it. Everyone made over him whenever they saw him—he had this aura about him that people loved instantly. All my sons were beautiful boys!

We left New York when Stephen was three months old, heading west for California via Dallas in that brand new, ordered from the factory, nine-passenger Chevrolet station wagon. Had to show off our new addition to his grandparents before the next duty station.

Oxnard AFB was a short tour. We got into base housing pretty quickly. I remember Scott disappeared one afternoon. I was frantic and searching the neighborhood, about ready to call the police when he showed up. Apparently he'd gone inside to play with a new friend and lost track of the time. The little boy's mother told me later that he was playing contentedly when all of a sudden he stopped, got up and ran out saying *I gotta go.*

We took the older boys to Disneyland and the San Diego Zoo one weekend. Stephen was too young to go that trip so we left him with friends. We stayed at the hotel there in the park. It was quite the treat for us all.

I shared with Dave how the magic of that fantasyland had evaporated by July, however, when Chuck received those first orders for Vietnam. I found myself filled with a sense foreboding that I quickly stifled. When those orders were cancelled and we learned he would go to Otis AFB in Falmouth, Massachusetts instead, I breathed a huge sigh of relief! Good friends of ours there at Oxnard had been transferred there a couple months before, so we had a place to stay when we arrived. We did not have to wait long for base housing and a place of our own.

We loved Cape Cod. Every time Chuck was off, we were exploring a new area of that wondrous peninsula. Tom Jones was all the rage then—and for my birthday, Chuck took me into Boston to see him perform. What a terrific evening that was! We'd had so much fun in fact that we forgot to get gas before we left in the wee hours of the morning. All the way back to the base, we went through our list of friends, wondering who would come out in the middle of the night should we get stranded. But, we made it home fine. Chuck took the sitter home. Then the next morning, on his way to work he ran out of gas at the bottom of the hill.

Chuck's parents came to visit us there around Stephen's second birthday. I know Chuck really enjoyed touring them around the base. There was an air show and event of some sort going on at the time. And we experienced preparation for a hurricane during this tour. Chuck was home for a change and helped secure everything down for our fourplex.

Then we waited behind the couch for it to hit. By some miracle, it turned and headed for Martha's Vineyard and missed us. As soon as it changed course, Chuck wanted to drive to the water and watch it. Though I thought he was crazy, I succumbed to his sense of adventure and off we went. As long as we were together, I felt safe.

After only 15 months Chuck received orders once again—this time for training in the F-4E for his Southeast Asia assignment. He was delighted to be staying in Fighters. For years now, the military had used two pilots in the F-4. Now they were opening that backseat up to radar observers. We were off to Tucson for the classroom segment, then on to George AFB, in the high desert area of California, for the actual cockpit training. And as usual, we came through Dallas again to visit family. We were in Tucson for Thanksgiving. I had the challenge of preparing turkey and dressing on a couple of motel stove burners.

We spent two months in an apartment in Arizona, and six months on base in California. I remember our washer and dryer were on the back patio and we had to be vigilant about black widow spiders. Our neighbor had gotten bitten and was quite sick. We all enjoyed the regular schedule training provided. Every evening after dinner we would all ride our bikes. Stephen was small enough so he was on a seat behind me. Then we'd have ice cream at home.

There was one really bad dust storm during that period. I never knew sand could seep through the windows and doors and walls. I thought I'd choke from the smell before it was over. And afterward everything was coated with sand and there were little piles under the windows.

Chuck graduated Top Gun from his class (not surprising!) and we all enjoyed watching him perform at the big base celebration in June of 1970. We made the trip back to Texas one big vacation, taking in Disneyland, the big meteorite crater in Arizona, the Grand Canyon and Carlsbad. Once back in Dallas there were hordes of family to visit with before Chuck's departure to Clarke AFB for water survival training before heading on to Korat AFB in Thailand.

The fear about this Southeast Asia tour that I'd felt at Oxnard two years earlier resurfaced with his new orders. And again, I could never bring myself to discuss it with Chuck. I remember him talking to me one night as we lay in bed about how the kind of war he fought from the F-4E was not like that of the ground soldier in hand to hand combat.

"While I'll be flying into a target area, dropping bombs in a matter of minutes, and heading back to air-conditioned hooch, I know the devastation and death left behind from my missions. I can't help but be changed by such an experience." He was telling me to prepare for him being perhaps different after his tour. Even with that opening, I remained silent. It was as if I was afraid that if I talked about this sense of foreboding, I would make it a reality somehow. So I would not give lend voice to this nebulous fear. Keeping it secret, however, did not eradicate its power.

Chuck had been in Florida TDY for over a month during the Cuban Missile Crisis years earlier, but the fear I felt then was about my safety, not Chuck's. During our interview, I told Dave about how, in contrast, I had immediately felt a deep angst about Chuck's first orders for Southeast Asia that never went away. It was different also from the fear I had felt at Griffiss AFB after the second F-101 crashed during our first three months there. That was about him flying. What I felt about his Vietnam tour was a deep foreboding, not that he would be killed, but that everything was not going to go as planned somehow.

My answer to pushing that fear down was to stay incredibly busy. I became active in my church, joined the PTA and served as treasurer, became a Cub Scout den leader so Charles could join the Scouts, took an art class at the YMCA, all while running the household and getting kids to and from school.

Those frenetic eighteen-hour days came to a screeching halt after Thanksgiving when I came down with Bell's palsy and couldn't drive because I had to wear a patch over my good eye that was not blinking due to paralysis on left side of my face.

By then I was beginning to feel less fearful about Chuck's safety and looking forward to Christmas with all the family. It would be the first ever with all the grandparents. Chuck's sister, Wanda and her two kids were living with the Strattons at the time after her divorce. My brother and his wife were coming up from Rice, Texas, so Olin could play Santa in Chuck's place, assembling toys that needed it.

Mother and I had great fun decorating the house. She'd not done much of that since my father died in '67. The boys and I thoroughly enjoyed preparing a Christmas box for their daddy. I'd ordered little lightweight metal Christmas ornaments—stars hanging free inside a wreath with our names on them to hang on this little artificial tree. The boys picked out a faux black lizard bedspread for his bed because he'd written about all the geckos that came crawling down the walls of his hooch to greet him. And they chose some Peanuts banners for his walls to remind him of them as well. We'd dubbed Charles as our Charlie Brown, Scott as Linus with his blanket sucking his thumb, and Stephen as Schroeder at his little play piano.

We celebrated Christmas Eve at the Strattons because Jean said they always went to her mother's on Christmas day. That was fine by me. Chuck and I always wanted the boys to be able to enjoy all they fun gifts from Santa on Christmas morning. Eurcil assured the boys he'd come by our house on their way home from Greenville to see their Santa haul.

Our Christmas morning was relaxed and great fun with just my immediate family. Mother and Olin thoroughly enjoyed seeing the boys' sleepy and surprised faces upon first glimpse of all Santa had left for them.

By early afternoon the boys started asking for their grandpa Eurcil. "When's Papa coming?" they asked me every hour or so.

When darkness settled in with no Papa in sight, I called. I was feeling worried at that point that something might have happened to them. But no, they answered the phone and come to find out had been home all day.

Jean had decided she didn't feel like driving to Greenville. I was stunned at that revelation at first, but by the time I hung up the phone, I was furious. That they'd never even called the boys to tell them Merry Christmas, let alone come to see them as promised. All afternoon I'd had to watch their disappointed little faces as I repeated over and over again, "I don't know," to their queries about their Papa.

I swore to myself that evening it would be a cold day in hell before I darkened their door again. If they wanted to see us they'd have to come here. I did not say that to the kids, or to Chuck in my nightly letter. I wrote only about the boys' delight with all their Christmas toys and mine with the gorgeous carved teak jewelry box and grape-cluster emerald ring he'd sent me.

We were already counting the days until his six month R&R in February. He wanted me to meet him in Hawaii for our tenth wedding anniversary. It was far more pleasant to entertain that fantasy than give any more time or energy to Jean and Eurcil before turning out the light that night.

At this point my mouth was quite dry from so much talking. I asked Dave if he'd like some tea or coffee or water. While I was in the kitchen I pulled out my scrapbooks with all the communications from the military that January to peruse until I was back with my tea. Then I resumed my story of that fateful morning I got the telegram saying Chuck was missing.

CHAPTER 7

ENTERING LIMBO

DAY 1 or Monday, January 4, 1971

Startled awake by the doorbell that first Monday morning of the New Year, I bolted out of bed. It was only 6 a.m. Mother must have overslept, I thought, and her ride had come to the door. I grabbed my robe and raced to answer it. As I opened the hallway door, I saw that Mother had beaten me to it. There *he* was—a looming figure in Air Force blues, so tall he was visible over Mother's head and outlined her silhouette. My heart stopped for a moment. How many times had I secretly imagined that figure in the doorway and wondered how I'd respond? Mother was unlocking the glass storm door, inviting him in when I entered the living room.

"I've come about your husband," he said, looking at me as I started to move forward a bit.

I thought to myself, *what a lame remark. What else would you be doing here this time of day? Just tell me what it is you have to say.* The only words that escaped from of my mouth, however, were a polite "Please have a seat," as I motioned to the couch.

He opened his folder and pulled out a telegram and read to me:

IT IS WITH DEEP PERSONAL REGRET THAT I OFFICIALLY INFORM YOU THAT YOUR HUSBAND

71

CAPTAIN CHARLES W. STRATTON IS MISSING IN ACTION IN SOUTHEAST ASIA.

3 January, routine mission, second pass, huge fireball explosion, no beepers heard, no chutes seen, extensive search—the words droned on in my ears which felt like they were filled with cotton. Strange, I knew something was wrong, but I also knew he was not going to tell me Chuck was dead, which is the first thing a military wife thinks of when she sees a uniform at her front door unannounced and he's flying.

In a protective shell of numbness past that first sentence, time stood still as I sat on that familiar turquoise '50s Danish Modern sectional—the very place where I'd so willingly surrendered my virginity to Chuck some ten years before. The sergeant sat to my right, Mother on my left. Emotion was frozen somewhere in my body, lost in the cold darkness of that awful morning. *Missing in Action. Missing. JUST missing. Good,* I thought. *Then there's hope.*

We talked a few minutes. He was trying to be as helpful as he could under the circumstances, but of course he couldn't answer the big question looming now about Chuck's survival. He re-iterated that within 24 hours someone from Perrin Air Force Base would call to assist me in any way possible. And there was a number in the telegram I could call if I had further questions.

"Have you notified Chuck's parents?" I asked.

"Not yet. I am on my way from here to do that," he replied.

"No, you can't go to the house now. His mother Jean will be alone and his father Eurcil is already at the Post Office sorting his route. Can you find him first? Let him be the one to break the news to her? I'm really worried about how she'll react. She went to bed and cried for days after Chuck left for Southeast Asia."

In the moment, I swallowed my anger toward Jean, feeling instead only compassion for her. Sergeant Morgan agreed and asked just where he could find my father-in-law. Then off he went with their telegram.

The boys were sleeping quietly in the front bedroom as I struggled to wrap my mind around the scenario. Mother and I decided to wake them at their normal time and get them ready for the day as usual. Why put them through this anxiety of uncertainty just yet? Maybe this afternoon we'd know what to tell them. In the meantime I needed to pull myself together, be strong for them, and carry on until we got more information.

Mother's mind engaged far more quickly than mine in terms of what to do next. She called her workplace to say she was staying home all day, then called my brother Olin before he left for work. Living only a few blocks away, he was there by the time the boys were eating their breakfast cereal. I was still in my robe, a wonderfully warm white furry winter favorite. Olin offered to take the older boys to school while I got dressed. I was relieved to have a few minutes alone. I couldn't let Stephen see me cry. Thank God Mother was there to help keep him occupied and unaware that his father's plane had crashed.

She called her closest sister, my Aunt Nita, for some moral support along with our nextdoor neighbor, Lydia. Lydia's husband Louis Canright was a minister, and God knows we needed all the prayers we could muster while we waited. From those two calls, the word spread rapidly amongst all our family and friends. Mid-morning the postman came, and there was my eagerly awaited daily letter from Chuck. It felt so strange, surreal and painful to hear his voice speaking from the page as I wondered where he was at that moment.

How I treasured his letters. I'd never have made it these last five months if I'd not been able to read them over and over again. I could hear his voice as I read each one. The first part was always newsy and written for the whole family, special greetings for each son, responding to their experiences here in Pleasant Grove shared in our last letter to him. He would warn me then when I was to stop reading aloud and retreat to savor his special loving words for my eyes only. He wrote very openly and explicitly about his sexual desires and fantasies.

By afternoon the house began to fill with concerned friends, many bringing food to sustain us as we waited. I learned from Jerry, my closest cousin, that his mother, Aunt Nita, hadn't been surprised to get Mother's call this morning. She had awakened in the night and knew Chuck was in great danger. She envisioned him in a small dark cell. Given that premonitions were nothing new to Aunt Nita and that her dream had occurred before we knew that his plane had crashed, I really latched on to the hope that he had survived. I certainly preferred to believe that he might be a POW than that he had gone down with that F-4. I had the utmost confidence that he could survive in a POW camp. I also believed that if he were dead, I would feel it somehow. No, I was certain that he was alive.

When it was time to collect the boys from school, Jerry volunteered to go so that I could stay by the phone. But it remained silent no matter how desperately I wanted it to ring with good news that Chuck had been rescued. Charles and Scott bounced in through the back door as usual, clamoring for their after-school snack and raring to get back outside to play after being cooped up in school all day.

By late afternoon I began to feel the urge to call them in to tell them about their dad. I didn't want them hearing the news from anyone but me—and especially not on television. We always watched the evening news, and I had no idea if there would be anything released to the media or not. I dreaded the task. After Chuck telling him he was the man of the house now and needed to look after the rest of us, I wondered if Charles would feel really burdened now. Scott was always so quiet. I never knew what he was thinking behind those big brown eyes. Stephen had tried to stop his daddy from leaving.

I interrupted their play with their neighborhood friends and led them into my small bedroom in the back of the house where I had been sleeping when the doorbell shattered my dreams. I sat down on the floor in front of the closet with them so I could look into their little faces.

"I imagine you are wondering why all these people are here this afternoon?" I started. "They've all come to be here with us because Daddy's plane crashed last night, and the Air Force is still searching for him."

Words tumbled from my mouth matter-of-factly without tears. I felt that I had to stay calm and positive with this scary news. More than anything, I wanted to instill them with the hope I so needed. I reminded them that their daddy was highly trained in survival and could take care of himself if he got out of the plane. We would just continue to pray for his safety and wait for further news. Given that I refused to let in the possibility that Chuck could be dead, I emphasized only the positive. I assumed that my strategy was successful. Charles' only response was, "Can we go back outside and play now?" Was he mirroring my denial? Had I not sent them off that morning as if nothing unusual had happened? He was certainly following my lead, being perfectly willing to carry on as always with our normal routine. And his brothers followed after him.

Eventually everyone was gone, and we were left alone to settle in for the evening. We had survived our first day of uncertainty. Maybe tomorrow would bring us welcome news. The boys bathed and put on their jammies, ready to climb into their beds—Charles on the top bunk, Stephen underneath him, and Scott in the trundle below. Stephen was the youngest, and should have been relegated to the trundle, but he feared an imaginary wolf dog that lurked there in the dark of night.

I can't remember just when he first encountered that wolf dog. Chuck had tried to convince him that the animal was just a bad dream, but he would have none of that. He was sure the creature was quite real. Charles fanned his fantasy by pointing out the little wooden ladder from Stephen's favorite Fisher Price Circus Wagon that was indeed out there in the middle of the floor where Stephen had seen the wolf dog carry it.

Chuck finally suggested that Scott switch beds with his little brother. Ever ready to please his daddy, Scott agreed to give up his lowerbunk for the trundle. Satisfied that he would be safe enough there in the middle, Stephen gladly agreed with the arrangement.

Mother had retired to her bedroom on the other side of the house, and I retreated to mine down the hall from the boys. I was more than ready now for my evening ritual—reading some of my favorite love letters that I kept in the headboard of my bed. Chuck was quite the romantic and freely expressed his love to me when we were apart. Often he closed with *more than yesterday, less than tomorrow, I love you.*

I actually chuckled at his admission in one letter that I had spoiled him by bringing him coffee in bed each morning. He apologized for taking me for granted and added that he hadn't been able to convince the Thai maid who cleaned his hooch to provide that service.

DAY 2 or Tuesday, January 5th

What's that noise? No—not yet—I see Chuck in the cockpit and want to stay with him… damn that alarm! It can't be morning already. I just fell asleep.

What day is it? My mind queries as I struggle to get my bearings, not wanting to leave Chuck in my dreams.

The unwelcome images from yesterday quickly jolted my groggy stupor. Chuck was missing. Surely we'd hear something today. Coffee—I needed coffee! I'd be making the school run that morning since everyone was going back to work as usual. I needed to keep things as normal as possible for the boys and for me. I told them the night before that everything would be okay. I needed to act as if that was really true.

Dear God, please give me the strength to carry on as we wait for news of Chuck. Protect him and keep him safe. May he feel our love and prayers wherever he is right now. Thank you for Mother and her unwavering calm support—for all my wonderful family and friends who are keeping us in their prayers.

It had been over 48 hours since Chuck's plane crashed with no more news. How I longed to be rid of the torture of this uncertainty. It took me longer to put on my optimistic face before waking the boys that morning. I was thankful for the small comfort of the school routine. It helped me forget, even so briefly, about that silent phone.

And so began day two, one I needed to treat as any other, taking care of all of my commitments, keeping myself too busy to dwell on the possibility of losing Chuck, just being a mom running a household. Mother and I spoke briefly before her ride to work came. I was to call her immediately if I heard anything, even though I might not, she told me. Good old pragmatic realistic Mom, trying to ward off potential disappointment.

The boys were unusually quiet at breakfast that morning. I doubted they had a clue about what to say or ask at this point. We just needed to keep up our normal routine while we waited for news, I told them. I assured them that if I did get any news, I would come and get them and tell them immediately. Right now, we would all need to be strong for Daddy, keep thinking good thoughts, and ask God to protect him. Good little soldiers that they were, they obediently got dressed so they wouldn't be late for school.

I dropped Charles off at Adams, then Scott at Little Folks. Stephen was in the front seat with me then, all strapped in with the seatbelt—his little head not yet high enough to see out the window. As we drove home he mumbled something in such a quiet voice I didn't understand what he said.

"What was that, sweetie?" I asked him.

"It's my fault," he said again.

"Your fault? What's your fault? What are you talking about?"

"I should never have unlocked the door and let him go," his sad and serious voice replied. I was so taken aback I had to pull over and stop the car after this stunning revelation. I looked directly into his little face with eyes down cast.

"Look at me Stephen. Oh no baby—it's not your fault. Daddy had to go. You couldn't stop that. Remember how he told you it was his job—just like Grandma has to get up and go off to work every day? So did your daddy. Stephen, it is *not* your fault—do you hear me?"

He nodded his little head, but his eyes still looked so sad, like his favorite Eeyore stuffed animal with the button-on tail. I hugged him and kissed his forehead and we sat there for another minute before continuing the drive back home to stay close to the phone.

It was shocking to me that Stephen could possibly think he was to blame for his daddy's plane crashing because he agreed to let him go away that morning. The limbo was taking its toll on the boys too it seemed. I was glad I would have more time with him alone that day to let him know I was there for him and he could always come and talk to me when he was feeling sad or scared, or to reiterate, if need be, that none of this was his fault. I would remind him that our job now was to ask God to take care of his daddy.

He brought his little circus wagon and animals into the den, as I turned on the television for my morning trimnastics with Jack LaLanne. Gotta stay fit, *young, youthful and beautiful,* as Jack was fond of saying, for Chuck. Continuing with my usual daily routine helped keep my mind off the anxiety of uncertainty. After my workout, I prepared for my Cub Scout den meeting that afternoon after school, but made sure I also took time to play with Stephen too.

Then the postman brought another letter from Chuck. He wrote to me every day, as I did to him. Mail took at least five days to travel from Thailand to Texas. Even knowing that it had been mailed well before his plane crashed, it still felt comforting to read his words, offering the illusion that he was still alive somewhere in the jungles of Laos and not lost to me forever.

The phone never rang.

DAY 3 or Wednesday, January 6th

My next official communiqué from the Air Force was another telegram, hand delivered, informing me that organized search activities were impossible due to the area being extremely hostile. Other aircraft traversing the area had been unsuccessful in picking up any signals. They would continue to make every effort to determine his status.

"Your husband's commander will write you a letter, which will contain all the known circumstances concerning the incident in approximately ten days."

By the end of the week, my final letter from Chuck was mailed to me by the summary courts officer appointed to pack up his personal belongings and send them home. It was still in the tablet on his desk, waiting for him to finish when he returned from that last mission. It was the one in which he described a big champagne celebration on the runway to welcome back a pilot and his back-seater who had spent the night on a hill in the Plain of Jars surrounded by the enemy until a rescue team got them out the next morning.

I had actually read about that incident in the newspaper here: "An Air Force F-4 Phantom fighter-bomber was shot down on a support mission near the Plain of Jars in North Central Laos on Saturday. The two crewmen of the $2.5 million jet that can carry seven tons of bombs at 1,600 miles per hour were rescued, the command said."

This party must have taken place the morning of Chuck's final mission. What I deduced from the commander's letter was that if Chuck had ejected before impact on Sunday night, his primary objective would have been to stay hidden from the enemy until daylight. He would not necessarily have set off an immediate signal, as the enemy would have been alerted to his location before any rescue attempt could be made.

I dreamed of Chuck again, a powerful dream that felt so real, it gave me comfort that has stayed with me to this day, the image as vivid as the first time I experienced it.

In the dream, Chuck was standing behind a barbed wire fence with concertina across the top. It was daylight. He was wearing a green camouflage flight suit and he looked tired, but also very much at peace, sporting a scruffy beard of several days. We were too far away from each other to speak, but our eyes met, and he communicated quite clearly to me—we'll be together again but it will be a long, long time.

After the dream, I knew in the depths of my soul that he was alive and would come back to me. Overflowing with hope, I waited.

CHAPTER 8

FINDING SUPPORT

From the Commander's letter the following week I learned the actual time of the incident. It was 10:30 p.m. when they commenced that first pass over the target area. That would have been 10:30 a.m. Dallas time. We had been in church at that moment. I had been notified in less than 24 hours of the crash. Col. Jarvis wrote that while no one witnessed any ejection or parachutes, *darkness could have precluded such sightings.* A detailed report was being prepared for forward to the Casualty Division, United States Air Force Military Personnel Center, Randolph Air Force Base in San Antonio.

Within days then, I received a call from the Casualty Office at Randolph that would be my contact point from then on. The officer wanted to make sure my needs were being met. He gave me information about the National League of Families of American Prisoners and Missing in Southeast Asia. Shirley Johnson in Plano was the North Texas Coordinator. He asked me if I would I like to contact her. "Absolutely!" I told him without hesitation.

I phoned her immediately and learned that there were eight other POW/MIA wives in the Metroplex area. Her husband, Sam, had been a POW for almost five years by then. Much to my delight, she set up a meeting at her home to acquaint me with the other local wives and the activities of the League. I felt elated after our conversion. Relating my story and hearing hers, talking to another woman who had survived this same limbo and remained positive in her attitude really lifted my spirit. I couldn't wait to meet her.

My hopes were further buoyed with that meeting at Shirley's. Three of the local wives knew their husbands were POWs, but that had not been the case when their planes were first shot down. The rest were MIA wives like me. All had been shot down in the late 1960s.

Military wives have always been a mainstay of support for one another. Our guys were away from home a lot flying missions and pulling alert. This was my not my first experience with waiting wives. However, I had been out of the military community for more than six months now, surrounded only by civilians. I felt connected to these women, and gathered courage from them and the fact that they had survived for years now with the fate of their husbands unknown.

Knowing your husband was a POW, I learned from these women, offered no certainty either. Communication with them was sparse and had only come in recent months. Bonnie Singleton had just received a letter from her husband in March of 1970, even though he had been a POW since 1965. Chuck was still in the 4452 Combat Crew Training Squadron at George Air Force Base in California at that time.

It was Joy Jeffrey's story that impacted me the most that evening. Her husband's wingman had told her that there was no way Bob could have survived. His plane had taken a direct hit from a strategic air missile in broad daylight over North Vietnam and blown up before his very eyes. No chutes seen. Yet his name appeared on a POW list sometime later. His back seater's name, however, did not.

Joy told me to never give up hope. Bob had miraculously survived when even his wingman that witnessed the hit and said it was impossible. I knew if anyone could survive in a POW camp, it was Chuck. Of that I had absolutely no doubt. The man had such a brilliant mind filled with all sorts of trivia, he could easily amuse himself for years, even if he were held in solitary confinement.

The known POWs had been held for years before being acknowledged by the North Vietnamese. No prisoners had ever been identified by the Pathet Lao, though it was known that they had taken prisoners. So how in the world could I not continue to hope that Chuck was still alive and being held captive? I had always believed in miracles, and if anyone ever deserved a miracle, it was Chuck. So that was the story I chose to inhabit, the story that would allow me to survive the not knowing.

Having Chuck with me daily in our three sons was ultimately the reason I would survive. How difficult was it for them? How do children cope with *missing in action*? They are such concrete, literal creatures. I reasoned that they could only follow my lead and live the story I chose to believe.

President Nixon was already talking about "the light at the end of the tunnel." I figured I would have to endure this status for maybe two years at most. If these strong, positive women I had just met had already survived for five years as POW/MIA wives, I could certainly handle two years. They hadn't had the support of one another and an entire League of Families when they entered those circumstances. I was so fortunate to have them in my life from the beginning of my ordeal. This was the story I told my sons—that we just needed to hang in there for a couple of years because it was going to take that long to get him back home.

The January 20th, 1971 issue of the *Air Force Times* listed Chuck and Jim in their brief Combat Casualties article as missing in action. The very next day, I received a letter from the Department of the Air Force that Chuck had been selected for promotion to major, though they did not know the effective date. I would receive a copy of the orders when they were issued.

"The announcement of his selection will not be released to the news media nor will his name appear on the list of selected distributed throughout the Air Force. Our rationale for withholding this information is to assure that it may not be used to subject him to any additional pressure or stress in the event he is being held captive."

But when I received my *Air Force Times* for February 3rd there was Chuck's name, big as life in the article "2470 Named for 0-4 Hike." 04 equals major in the Air Force ranks.

Within the week I received a letter from PJ, the officer and friend who had gathered Chuck's belongings together to return to me. He said I should be getting the stuff soon if I hadn't already, and he didn't think he'd missed anything.

"I don't know exactly what they told you, but they went down in enemy territory north of Tchepone near a truck storage area. Nobody on our side has had ground troops in that area in a long time. I don't know if they will get that far north on this drive. A S.A.R. wasn't started because there was never any radio communications or any sort of signal.

"The crash site was photographed, but as I've said above, there is no way to get enough ground troops there long enough to make a conclusive search. You asked what the chances are that he got out… very slim. I hope and pray that there is a chance, but in all honesty, I don't believe there is…I'm not sure how long he'll be listed as MIA, it could take as long as seven years or as short as 90 days, but you'll receive his full pay as long as he is listed as MIA.

"I'm sure I haven't answered all your questions. If you have any more, I don't think they're so jumpy now. Security plays a role, but it's ridiculous to think that we aren't in Laos. They're also trying to give the facts, which can often be confusing. If you have any questions or problems, please write me."

I was filled with questions and had already written to another of our friends there at Korat who had been in training with us stateside. I thought he might give me answers that had not been forthcoming from other authorities. But weeks passed, and I received no reply from him.

When Chuck's letters stopped, others began to come in from old military friends who had heard the news, all offering support and prayers. My favorite came from Lynn, the first military wife I had connected with at James Connally in Waco when Chuck was training as a RIO. We had then gone through our first two pregnancies together at McClellan Air Force Base in Sacramento, and then Griffiss Air Force Base in New York. Her husband, Nobby, had been transferred to the Philippines two years before we left Griffiss. She wrote, "Know lots of 'no chutes seen' survivors. Our tour at Clark taught us never to give up hope when there's no proof. Chuck is probably swearing at the USAF for assuming they can't get in there easily—probably been sleeping and eating rice and playing it cool. God we hope so."

Simultaneously I received another note from a military wife I'd also known in New York that began, "There are no words to express our sorrow over Chuck's death. Dick was stunned to hear of it when he arrived at Korat. I know you are devastated but also know you will pick up the pieces and carry on." She included a poem that had appeared in the *Air Force Times*, "To a Pilot's Widow."

My overall reaction to her letter, however, was anger. I knew in my heart that this wife was relaying what the guys at Korat thought—indeed what Chuck himself would have said to me, given the report of this incident. I could almost hear him giving this same conclusion thus: *so-and-so bought the farm today.*

But that was not the stance I was going to take now, no matter how bleak the few known facts read. Chuck himself had come to me in my dream to tell me otherwise. I would not let go of that hope.

I finally received a detailed letter from Chuck's Squadron Commander dated February 18th, 1971—our 10th wedding anniversary. It was obvious he had been given my letter to the so-called friend that had never been answered. Every question I had posed was covered systematically. I felt even angrier when I later learned that it had been forbidden for any of the others there to write to me. Colonel Stewart introduced himself as a "personal friend of Chuck's" and reiterated that the "Men in Black [his squadron] shared my grief and hope." Actually there was no grief yet from my perspective—only hope—and therein lay the crux of any "normal" resolution.

After the usual assurances that our missing men were not forgotten, he prefaced the account with, "No positive facts are known about the details of Chuck's accident. I was assured that his pilot was one of the most highly qualified...yet to be assigned to this unit." He then proceeded to explain to me the normal procedure for night missions.

"The dry pass is not mandatory but used by many pilots, especially at night, when target identification is difficult." January 3rd was a moonless night to boot. Well, that certainly cleared up the question of no ordinance being dropped on that first pass. It did not necessarily mean there was a problem with the aircraft. But, of course, mechanical failure was still a possibility for the crash on the second pass. Enemy ground fire was another. While none was observed from either the Forward Air Controller in the area or the second F-4, random small arms fire through the jungle canopy is practically impossible to detect and was capable of bringing an aircraft down.

Pilot error such as target fixation was also a possibility. In a two-seated aircraft, both crewmen are aware of the minimum altitude from which a safe recovery can be made. Chuck's primary job as the back-seater on a bomb pass was to monitor altitude, dive angle and air speed. "I have flown combat missions with Chuck in my back seat," he wrote, "and I feel very strongly, based on Chuck's superior performance, that unless he was distracted by some extremely critical occurrence that he would not allow any pilot to just fly into the ground. But, no matter how we feel about pilot error, the possibility must be considered."

The crash site was near the target, definitely in the target area, and was fixed by the number two aircraft that remained in the area without dropping ordinance until fuel dictated its return to Korat. The Forward Air Controller plane remained in the area for about two and a half hours, monitoring for any signals from the crew.

Neither aircraft observed an ejection or parachutes. All radio attempts at contact after the crash were unsuccessful. "All crew members are equipped with survival radios and beeper capabilities. The automatic beeper is optional. Most crews choose not to use the automatic beeper for two good reasons. It blocks out all other transmissions, especially if there is no time to turn it off, and secondly it could pinpoint your position to the enemy. On flights I had with Chuck, he chose not to use the automatic beeper. I can assume he did the same for every mission."

I certainly concurred with his assessment. His answers were exactly what I had expected them to be. You can't be a military wife for ten years without having a pretty good idea what your husband's missions entail. I had a map of Southeast Asia over my bed, and Chuck would write me coordinates I could look up and mark.

Commander Stewart said he'd put off writing sooner, hoping they would have more facts. I could understand that logic. It was mine when I sent my sons off to school that morning I received the news. He summed up the reality I would have to live with, like it or not—lots of questions deserving of answers that were unfortunately unavailable. He only had theories and speculation.

A couple of weeks after that letter from Col. Stewart, I received two letters, both written on March 5th, one from Hippy, the friend I had written to for answers, apologizing for being so long answering my letter and explaining that he'd had no alternative but to turn it over to the Squadron Commander.

"PJ said he's written to you and that he had a letter disapproved.

So he wrote another one anyway. Guys have gotten in deep trouble for writing to next of kin on any information regarding incidents whether the information was true or not. Such a great guy like Chuck will never be replaced in our hearts. All of us guys here at Korat miss him dearly and have deep sympathy for you and family."

That explained why PJ's letter back in February was posted from his stateside residence and not Thailand. He'd sent it through his wife after his first one had been disapproved.

The other was a lovely letter from Brenda Ayres. I had called my Casualty Officer after learning who Chuck's pilot was to make contact with his family. Brenda was amenable to me calling her. Both she and her husband Jim were also native Texans. They had met in Lubbock, her hometown, when he was at Texas Tech.

Our life situations were similar on many levels. They, too, had three children—they had two boys and a girl. Jim's parents lived close by in Pampa. She had felt there was something wrong before she was notified of the crash. She now shared what she had learned from a friend at Korat who had been Jim's regular GIB—guy in back. He'd been to Taiwan over the holidays and was out on crew rest so didn't fly that night. He told her that the circumstances weren't good, but there was always a chance.

"We can't give up hope," she wrote. Her biggest worry was that there were no beepers. "We'll just have to keep our fingers crossed. One day I feel that Jim and Chuck are alive and then the next day I'll feel just the opposite. I'm sure you know what I'm talking about. I've never had such mixed emotions."

Actually, I had never thought that Chuck was dead. My head told me that was a possibility, but my heart wouldn't entertain the notion. That's how strong my connection with him was from my dream.

I thought back to that awful foreboding I felt each time he'd received orders for a Vietnam assignment. At the military briefing for the wives before we departed George AFB, they had prepared us regarding what documents we would need to keep while our husbands were overseas and what we needed to know if they should be killed or possibly captured.

Oddly, I asked specifically what to expect if we didn't know for sure, though I had no conscious premonition about a missing in action scenario. Perhaps knowing that my only cousin on my father's side of the family had been MIA in WWII brought that to mind.

Obviously, somewhere deep within my psyche I knew.

This was Jim's second tour in Vietnam. He'd flown C-123s out of Saigon in 1967. He was thrilled to be flying the F-4E and considered it the only airplane to fly. He and Chuck were alike in that regard. She told me she'd just received a notice that Jim's personal effects had arrived, and she was going to pick them up that afternoon.

We both received the guys' belongings that first week of March. Each had purchased tape decks and speakers while in Thailand. In Chuck's footlocker were other local purchases he'd made—a couple of large velvet wall hangings and a new camera, plus his clothes and personal items, including his wedding ring. Chuck never flew with it on, not since he caught it on an F-101 canopy once at Griffiss Air Force Base and cut his ring finger.

Also there were all the things we had sent him for Christmas to brighten up his room. The boys had thought he'd love Snoopy flying his doghouse on the wall over his bed.

I received another letter from the Washington, D.C. Personnel Directorate around mid-March recapping the known details of Chuck's incident and officially acknowledging the actual location of the crash site 28 miles northwest of Tchepone, Laos. I could now circle that spot on the map over my bed. I had a visible place for Chuck. So close to the DMZ, it was easy to imagine him being taken north to Hanoi via the Ho Chi Minh Trail.

No other communication from the Air Force the rest of that year added anything new to the information I had now been given.

The National League of Families, incorporated only the year before, however, added lots of information new for me, stories and facts that convinced me of the necessity for activism. I was embarrassed to admit, as the wife of a career military officer who most certainly would eventually be called to serve in Vietnam, how little I knew of our history in that country or the plight of our POWs and MIAs when Chuck received his orders for the F-4 assignment.

CHAPTER 9

A NEW MISSION

I joined the National League of Families of American Prisoners and Missing in Southeast Asia after that meeting at Shirley's. I wanted to be a part of the action these amazing women who advocated for their husbands, fed up with just sitting and waiting, of being quiet about their husband's plight. "Don't do anything to jeopardize either the delicate negotiations being conducted or the lives of your loved ones"[6] had been the Administration's policy for POW/MIA families in the '60s.

Wanting a communications network for greater exchange of information amongst the families, Sybil Stockdale, wife of a senior naval Officer held in North Vietnam since 1965, began contacting wives across the country asking them to serve as area coordinators and seek out others to affiliate with them. By 1969, her perseverance led to the formation of a National League of Families that was officially incorporated on May 28th, 1970.

Chuck was just finishing up his F-4 training at that time. I was incredibly fortunate to have had the already organized Dallas wives take me under their wing within a week of my learning Chuck was MIA, so I never felt the isolation my predecessors experienced in the early years.

I was immediately given the opportunity to participate with our North Texas chapter. February 12th, 1971, some one hundred Texas family members convened at the State Capitol in Austin to visit the Texas Legislators. It was the first such meeting of its kind for families to discuss future activities to help free POWs and focus public attention again on the plight of POW/MIAs. Bonnie Singleton addressed the joint legislative session, along with Ross Perot, founder and board chair of United We Stand, Inc. I met with Congressman Olin Teague that day and still have a little penknife he presented us that afternoon. I had never done any sort of lobbying before and found the experience exhilarating. It really did lift my spirits to feel as though I was "doing" something to bring about an answer regarding Chuck's fate.

The first National Week of Concern for Prisoners of War-Missing in Action was set to begin Sunday, March 21st, 1971, six years and 361 days since the first U.S. serviceman was imprisoned in Southeast Asia. The League asked Americans to show their concern through specific daily activities, the very first one urging the public to write letters asking for POWs release to Mrs. Nguyen Thi Binh, South Vietnamese Liberation Front (Viet Cong) and Xuan Thuy, North Vietnam, both in care of the Paris Peace Talks.

The *Dallas Morning News* ran feature stories every day that week covering the issue. Monday morning the headline read: "Flier's Family Maintains Hope," our story made public for the first time. There we were on the front page, standing on our front porch, the American flag flying behind us, me in a patriotic red, white and blue jumpsuit, hair piled high on top of my head, holding Stephen, who was not at all a happy camper about being photographed in my left arm, my right around Charles Jr. with a happy smiling face, and Scott, more pensive, in the foreground sporting a USS Galveston cap, playing with a GI Joe doll perched on the handlebars of his tricycle. And Doug Domeier captured the essence of the path I had chosen to follow in his title: one of *hope*.

Mayor Jonsson proclaimed this week as Dallas Week of Concern as well, and I was a spokesperson to the City Council that Monday morning, reminding them that almost 75 service men from North Texas were listed as missing in action or prisoner of war. That March event thrust me into the public eye of the POW/MIA issue and set my course of action for the next two years. I wanted to awaken Dallas to action as I had been.

Tuesday the headline read: "Dallas Cares to Be Launched As

Local Aid in POW Fight." Bonnie Singleton told the reporter, "It's hard for the POW wives and families to know what's right and go about things in an effective and efficient way. The organization, run and staffed entirely by volunteers, will coordinate the city's efforts to free the POWs…to oversee projects (as drives, observances and campaigns). Also envisioned is a speakers' bureau…."

I knew I wanted to be a part of that speakers' bureau when Dallas Cares was officially launched. I had taken speech in high school and done relatively well in extemporaneous competition. But I had my work cut out for me then, lots of homework for me to be able to present an accurate picture of the current state of affairs. I could certainly field questions from a personal perspective, but tended to present a more factual, objective view, holding my personal feelings or emotions at bay.

In April the Delta Zeta Sorority at Southern Methodist University organized an Easter Egg Hunt and party for the children of the area POW/MIAs featuring an impressive seven-foot tall Easter Bunny to fill in for the absent fathers. Stephen was the baby of the hunt. This was the first of many wonderful gestures my boys received from organizations wanting to help make up for their dad's absence. A very memorable occasion was when the National Guard at Navy Air Station took them on an overnight camping trip. The general himself took Stephen under his wing because he was so young.

Come nightfall when they were bedding down for the night, the general told Stephen good night and proceeded to carry the lantern back out of the tent. He was stopped and completely taken aback when Stephen said, "I guess you know I sleep with a night-light." We had quite the chuckle as the general related that story to me afterward.

Dallas Cares held their very first meeting on April 21st at the Lovers Lane United Methodist Church. A ticket committee was formed immediately to handle its first big benefit project—the opening of the new Barn Dinner Theater still under construction. They were donating the proceeds of their first performance to Dallas Cares, the play to be announced later. By the time *Plaza Suite* opened on May 26th, Dallas Cares was some 500 members strong and growing. The funds raised that evening were earmarked to send two delegates to Paris, Stockholm and Moscow on a Flight for Understanding with Lt. Gov. Ben Barnes in August. Some 1,000

Texans were slated to make that trip to speak with representatives from North Vietnam, the National Liberation Front and the Communist embassies.

Our first public booth for disseminating POW/MIA information was at a 30th anniversary open house at Navy Air Station (NAS) on May 15th. The Thunderbirds dazzling teamwork in their F-4E Phantoms was the highlight of the celebration. Watching them brought back fond memories of watching Chuck perform bombing patterns across the airstrip at George AFB at his graduation. "Every team member personally knows at least one American prisoner of war in Southeast Asia and Saturday the 'missing man formation' will be flown (Lt. Col. Samuel R. Johnson of Plano, now a POW is a former Thunderbird)," a reporter wrote.[7] The boys and I had our picture taken with that Thunderbird team, a treasured keepsake from that afternoon.

May 26th was designated Dallas Cares Day by the County Commissioners and began with a special flag raising ceremony at the Dallas Historical Plaza downtown. Dallas Cowboy Quarterback Roger Staubach read from the proclamation that urged all citizens to fly their flags that day in honor of our POW/MIAs. Reflecting on his own military service, he said lack of hope would seem to be the most difficult aspect of a prisoner's experience. "Hopefully they will have God and their families to think about" and they will know that "people in Dallas and all over the United States care about them."[8]

On the national level as we were getting Dallas Cares off the ground, North Vietnam and the Viet-Cong rejected President Nixon's proposal for sending all prisoners of war to Sweden. They insisted he must set a troop withdrawal date before the prisoner issue could be solved. Some 2,000 anti-war protestors were reported arrested in Washington D.C. the same day the rejection of that POW plan made the news (May 5th).

Within a month then The National League of Families urged the president to take new initiative to end the war and bring our men home, to be willing to set a date if the Vietnamese would agree to release prisoners when he did. But mid-June front page headlines blasted the North Vietnamese with accusations of using our POWs to blackmail the United States. Secretary of State William P. Rogers blatantly announced in a press conference that President Nixon would remain firm in his determination to leave South Vietnam strong enough to defend itself against a Communist takeover. "We cannot abandon our national objectives to pay ransom," he said.[9]

Like the League, I really wanted our government to bring an end to the war and bring our men home, I wasn't sure setting a date was the way to do it. I was still trusting Kissinger to negotiate a reasonable solution without abandoning South Vietnam.

In June, Dallas Cares began a major campaign to write letters to the ambassadors of countries who had signed the Geneva Convention, demanding humane treatment of our POWS until they were released. I was getting pretty adept at letter writing by then and both my mother and mother-in-law wrote letters too.

Father's Day brought another sad reminder of our prisoner's absence. The *Dallas Morning News* ran a poignant article by Doug Domeier who had covered the Week of Concern. "While the wives of POWs and missing men have spoken about their husbands, the children in the families have rarely expressed their feelings," he wrote. "One school age girl, whose father is missing, went to her room and cried when asked to comment. 'I just can't do it.' She told her mother afterward. But the crying may have been good, her mother believes. 'She's had it bottled up inside for four years.'"[10] Some of the children didn't even understand Father's Day because they've never celebrated it. Bonnie Singleton's son was born after Jerry was shot down. He had asked his mother what a father is and didn't understand why his father didn't return to them in the helicopter he had flown.

My sons hated the publicity aspect of my becoming active in the POW/MIA issue. They didn't like to talk about their dad with anyone outside of family either. We celebrated that special Sunday with Chuck's dad. Eurcil was a real father figure for the boys. They loved being around him. My brother, Olin, and brother-in-law, Tommy, were also stand-in father figures. They both did things with the boys and were important male models for them. I felt incredibly lucky and grateful to have them for that loving male presence in my sons' lives.

July 1st the North Vietnamese offered a new peace proposal that Senator Muskie, leading contender for the Democratic presidential nomination, thought was the best offer yet. We local wives were still quite skeptical, refusing to get excited only to have our hopes dashed once more. "We've been let down so often," sighed Bonnie

Singleton. "Someday this will all be over, but we can't anticipate it. I'd like to see more interpretation of the North Vietnamese demands. It's of utmost importance that all prisoners, not just the 369 they admit to having, be released. Only one prisoner of the Viet Cong has ever written," she noted.[11]

In late August, Dallas Cares brought in Steve Frank, a law student who had taken time out from his studies to travel around the country for VIVA to speak about their bracelet program. The brainchild of Voices in Vital America (VIVA), the first POW/MIA bracelet made its debut at the founding meeting of the League in May of 1970. They were proposed as an awareness tool, a conversation starter, a connector on a personal level, these simple nickel or copper bands engraved with the name of a serviceman who was a prisoner or missing in Vietnam and the date he was lost. Families would need to give permission to use their loved one's name. Because the League wanted to remain independent of all other POW/MIA organizations, they never actually endorsed VIVA, but they did disseminate the information to their membership so families could participate as they chose. I gave them Chuck's information as soon as I learned about the bracelets.

Several Dallas Cowboys were there that day to help promote the bracelets in the Dallas area. I had quite the challenge to open a bracelet out far enough to fit over the wrist of offensive tackle, Rayfield Wright, for a photo op. Many of the Cowboys not only wore bracelets, they gave of themselves to my sons in ways that meant so much to them—especially Charles and Scott who were avid Cowboy fans. They provided tickets to games on occasion. Danny Reeves took us all to the Mesquite Rodeo with his family one night to see Walt Garrison perform. Mike Clarke took the boys out to Texas Stadium one New Year's Day for their practice session. They got to go into the locker room and see all the players for both teams who were to play that game. These gestures meant so very much to my boys.

POW/MIA bracelets created a relationship to a particular person and family. It gave a face to a number, so to speak, making the issue personal for those who wore them. *Links of love*, they were dubbed. With their purchase an individual vowed to wear that bracelet until their man came home or was accounted for. Dallas Cares sold bracelets with the names of all our local area POW/MIAs.

I chose to wear a copper bracelet engraved simply, *Capt. Charles Stratton, 1-3-71.* Most people wore a nickel one. The bracelets were purchased for $2.50-$3.00, the cost of a movie ticket in those days. These simple bands were strong links of caring and concern that transcended the political division within this country on the war itself. I dare say, they were *the* most powerful tool ever used in seeking humane treatment and ultimate release of our men held captive in Vietnam. Wearing a man's name produced a bond that no written appeal could match. I sold hundreds of Chuck's bracelets when I went out to speak on the issue.

The first letter I received from a bracelet wearer was postmarked April 15th from Hamilton Ohio and sent care of VIVA:

> *To the family of Capt. Charles Stratton,*
>
> *Because I am concerned with the treatment of men missing in action and prisoners of War in Southeast Asia I decided to write to Voices In Vital America to see what I could do to help. I received a P.O.W.—M.I.A. bracelet with Capt. Charles Stratton's name on it.*
> *I would like to know more about the man whose name I received and would appreciate hearing from you about him. My address is— Thank you very much.*
>
> *Sincerely, Robin...*

I wrote back to Robin and learned she was a sophomore who had heard about the bracelets from a friend at her high school.

The second letter I received was from a 22-year-old woman in Minneapolis whose brother had read about VIVA in his ship's plan of the day and ordered two bracelets before his discharge from the Navy in April. Then came a letter from Vietnam itself, an Air Force sergeant who learned about the bracelets from his wife back in Tacoma. He arrived at Chu Lai about the time Chuck was headed for Thailand. I enjoyed answering their questions and telling them about Chuck and our family. It was the caring and prayers of so many that made each day a little easier to face.

The Second Annual Meeting of the National League was being planned for September. A new board of directors was to be elected. Shirley asked if I would be willing to run for that new board. It would mean a trip into D.C. every other month for a long weekend. Dallas

Cares would help cover any other costs. My mother had been very supportive of me being gone for speaking engagements in an evening, but was she up for an entire weekend with me gone? She was, so I submitted my bio and statements about why I wanted to serve on the board to the League's Nominating Committee Chair.

The summer months passed quickly with all the new Dallas Cares activities added to my other volunteer work—Cub Scouts and vacation church school at Pleasant Mound United Methodist Church. I did take time for a vacation to enjoy some family fun in the midst of the uncertainty of Chuck's fate and the efforts to find an answer. With the boys so young, Mother and I decided we would just explore some of Texas' attractions, not spend too many hours on the road in a day. San Marcos and Aquarena Springs fit the bill for our first leg.

Then we took in Natural Bridge Caverns on the way to San Antonio with all its missions and wonderful Tex-Mex at Casa Rio on the River Walk. We'd gone there with Chuck after our Galveston excursion before he left for Thailand. In fact, at some point during that visit, Chuck had taken the two older boys into this hotel to find a bathroom while Mother and I stayed outside with Stephen, and came out laughing. It seems he lost Scott briefly on the elevator. But they had managed to reconnect and all was okay.

From San Antonio we headed due west for Laredo for a couple of nights. The boys' first experience of Mexico into Nuevo Laredo was a great finale. They found it quite fascinating. That vacation was a rejuvenating two weeks that would tide us over until next year.

For the fall Dallas Cares had begun a letter campaign asking our congressmen to "insist that the inspection determining the status of MIA's-POW's be an integral part of any negotiations toward the settlement of this war and that our government give top priority toward a full accounting of these men."[12] SMU fraternities and sororities, some 143 churches and various shopping centers helped us collect around 60,000 letters, including one from County Judge Lou Sterrett, to be hand-delivered by the POW/MIA wives attending the National League of Families Annual meeting.

I had never been to our nation's capital before this League meeting. Nor had I ever been to a convention of any sort. It was a new experience on many levels. Registration began Sunday September 26th. State and Regional Coordinators and the current Board of Directors held meetings that day as well. The first General

Session for all the League membership began at 8:50 Monday morning with political and psychological seminars to update families on all pertinent aspects pertaining to the POW/MIA issue.

I was like a sponge soaking in every bit of data presented that day. The presentation that stands out in my memory the most, however, was that made by Martin T. Orne, M.D., and Chairman of the Department of Psychiatry at the University of Pennsylvania. He related the stages a prisoner would go through after capture. I was struck by what I heard, recognizing similarities in their process to what I had also experienced. First there is shock from the initial incident and then their capture. The body responds to the trauma with numbness. Then they are faced with the decision to live or die. If their decision was to survive, that's when things really got tough, he told us. He would then do or say whatever it took to survive from that point onward.

I had experienced those same adjustments, the difference, of course, being that I was home, surrounded by loved ones to help me cope, while Chuck would have been isolated, possibly wounded and in for physical as well as emotional torture. I too experienced shock and numbness. My decision about how to proceed for the future was based on believing Chuck was still alive. In order to survive, I chose to hope against all odds that Chuck had survived and was a prisoner of war. I did not believe I could live without him. My every action from that point onward was to do whatever I could to ultimately bring him home. I found it comforting to understand my own reactions to the limbo I had entered.

To my great surprise I also learned that I had been elected to the new board of directors. When I had agreed to run I never really thought I would actually be one of the fifteen to be elected. I am convinced it was only because of the name Stratton. No one knew who Chuck was, but Lt. Cmdr. Richard Stratton was a familiar figure. He had been captured January 5th, 1967 and his picture used in the media by the North Vietnamese. I will always believe that was why family members voted for me. They thought I was related to him. Whatever the reason, I was elated at the prospect of serving in the coming year, already totally enamored with the Washington scene from the little I had observed thus far. That evening I attended my very first official meeting with the outgoing board and we elected officers for our new team.

Day two began with a Congressional coffee. The four military services hosted luncheons for their members providing a more informal atmosphere for questions and getting to know personnel and other families from one's particular branch of service. Throughout the convention there were opportunities to consult with the service representatives about one's particular case. Champus, the insurance for military dependents, was also available for consultations. The League's first business meeting was held that afternoon.

Tuesday evening wound down our activities with a reception, followed by a formal dinner where The Honorable Melvin R. Laird, Secretary of Defense was the guest speaker. President Nixon surprised us all when he popped in unexpectedly. I will never forget that moment when "Hail to the Chief" began to play and we all automatically stood as if called to attention. Tears welled in my eyes as I felt the power of the office of President. It doesn't matter how you feel about the man who holds that title—being in the presence of your Commander in Chief is a moving experience. He assured us that evening that they were checking every possible lead... and there was every indication that POWs might be released.[13] Without elaborating he alluded to private undisclosed channels in that promise.

I felt encouraged after hearing him speak and trusted he was being honest about some sort of progress being made in private negotiations for our guys' release. We just needed to be patient a little longer.

Early Wednesday morning we resumed the business meeting. I learned during these sessions that there was growing dissention amongst League members. There was a group there who actually picketed the White House during the convention, urging that a date be set for the withdrawal of our forces from Vietnam as well as an immediate bombing halt in Laos.

All this unrest amongst some of the League members led to a directive to the incoming board to hold a special meeting in May rather than waiting another twelve months for the next annual meeting. They wanted the incoming board to re-examine what additional steps needed to be taken by the League and our government to foster a more rapid resolution of the prisoner/missing issue.

It was apparent that some members had reached the conclusion that the only way the League could successfully achieve its goals would be through the adoption of a more militant, political stance. I sided with the old board's commitment to continuation of the League's humanitarian stance, stressing the adherence to Geneva Convention standards versus any political stance.

After three intense, packed, eye-opening days, I was definitely ready to head home. I needed some time to digest all the information flooding my mind. I had so enjoyed meeting with wives and family members outside of my own local group, regardless of their differing opinions. It was invigorating to be a part of the inner controversy and arguments, and I returned to Dallas inspired by the commitment of this amazing organization of dedicated families who shared my hope. I felt grateful to be an integral part of this awesome group of activists.

Six of the Dallas area wives had gone to this convention. Two of those expressed concern over troop withdrawal without a full accounting of the 1,300 MIAs. At the same time, they both felt that the U.S. government was doing everything possible to win an accounting and release of the POWs. "Before I went to the convention I wasn't satisfied [everything was being done]," said Mrs. Klem. "Personally, I'm satisfied now. What the President said came straight from his heart.... I feel the President has a working plan—a step-by-step plan—that will probably take time," said Mrs. Whitford.[14] Marlene Klem's husband had been shot down over North Vietnam in 1967, and Jo Whitford's over Laos in 1969.

They had come to the same conclusions I had after that Washington trip. However, there were local wives who were not as trusting as we were at that point. We were as diverse in our opinions in the Metroplex as the general League membership. No one seemed ready, however, to abandon the humanitarian rather than the political focus of the League just yet.

Locally it was time to look at the possibilities of the State Fair again. The previous year, in October of 1970, the Dallas League of Families had a booth in the World Exhibit Center and collected some 15,000 signatures on a petition to release our POWs that would be sent to the North Vietnamese Delegation at the Paris Peace Talks. "There are very few people passing by that won't stop and aren't interested in our effort," Mrs. Shirley Johnson said. "Many of the young men who sign petitions are anticipating a tour in Vietnam soon." When asked whether such efforts are effective, she replied, "I feel it's because of the American reaction that North Vietnam has let some of the POWs write home. I received my first letter from my husband last April. I believe this was the direct result of the concern of the American people."[15]

The Dallas Cares booth this year would feature an original painting of the POW sitting disconsolately on his cot. Literature regarding the plight of our men and orders for POW/MIA bracelets would be available, as well as a volunteer who could field questions. In addition, coins tossed into the wishing well in the Women's Building were to be given to Dallas Cares for their ongoing projects. The State Fair provided an excellent opportunity to reach people from all over Texas.

CHAPTER 10

SERVING ON THE BOARD

My first official board meeting in D.C. was held November 20th and 21st at the Family Service Center at Bolling Air Force Base. Obligations of board members were reviewed along with the reorganization of committees. The Ad Council Campaign that had been in the works was a top item on the agenda. The FCC was now requesting a ruling as to whether the ads were controversial. The Families for Immediate Release were requesting equal time for their anti-war position. Could we risk such a large expenditure given that the ads could be cancelled out or not even run at all? Most of our contributions at that point were from fund-raisers and foundations. I agreed to pursue the foundation resources to cover the costs for the ad campaign. I also volunteered to work on a brochure for the League with Dallas Cares.

A special report concerning problems that had arisen after the recent October 8th release of POW Staff Sergeant John Sexton was brought to the board by the Michigan State Coordination for our consideration. After much discussion, a committee was formed to investigate the issues raised by the Sexton case: a so-called "propaganda" leaflet he wrote while a captive of the Viet Cong; a remark made by the Army Sec. raising the question of punishment for SSgt. Sexton for speaking with a reporter while he was in the hospital; and concerns about the way his release came about.

His parents who lived in Michigan had requested a review of their MIA son's case in July of 1971. It was discovered then that the Pentagon had gotten a letter from SSgt. Sexton was released by the Viet Cong on the 8th with no explanation as to why. He walked barefoot some eight hours to freedom. The Allies then released a North Vietnamese lieutenant as a reciprocal gesture for Sexton's release. That letter incident was being called a bureaucratic foul-up.

New business suggestions were proposed, including a nationwide candlelight ceremony in all big cities during the approaching Christmas season and League action requesting that President Nixon discuss POW/MIAs in Moscow and China. There was also discussion on a symbol of barbed wire to be used for the League, but the board rejected it and moved to pursue another symbol. We adjourned after setting January 22nd and 23rd as our next board meeting dates.

There were already Gallup polls being taken rating the leading contenders for the next presidential election. Thanksgiving weekend in Dallas a national convention for the coalition of peace and civil rights advocates formed a fourth party option they dubbed the People's Party, nominating Dr. Benjamin Spock, the renowned pediatrician, as their stand-in candidate for the next Democratic Convention. An amusing moment for the delegates of this meeting was the reading of a telegram from Georgia's Lt. Governor which read: "Whether you call yourself communists or not, you are acting like communists. You are making the same demands of America as the communist enemies...."[16] The political fervor was heated and building for new choices in '72.

Mother, the boys and I drove to Aransas Pass, 20 miles northeast of Corpus Christi and some 450 miles south east of Dallas, for the Thanksgiving weekend to visit a favorite aunt. We had planned to see her last summer before Chuck left for Thailand. However, Hurricane Celia hit the coast badly damaging the Corpus Christi/Aransas Pass area. We had gone to Galveston instead. I had stayed with my Auntie Merle the summer before we married so I could drive down to see Chuck in Harlingen on his off weekends. It was a lovely mini-vacation for us all.

Dallas Cares continued to keep the POW/MIA issue before the public. In mid-December our men were the focus of a program at Dallas North Shopping Center in Plano. Inserts for Christmas cards were made available throughout the metroplex. "As you celebrate Christmas in the joy of your home, surrounded by your loved ones, remember those Americans who are missing or prisoners in Southeast Asia. If you want to offer them a gift, send a letter showing your concern over their plight."[17] The address given was to President Ton Duc Thang in Hanoi. Ross Perot was the principal speaker for Dallas' special area wide Candlelight Ceremony December 22nd at Highland Park Methodist Church. Invitations were sent to all city, county and state leaders for this major Christmas observance. A candle was to be lit for each of the 55 men from the North Texas area in an affirmation of loyalty to our American POW/MIAs.

The boys and I were on the front page of the *Dallas Morning News* again that Christmas in an article titled "Yule Tapes Tell POW Tale."[18] Four of us area wives and families were given the opportunity to record our first visual Christmas greetings to our guys in a television studio at East Texas State University. TelePrompTer Corporation, headquartered in New York, was sponsoring a nationwide series of such yule tapes with the National League of Families. "Honey, it's Christmas and though we're miles apart we can never be separated," I told Chuck. We all poured out messages of love and wishes that they would be home soon. The ever-present question of whether or not Hanoi would accept the tapes failed to diminish the feeling and spirit of our messages. This was only my second Christmas without Chuck. I felt certain that it would never become seven Christmas' like two of my "sister-wives" in the studio that afternoon.

Christmas that year felt very different from last year. It was the first we celebrated with Chuck missing. His absence the second year was a much darker gaping hole than the previous year when we knew he was alive and with his fellow airmen of the 34th Tactical Fighter Squadron. It was nonetheless still a joyous family time for us. My brother and his wife spent Christmas morning and day with us. We had our traditional Christmas Eve with Chuck's family.

January 3rd fell on a Monday and brought back memories of that early morning notification just a year earlier. Instead of being on a new assignment in Europe with Chuck, I was still in Dallas living with my mother. We knew no more this morning than we did this time last year. Chuck was a major now though. I knew he would be so happy to pin those maple leaves on his new uniform when he came home. I was keeping the pair that were in his belongings, looking forward to the story of the man who had given them to him. I suspected he knew about the promotion, even though the official list was not released until after he was missing. That kind of news can travel fast through unofficial channels amongst the guys.

I missed the January board meeting much to my disappointment. The flu slapped me into bed, rendering me totally out of it that weekend. Thank God my mother was there to care for the boys—and me. All I could do was sleep under piles of covers. I had sent my voting proxy to the board chair Carole Hanson along with a copy of the brochure we'd worked on so it could be discussed. I learned later from the minutes sent to me that the Ad Council had received permission to proceed with the production and distribution of the 30 and 60 second TV spots.

Among other business items, the board resolved to send a representative to the VIVA Symposium to present the League's plans for the next Week of Concern and ascertain proposals made by other organizations. Of greater significance was the adoption of a symbol for the National League of Families designed by Mary Hoff, an MIA wife, and to pursue making a flag with that symbol.

Within a white circle on a black background is a head and shoulder silhouette of a POW, his head slightly bowed. Behind him stands a simple guard tower and below his profile are two single strands of barb wire extending from below his neck brought together in a small star shaped connector below his chin and ending at the circle's edge. The letters POW MIA separated by another 5 point star arcs over that white circle and rounding below, the words: YOU ARE NOT FORGOTTEN.

The proposed brochure was also accepted with the incorporation of our new symbol if possible. That moving symbol stands out on paper or a flag. It's simple but speaks volumes, far more than just barbed wire alone.

Days after that board meeting, the newspapers carried stories that President Nixon's peace plan was rejected by the North Vietnamese Delegation in Paris. The League then announced the formation of a "non-partisan political action committee" to maintain pressure on all presidential candidates, President Nixon included, to resolve this conflict so our POWs would come home and the missing be accounted for. Bonnie Singleton became the Texas chairperson to ascertain statements from congressional candidates regarding their stand on the POW/MIA issue. As family dissatisfaction with the results of the current Vietnamization policy was growing ever more heated, the League as a unified body gave a qualified endorsement of President Nixon's peace plan.

I eagerly awaited the March 10th board meeting. In addition to the board members in attendance were office staff, regional coordinators, several advisors and numerous League members, forty-one people total, which was definitely out of the ordinary. The agenda was filled with increased activities and projects. That morning President Nixon had signed the proclamation for the Week of Concern to begin later that month. It was resolved that the special May meeting requested by the membership at the annual meeting would be a symposium with panel discussions involving family and board members from the League, POW/MIA Families For Immediate Release, Rescue Line, and other POW/MIA groups. May 5th, 6th and 7th were reaffirmed as the meeting dates.

A letter was to be sent to Secretary of Defense Melvin Laird requesting Space-Available travel implemented by the National Guard. There was discussion about meeting with Dr. Kissinger and participation in both the upcoming political conventions, both subjects the visiting League members wanted a voice in. It was resolved by the board to submit names of members using a lottery system for 25 members of the League for the Kissinger meeting in addition to the board. And it was resolved that we would participate in both the Democratic and Republican Conventions in a manner consistent with our purposes and objectives. On a more mundane new business item, I was appointed Nominating Committee Chairman to work with the regional coordinators to develop recommendations and nominations for the next slate of officers. Our next board meeting was to coincide with the next Kissinger meeting in April.

Dallas Cares brought returned POW John Sexton in from his hometown of Warren, Michigan to share his experience with us in late March. He was welcomed to our city and made an honorary citizen by Mayor Wes Wise when he arrived at Love Field. Held in 3' x 7' Viet Cong bunkers in the South for over two years, he reached times when he no longer cared and said to himself *let me die,* but his desire and will to go home sustained him in those dark moods.

All political candidates should stand united on the POW issue and come up with a solution, he told the audience that night. He assured us that POWs know we care about them. When asked about the draft dodgers fleeing to Canada he responded, "Is that what this country's based on, people taking the easy way out when faced with something tough?"[19] Indeed, I thought to myself. I would have disowned one of my own sons if that were a choice he made. I took heart knowing that this young man was now a civilian back in college in Detroit, struggling to integrate back into society after his ordeal.

The North Texas Chapter of the League invited Dolf Droge, a special consultant on Vietnamese Affairs to the National Security Council, to speak to the families April 7th. Due to illness, Mr. Droge could not make that meeting. A record from Congressman Philip Crane's interviews with him for Conservative Viewpoint was played instead. I too was absent because my son Scott was having surgery that afternoon to have tubes put back in his ears. There was a big Scout Exposition the next day and I was preparing to leave again for D.C. the following Monday.

That flight into D.C. was perhaps the most memorable I ever experienced. I left Dallas Love Field Sunday evening to spend the night at Randolph AFB and fly space-available to Washington for the big Kissinger meeting. The "April showers" that night were anything but. I had never flown in such turbulent stormy weather and certainly hope never to again. I love to fly, but by the time I got to San Antonio I was seriously considering renting a car and driving back to Dallas the next morning. The prospect of meeting personally with Dr. Kissinger in the White House, however, was a powerful incentive to get back on a plane the next morning.

That military flight was late taking off because the severe weather the night before had delayed the plane and thus interfered with the necessary crew rest time between flights. It was after noon before we were airborne. I became concerned after a couple of hours that we weren't going to make it in time for the meeting and expressed that to the pilot. When we finally landed, they had arranged a limo that met me on the runway and drove me directly to the White House.

Cheeks red with embarrassment at being a little late, and coming into the West Wing with overnight and garment bags in hand, I smiled at the guard at the door and, nervously making light of my predicament, announced, "I'm moving in." He did *not* seem to appreciate my humor. He reminded me of the totally stoic, no-nonsense guards of Buckingham Palace. When the door was opened for me into the cabinet room, Dr. Kissinger got up and personally pulled a chair over next to him where I sat at his elbow for the entire meeting. I found Dr. Kissinger to be a charming, soft-spoken, very confident man. He assured us any agreement reached with the Vietnamese would be a package deal, including the men from Laos and Cambodia. He took us into the Oval Office after we had concluded our business that afternoon. I was duly impressed by his demeanor and trusted his promises.

We convened the board meeting that evening at the Army-Navy Club in Washington, D.C. at Bolling AFB and worked until after 10:00 p.m. The return trip home was uneventful beyond my head still swimming from the White House meeting. I felt encouraged that President Nixon and Dr. Kissinger were doing everything in their power to bring our men home honorably. I trusted that Dr. Kissinger would be a man of his word and refuse any settlement that did not secure the release of prisoners taken in Laos and Cambodia—that the peace would be a "package deal," no man left behind, as he promised.

At the May meeting emotions were intense and families were as diverse as the rest of the nation in their support of the current administration policies versus setting a date for withdrawal of troops immediately to bring out men home. Strong opinions fostered heated debates. The format for both the symposium and the separate caucus meetings was structured to assure that everyone would have an opportunity to make a contribution to the discussions.

One of these caucus meeting was for the families and wives of those missing in Laos. We were becoming more concerned that our men would be swept under the rug with all the emphasis on the prisoners in Vietnam. We voted to send a delegation to Laos in December. Also there was a suggestion about posting ads in the Bangkok News seeking information on our guys.

After dinner on Saturday evening there was a presentation by Dolf Droge, the Vietnamese expert and historian on leave from AID (Agency for International Development) to the Nixon administration who had missed our North Texas Chapter presentation weeks before. I was eager to finally meet this man. He spoke to us about the "gigantic homework gap" evident in United States dialogue on the Vietnam War. All discussions had been from either hawk or dove position, both of which were totally irrelevant, he told us. What was needed was the "owl position," one based on an understanding of the Vietnamese people and their long history.

Much of Mr. Droge's presentation was through songs he had written to relate that history, particularly to young college students. His casual appearance was geared toward the youth as well. He was an obviously brilliant and talented man who looked quite ordinary—gangly even—glasses, tall, huge hands, strumming his guitar, imparting facts in the most entertaining way. It was one of the most enlightening two hours I believe I have ever spent.

Granted, his intention was to sell us on President Nixon's Vietnamization program. But it did far more than that for me. I will never forget him saying that the Vietnamese were a 2500-year-old people who would consider us a 200-year-old experiment doing rather nicely. That statement went into the depth of my being and seemed to me the crux of the problem with much of our foreign policy. "The Vietnamese believe there are 58 shades of good and evil in every situation," he said, "while Americans are monistic people who want to choose good over evil." This made me want to know more about their Taoist perspective.

I was also struck by the fact that Ho Chi Minh had changed his name 22 times to survive politically, not becoming the beloved Ho until 1941. Dolf Droge's take on the Vietnam conflict felt truer than any I had heard to date. His presentation, for me, was *the* greatest gift of this special League meeting, on par with that of the psychologists at the annual meeting the previous September. His songs entered my soul in a way that reading about that same history could never have done.

He had even written one about our guys that he introduced thus: "There are government policies that say we care, but there is no book, no song, no movie, no poem, no play, no drama in this country that says we care, so I've written one that says we care—and not just that our men are being mistreated by our standards of Western behavior, but they are being mistreated in violation of 2500 years of Vietnamese culture and tradition. The Communists are really out of step in Hanoi and we should call their attention to it. I symbolize all our men—airmen, soldiers, sailors, marines—as Eagles."

I can still hear his voice singing verse after verse as he strummed his guitar and wish there was a way to transmit them from this page. And I have a record, an LP entitled *Vietnam: The Hawk, The Dove, The Owl,* with Dolf Droge and Congressman Philip M. Crane that I still play occasionally to hear this and his other amazing songs he wrote about the history of Vietnam.

The general League membership seemed not as impressed as I had been, however. The resolutions reached on May 7th of that meeting were concerned with the failure of our government's Vietnamization policy to provide adequate results toward resolving the MIA/POW issue. Three family members who held the confidence of the League majority would be elected to meet with President Nixon to reaffirm our extreme distress and our expectations that an immediate policy be adopted that would insure an accounting of our missing men and the release of our POWs, not just the withdrawal of combat troops. We wanted the Paris Peace Talks reconvened simultaneously with inspection of POW camps in South Vietnam, Laos, Cambodia and North Vietnam.

We wanted a show of unity in the MIA/POW families, the American people, and our congressmen and senators behind our government in their efforts to gain identification and release of our men before the 1972 elections. The League would compile a list of neutral countries to be presented to the Paris Talks (or other suitable place) for them to choose a medical team to inspect all POW camps in South East Asia. Furthermore we urged the government to use the word *presumed captured* when referring to the MIAs to avoid the association and assumption that POWs are living captives while MIAs are dead. A Committee On Identification and Discrepancies was to be established in the League to publicize the dozens of American servicemen captured alive that appeared on no POW list to date.

I wanted to be nominated for a second term on the board. I loved those trips into Washington. I loved being privy to the briefings and business of this dedicated group of family members who had decided the government's policy of keeping a low profile and not speaking out publicly on the POW/MIA issue was not working to bring our guys home. There's no question that treatment improved because of the efforts of the National League of Families. I really began to understand the workings of my own government that year and to question rather than blindly trust.

I returned home to learn that my sons were terrified every time I flew. Mother was listening to their prayers one night and they closed with "please don't let mommy's plane crash." Strangely, it had never occurred to me that they would be afraid for me to fly. The fact that their dad's plane had crashed would certainly be impetus to develop flying fears—or worry that you might lose the only parent left to take care of you. Because I had no fear of flying myself and had so enjoyed my trips into D.C., I had been blind to their angst.

I sat down and talked to them about their fears, trying to assure them that I was perfectly safe. I told them that I believed the work of the League was the only thing we could do right now to help bring their daddy home. I asked them if they thought they could tolerate me finishing out this one term of office—that would mean, only an overnight trip to the State Department, and the July, September and October board meetings left. "If you can handle those last four flights, I promise I won't run again. I will confine my work locally through Dallas Cares," I assured them.

They were little troopers and all agreed they could handle the remaining trips. It would be their contribution for their daddy. From then on it was *Countdown, 4, 3, 2, 1.* Much as I wanted to continue my stimulating participation on the board, my sons were far more important. However, my decision not to run again did not mean I had to resign as the chairman of the nominating committee.

My family had gotten more than they bargained for when they first agreed to me serving on this board. In addition to the every other month regularly scheduled board meetings, I had flown in for the special meeting with Dr. Kissinger in April and another special meeting at the State Department for families with men missing in Laos, an outgrowth of the special caucus in May.

I did decide to post an ad in the *Bangkok Post* after returning home, which Dallas Cares gladly funded. I had no idea if it would produce any results, but was willing to explore every possible avenue.

… MAYDAY SOS! … Pathet Lao, NLF, North Vietnam…
American Family Seeks Information
CHARLES W. STRATTON

MISSING IN ACTION ... JANUARY 1971
... CONTACT ARC, VIENTIANE, LAOS

The overnight to the State Department in June was made even easier when a staff member picked me up at the airport and let me stay with her to minimize costs. We drove straight to the meeting. Upon arrival, our purses were x-rayed, and we had to go through metal detectors. The White House had been easier to enter than the State Department.

They had prepared a nice lunch for the twelve family members before the meeting began. There was no real new information given us that afternoon. They definitely felt that the men captured in Laos were in North Vietnam and believed that when they came home we would learn some had actually received mail. They estimated 50-100 men were being held captive of those missing in Laos and expressed frustrations at not having intelligence information about the men. They were very aware of the problems of accounting for all the missing. Teams were being prepared for crash and gravesite inspections. We requested that wives not be suddenly dropped from emotional help in the event they might need it should their husbands not return.

By the July 7th board meeting, our Nonpartisan Political Committee chairman was in Miami to cover the Democratic National Convention. She would continue to pursue the purposes of that committee in August at the Republican National Convention as well. The board discussed the Democratic platform, of course, along with our own internal upcoming election. I reported having received nomination acceptances for the next board from 39 of our members. I was given another 15 nominations for follow-up at that meeting. Nominations were then closed by motion and vote of the board. Ballots were to be mailed out to the membership by September 1st with a return date of later than October 1st for the casting of their votes.

I was also working with the Committee on Discrepancies and Identification on a new brochure for the League as directed by the membership at the May meeting. We were waiting on DOD to give us better photos and updated evidence. There was some question of two more pilots believed captured who were not on the current list of

24 absent from Hanoi's list. Discussion was raised again about holding the October annual in Omaha to accommodate our western and mid-western members, but voted down by the board because of the upcoming election and need to remain in D.C. for access to officials here. It was the sense of the board that should another annual meeting be necessary next year, it could be held elsewhere.

I returned to Dallas in time for Vacation Church School week. At least this year I was not teaching one of the age groups as I had done last summer. Mine was a more overall supervisory role, getting others to volunteer to do the teaching. I just had to be present to make sure all went well during the week and prepare for the graduation program for the parents and congregation at the end of the week.

I had no more trips to D.C. until the fall after the kids were back in school. Was it just a year ago I asked to run for the board? Seemed like I'd been crusading for the POW/MIAs forever; Chuck had been gone a little less than two full years at this point, yet it felt like a lifetime. In my second letter to him via Hanoi in April, I wrote that Charles was getting his Wolf Badge and a gold and silver arrow and we were ready for a summer vacation.

This summer's letter reported that Charles had moved up to Webelos in preparation for Boy Scouts, which meant he had a male leader. Scott wanted to follow in his brother's footsteps, so my den mother days were not over.

Mother and I had found a guest ranch in the piney woods of East Texas that we thought would be a perfect place for rest and relaxation this year. The Alabama-Coushatta Indian Reservation (Texas' oldest) was close by and well worthy of exploration. I had always felt a kindred spirit with Native American Indians, so much so that I fantasized being raised by them as a child, and preferred to be an Indian rather than a cowboy when my brother and I played. My maternal great-great grandmother Abigail was full-blood Cherokee, or so I had been told, and she hailed from Alabama.

The Triple D Ranch was sheer heaven for me—no television, no newspapers, no telephone. I really needed that—to be totally out of the loop of all the Vietnam news of the day. The August 1st newspaper I'd read the morning before our arrival reported that the Air Force had lost two more Phantom jets. Hanoi claimed that they had captured two airmen, one suffering head and leg wounds. My heart went out to the crew *not* claimed—for surely it meant that two more fliers were added to the MIA rolls. Even with the news shifting almost daily between positive and negative assessments of the ongoing peace process and troop withdrawals, we continued to lose more of our finest.

I wanted just a few days off the busy highway of my life, surrounded only by pine trees and horses, quiet but for the sounds of nature and a dinner bell announcing the time for a wonderful home-cooked meal prepared by someone else. I wanted *not* be reminded of the Vietnam War or politics, just for this week.

The boys certainly had plenty of activities available to keep them entertained and happy. What boy wouldn't be content in such a great outdoor arena that included a stable of horses to pick from for a daily ride, a stagecoach to ride in if you weren't up to horseback that day, a swimming pool to cool off in from the August heat of Texas, a recreation room off the chow hall with pool tables and other fun games to play, and a night sky full of stars you never saw in the city?

They delighted in actually having their picture taken with an armadillo the ranchers had caught. It was the first time they'd ever seen that critter in the wild, outside the confines of a zoo or what was left of road kill. It was pretty much paradise for them too.

There was only one minor upset that week. Charles and Scott's horses decided to race back to the stable one afternoon, and poor Scott couldn't hold onto Phoebe's reins. He sprained his wrist in the fall, but not badly enough to require a doctor, thank goodness. He was quite the little trooper—back on another horse the next day.

I soaked in the simple serenity of that place, as did Mother. Feeling rested, we set off to Galveston for the second week of our vacation adventure. We stayed at the Sandpiper, the only motel on the gulf side of Seawall Blvd., adjacent to Stewart Beach. While the Gulf of Mexico is not the ocean per se, it has sand and waves like the ocean and is another of my favorite places for rejuvenation. We had come to Galveston the July before Chuck left for overseas, so it was not the boys' first time to see this Texas "ocean," but it was their first time to stay where we could just walk out across the dunes to the water, and see it from the balcony of our room.

Again, there was lots to do there besides play in the water—Sea-Arama SeaWorld, putt-putt golf, the ferry over to the Bolivar peninsula, a trip the Seawolf Park to see the ships. Feeding the gulls out over the pier after we ate was fun for all, and Mother and I thoroughly enjoyed the seafood at Guido's. Riding the little tram around the city of Galveston was both entertaining and informative, and the visit to Bishop's Palace was amazing.

After another fantastic week spent soaking in lots of sun and fun, none of us was eager to return to Dallas. However, both money and obligations dictated that we must. School would begin again soon and there was much preparation for that.

Dallas Cares had become extremely active in helping other cities form similar non-partisan, non-profit groups seeking the release of the POWs and accounting of those missing. In addition to continuing a letter-writing campaign to the heads of state of the 100 nations which had signed the 1949 Geneva Convention, reminding them of North Vietnam's violations of POW agreements despite their having been one of those signatories, we were also sponsoring billboards throughout the city asking people to remember our men.

Each billboard had the photograph and information of one of our local POW/MIAs. At that point we were also selling some 9000 POW/MIA bracelets and preparing biographies of each man to be available on request. I knew I would have this group still available for my energies after my League board membership was terminated, and that helped soften the loss of those amazing meetings and contacts in our nation's Capital. I felt grateful that my sons were willing to withstand me finishing out the one term. Honoring their feelings was more important than any pleasure I gained from being at the center of the action. It was far more important that they not feel abandoned by me.

I shared all of this with Dave in three hours of non-stop talking, telling him about our early life together and that awful week I learned he was MIA; my finding of support from the local POW/MIA Wives and then the League; and all this information about my history on the board. Dave scheduled another morning in two weeks so I could continue filling in the details of my long journey.

Was I ever primed then for the TV interview later that evening!

Chris Salcedo was as wonderful as Charles had said and he did a really lovely piece for his newscast. I was particularly struck by one unanticipated question he asked me off camera: "Would you change anything if you could?" No one had ever asked me that before and I stammered for a response initially, as I realized, no, I wouldn't. I had just spent a good half hour raving about this man I adored, but the truth was that because of Chuck's MIA status, my whole world had expanded such I could not imagine going back and being that same woman he left in Dallas thirty-six years before. I answered him honestly, but was very relieved he'd asked after the cameras were off. It was a very sobering moment for me.

BOOK II

WEAVING PAST AND PRESENT

"I weave my own wiles. First the divinity put the idea of a web in my mind, to set up a great loom ...and start weaving a web of threads, long and fine. Then I said to them: "Young men, my suitors,... wait, though you are eager to marry me, until I finish this web, so that this weaving will not be useless or wasted. This is a shroud for the hero...."[20]

Penelope to Odysseus after he has returned to Ithaca
and presented himself as a beggar

CHAPTER 11

MEMORIAL PREPARATIONS
AND REMORSE

In between my meetings with Dave, my work schedule, and other television interviews, I continued to pursue Pleasant Mound United Methodist Church as the location for Chuck's service. I did learn from an old friend who was still a member there that the building was also being used as an elementary school during the week. Use of the kitchen for guests to congregate afterward and have a bite of lunch together before the group burial would pose a big challenge. I was also concerned about the media that I knew would be a sizable presence. There were definitely some difficulties that would have to be overcome if we had the service there.

At some point I received a call from Tim in Mortuary about a bracelet wearer in Austin named Ellen who had wanted to contact me after seeing the DOD-released statement in her newspaper. He gave me her phone number if I wanted to call her back. I certainly did, but would wait until evening in case she was working then. I gave him requests for contact information of old military friends I wanted to reach out to and share the news, but had lost touch with over the years.

After speaking with Ellen, I knew I wanted her to represent bracelet wearers during Chuck's memorial service if she would be willing to do that. She'd had a phenomenal experience at the traveling wall just after Memorial Day that she shared with me, and I felt it would be a perfect story to share with all who came to say goodbye to Chuck.

Brenda and I finally met again for dinner after Jim's funeral. I'd been unable to attend because my colonoscopy had been scheduled for that day, so I was anxious to hear all about it. I also wanted to hear more about her experience picking up Jim's remains in Hawaii, which she had described as intense in our earlier conversation. She and Tim (our mortuary officer) had arrived late on August 2nd and were at Hickam AFB by 11:00 am the next day, and then flew back to Texas that night. I knew that would be too much for me and I had told my mortuary officer I needed a down day after we arrived in Hawaii before picking up Chuck's remains.

She told me that actually holding Jim's remains was very emotional. She felt him there and had no doubt whatsoever that those bones were his. She had shed a lot of tears, and had been carrying his picture in her wallet ever since. She had not expected that kind of reaction and realized she'd been married to him all these years, unable to really commit to another, so it was no wonder her subsequent relationships and marriages had failed. I was not surprised to hear this, and was really happy that she was finally grieving Jim. Sure it was hard, but far more healing than simply avoiding the grief.

In terms of the funeral itself, she had only one regret and that was about the music she chose. No one knew the Air Force hymn, "Lord Guard and Guide the Men Who Fly," to sing it. I was already struggling with the music aspect of the service, so that was good to know. Maybe I would choose to have the songs played rather than have us sing them. She was in agreement about the Patriot Guard participating in the group service. They had been at Jim's funeral too.

She'd chosen to bury the urn she brought back with Jim's identified remains. I was not sure I wanted to bury Chuck's urn. We agreed to bury the remaining unidentifiable bones at the DFW National Cemetery. I reminded her we needed to choose the last time slot available so I would have time to get there from Mesquite which is just south east of Dallas. We talked for over two hours over pasta and salad that rainy evening.

My journaling that weekend focused a lot on Brenda's revelation about being married to Jim all these years. While I had never remarried, I became aware of my own reluctance to really commit in relationships over the years. Brenda and I certainly had been severely affected in terms of commitment in future relationships as a result of a deep love for our husbands. And I imagine other MIA wives did as well.

My first relationships after 1977 were with men who lived far away or were already married, or much younger. There was an odd comfort knowing these were never to be lifetime commitments. I was enjoying reconnecting to my sexuality without feeling guilty.

But eventually I began to question why I was drawn to men who were unwilling to commit to me. It took a while before it dawned on me that the finger pointing to their inability to commit left the other three fingers pointing squarely back to me. I was the one who was unable to fully commit to another man. Then, the one man I did actually commit to emotionally and financially, even thinking of him as a husband, turned out to be another painful, devastating and transformational experience of my life. It brought me to my knees and into therapy.

I had begun my first day at Routh Street Women's Clinic on February 2nd, 1982, the beginning of a remarkable vocation. I was just beginning a career as my oldest son was about to be 20. His birthday fell on a Monday that year, my day off. I found myself crying most of the day. I felt unbelievably sad that Chuck was not there to see his number one son transition from teenager to adulthood. I relived the day he was born, how happy we both were, Chuck insisting the nurse show him that he really did have a son. So many images of Chuck with him over the years flashed through my memory. Every time I would regain my composure from an onslaught of tears, another image would bring on more. When I left the house to run errands, I even encountered a funeral procession. In pulling the car over onto the shoulder out of respect for the family of the deceased, the tears flowed again as if I knew them all personally.

When Charles came home that afternoon, I sat down with him at the kitchen table and told him what my day had been like, how proud I was of him and how sad that his dad wasn't there to share this special birthday with him. We *both* cried then, and he reminded me that his dad was there with him, that he'd always felt that his dad had his six (a military term for having someone's back). I knew he was right. I too felt that Chuck was indeed watching over his sons and me over the years. Believing that, however, did not erase my wish that his presence could have been more tangible, in a physical body we could embrace.

Working full-time now enabled me to look for a place of my own at long last. I found a two-bedroom condo that was perfect for Stephen and me within ten minutes of Routh Street. Scott had decided he wanted to stay with Mother, and Charles was already sharing an apartment with old high school buddies. Leaving my mother's house after twelve years of living together was like a painful divorce. Mother felt abandoned, that I was leaving her with this huge house to manage now. I had added on a double garage with a bedroom suite above it for her after having Chuck's status changed in 1977 rather than buy a house of my own then. The boys and I occupied the rest of her home, with its three bedrooms and a den.

While living together had been most beneficial during those years Chuck was missing, it became harder emotionally after I returned to school and began to create a new life for myself, especially after I was free to date again in '77. I wasn't interested in finding another husband, but after seven years of celibacy, I was interested in being sexual once more. I wanted to explore those options without any goal of marriage. I fell in love with Chuck at seventeen and married before any such exploration. Mother and I did not see eye to eye on my desire to explore my sexuality. It became a morality issue that caused much friction between us.

We were really getting to experience all the trials mothers and daughters normally go through during the teenage years. I never pushed the boundaries or sought to separate from her to become my own woman then. I went straight from being Mother's daughter to Chuck's wife without that identity struggle. I had idealized my mother, wanted to be just like her. Living with her as an adult, I realized how very different we were in many ways. I'm afraid I became quite the dissident daughter before I gave up trying to sway her to my way of thinking. Mother had told me she just wanted us to be friends—live together woman to woman. Yet every time I wanted to act in a way she didn't like, she pulled out the Mother (martyr?) card. For example, if I stayed out past 10 or 11 on a week-night, I was the cause of her being tired at work the next day because she was unable to sleep until I was home. I asked her once if she'd treated my brother that way when he lived at home after he got out of the Navy. No, He was a man. I was her daughter. It was different. There was definitely a double standard.

I really pushed it one night when I brought George home with me after a party at the University of Dallas. He was nine years my junior but had been flirting with me the whole semester and after a few drinks I told him to put up or shut up.

I celebrated my 40th birthday gainfully employed at my ideal clinic and living in a space of my own at last. There were several men in my life but none serious in terms of any long-lasting committed relationship. I was quite content to just have fun, playing the field so to speak. Mother and I did mend some of our fences over the next few months. Most of my energy, however, went to developing my counseling skills and focusing on my new career.

I was as interested in the history of reproductive rights as the counseling components of working at the clinic. I was amidst the leading feminist activity of our city right there at Routh Street with the volunteer group called appropriately, Choice. This organization helped co-ordinate local activities and projects of national groups like NOW (National Organization of Women) and NARAL (National Abortion Rights Action League). Stephen and I participated with Choice members in an ERA rally in Oklahoma that June of '82. Not only was I deepening my own feminist roots, but I was introducing my youngest son to that philosophy as well.

While my external world was quite busy in all these new pursuits, I continued exploring my own internal process via dream work with the Jungian psychotherapist Thomas Moore. And though no longer living with my mother, the mother archetype appeared frequently in my dreams during that summer, indicating that I was still in an ambivalent place with "the mother" in me as well as my own biological mother. Tom pointed out after one session that my "mothering" others was an indication that I was looking for mothering for myself. Another dream reflected that "Mother" was not the vehicle to get the help I was seeking. I dreamed of an abortion clinic that catered to children and play—a place where mothering could be rejected while children were celebrated. It was the paradox of the worlds in which I was living.

November initiated a huge shift in my life. I was feeling more and more comfortable with my counseling abilities and my newfound women friends. Willie Nelson came to the Sportatorium for a concert the 22nd and a group of the clinic staff thought it would be a fun thing for us to do together. I had never been much of a country western fan, but did like Willie, and had never been to the Sportatorium. I knew Elvis had played there before he'd become famous, but I'd never been much for concerts and crowds as a teenager. Other than that, I thought it was the place they held those ridiculous wrestling matches. It would be a night of firsts for me— including one of beer drinking. Wine was my drink of choice as a rule, but beer seemed to be the choice at the Sportatorium. And I made up for years of lost opportunities to imbibe the hops.

After the performance, one of our administrators suggested that we go to the stage door and see Willie as he was leaving. I thought that was a great idea. There were huge bear-like body guards keeping the crowd of women at bay as he came out the door. I was drunk enough to not care what anyone thought and began to scream over the noise of the others—"Willie, Willie, over here"—as I was jumping up and down trying to be seen over the burly chain. Sure enough, he heard me and came to where I was, leaning over muscle-men's arms to kiss me.

Well, that just made my evening. When Connie drove me back home that night, poor Stephen had to let his silly drunken mother in the door as she was blabbering on and on about how Willie had kissed her. He ushered me to bed that night reminding me that he had to be at school the next day and needed to get some sleep, as did I for work. I don't have to tell you that I was not feeling my best that next morning and drove to the clinic vowing never to party like that on a work night.

George had dropped out of my life with no explanation by then and I began a two year relationship with another man with a checkered past that included angry ex-wives and time in prison for a blue-collar crime. My fantasy was to bring this prisoner home and help him adjust to the current world. In the ensuing year I came to think I might love him.

Then my mother died suddenly on February 2nd, 1983, almost nine months to the day after I moved out. Scott found her dead on the bathroom floor after he noticed the light on as he was going to bed. He called me in a panic and Stephen and I raced out to Pleasant Grove after calling 911. She had been home sick with the flu for a couple of days, but no one had called me to tell me she was sick.

Mother never missed work and she never went to doctors. I was furious with her for not taking care of herself, and for putting Scott in this position of feeling guilty because he'd not checked on her sooner. Stephen began to blame himself as we drove out there late that night because he hadn't called his grandmother more often. If he had, he'd have known she was sick. I told them both that they were not to blame for her death in any way. It was she who was at fault for not taking better care of herself. I let my anger toward her block any grief. Yet the truth was, I'd lost my anchor.

All the funeral arrangements were made with me on autopilot, putting one foot in front of the other mechanically, in a fog of denial. And this new love was there to support me during this most difficult passage. I had brought him out to meet Mother one time after the holidays, so she knew I was seeing him. But we'd never really discussed her reactions to him. As in every crisis of my life, feelings were shoved down deep inside, put on hold so I could function and do whatever had to be done in the moment. Beneath the calm exterior however, I felt abandoned. Was she still so angry because I had moved out that she no longer cared to stick around to see my new life unfolding?

I shared my house with him for a while, becoming entangled financially and accruing a great deal of debt. He had several children who lived with us on and off, and I enjoyed being a mother figure for them. But that relationship became an on-again, off-again one too because of his anger issues and violent tendencies. Living with him was a whole different ballgame than dating him. His true nature, the one his ex-wife knew, revealed itself. I tried to extricate myself, but it took me landing in the hospital with a black eye and broken arm to totally sever the relationship.

George had popped back into my life a couple of months before that big fight. He called and wanted to meet and talk about an idea he had about setting up a counseling practice with me. I agreed to meet him for lunch. I could totally see working with George. Our counseling philosophies were very compatible. I learned at that lunch that the attraction to George had not vanished when he did.

We began to see one another again romantically. It certainly boosted my morale to feel that I was still a desirable woman. George went all out to bring me pleasure. Ours was not just a sexual fling. He cooked for me. He stimulated me intellectually. We talked for hours. I was able to just be me with him.

George helped me gain some perspective that November, as did Tom Moore. I had a few sessions with him again to help me sort out my attraction to George while still caring deeply for an abusive man. We talked about me surrendering to whatever this relationship with George was. But that surrender did not mean giving my power to him. If I was connected to the power inside of me, I wouldn't need to project it out there onto any man, Tom reminded me.

I had done that with Chuck too. The difference was that Chuck was connected to his own power and didn't need mine. Our marriage was harmonious, a partnership based on accepted and defined "roles." Mine was running the household, caring for the children. His was to provide for us. Life was simple then. There was no power struggle. One thing for sure, my relationship with George was based on mutuality and pleasure, not control and pain.

It was Saturday evening, August 16th, 1985, and I'd had a very hard day at the clinic and went to George's to have drinks with friends after work instead of going straight home, where this man was living with me. When I did, all hell broke lose and the fight ensued. Picking myself up off the floor and spitting up blood let me know I was not going to win here and just needed to leave. I got my car keys and drove off, headed back to George's.

I refused to go to the emergency room that night or the next day. I kept insisting my arm wasn't broken because it didn't hurt, at least as long as I didn't move it. George made a sling for me.

I saw an orthopedic specialist who my boss, Dr. Lea Braun, referred me to on Monday. I looked at the x-ray and was sure he had mixed my film with someone else's. That bone, broken completely in two, couldn't possibly be mine. But of course it was. The break couldn't just be reset and cast; it required a plate to repair. I was scheduled to go into St. Paul Hospital the following night to prepare for the surgery Wednesday morning.

I went out that night with one of the nurses from Routh Street and got smashed on margaritas chased with peach schnapps. She and George poured me into bed and then George took care of me when I threw it all up shortly thereafter. Talk about a true friend!

I was still in denial all the way to the hospital. I made George promise me he would keep my sons under control and not let them seek revenge. My fear was they would wind up in jail and the culprit would walk away free. He wasn't worth it. All my boys really liked George and I knew they would listen to him.

Charlotte and Becca (the business administrator who had been on maternity leave) came to see me in the hospital that night. I thought they might be there to fire me, but instead they had an incredibly generous offer for me. The surgery would fix my physical brokenness. They wanted to help me recover from the emotional brokenness. The clinic wanted to pay for me to see Ann Worth for a month. She was a therapist whose specialty was family systems therapy and particularly co-dependency.

Pia Melody, a pioneer in the field of recovery who had developed theories on the effects of childhood trauma that became the foundation for The Meadows, a multi-disorder facility specializing in the treatment of trauma and addictions, was coming to Dallas the last weekend in September to facilitate a victim's workshop. One had to be in therapy to attend. The clinic would cover that cost as well. After that I would be on my own in terms of therapy. They would support me in putting myself back together, but not in further destructive behavior.

My job was secure as long as I was healthy enough to handle it. I was feeling so much shame for having gotten myself into this situation that their outpouring of love was hard for me to take in. It was the rainbow of hope that sustained me over the next couple of months.

When I woke from the surgery my arm really hurt. I found that surprising, since it had not been painful before. I rang for the nurse who then gave me shot of Demerol. I was on that buzzer as soon as that shot faded, wanting another. I had never experienced pain that severe before, and I have a pretty high pain tolerance. It helped me stay in touch with some healthy anger that squelched any desire to ever mend that relationship.

When I was finally released from the hospital, Stephen took me home. He'd spent days cleaning up the place, washing the walls with bleach to get the soot off them. The house looked pretty decent when I first saw it again. He had taken all the linens, all my pictures of him, too much for me to take in as I walked through the place. He had slept in my bed too, and I couldn't help but wonder if he had been alone. I felt tremendous sadness, but also relief. *How can he care so little?* I asked in my journal.

One of the most humiliating experiences of my life occurred the day Stephen and I went downtown to try and get the gas company to replace that meter. I didn't have the money to pay the arrears charges and wanted to appeal to them to have mercy on me, to see that I was a victim of the man who had necessitated their drastic action. Sitting there, my eye still very black, my arm in a cast, filled with shame already in having to plead for some leniency, this was to no avail. The woman was unmoved by my pitiful presence and would not budge an inch. No payment, no gas. I left feeling very angry with her and the gas company.

My humbling process was just beginning. How I hated having to be so dependent upon others while my arm healed. Of course it had to be my right arm. Even the simplest task, like brushing my teeth, was difficult because of the shape of the cast and the angle at which it held my arm and hand. It took me forever just to dress. I would have to lie down across the bed to fasten my pants. It was awful.

Stephen was an angel those first couple of weeks home. He even considered not going to college that fall semester to stay and take care of me. I said no way. George took over when Stephen left. I had lots of friends all willing to help get me to work and home, etc. The clinic let me work in the office, away from all patient services, while I was recovering.

Through my work with Adult Children of Alcoholics, I came to see how the Universe had brought this man into my life to give me the opportunity to work through some unfinished business of Chuck's absence. For years I had lived with the fantasy of welcoming the prisoner home and helping him adapt as he re-entered the world again.

The night I got into the fight that left me with the broken arm was a replay of what I witnessed when I was about four. My father had come home drunk and he and Mother had words. Daddy, in his rage, picked up the bowl of gravy on the table and threw it against the wall and had given Mother a black eye.

And that was what had happened that night I came home late. He threw a container of fast food across my face in his rage. Instead of the fear that I felt as a child that made me run and hide, the anger of my mother that night surfaced. I really was trying to kill him. I didn't see what my mother did after the gravy episode, but my brother told me years later. She went into the kitchen and came back with an iron skillet and knocked Daddy out. That night, I found my own anger that led me to stand up for myself. However, I felt terrible shame that I had put up with this abusive behavior for so long.

After a couple of years of therapy with the twelve-step work, I came to be grateful for learning about my own co-dependency and how I was in denial for so long. I wasn't in love with that man. He was more of an addiction that I could now recognize and avoid repeating, Even so, it's still one aspect of my shadow I've found reluctant to reveal.

The other aspect I was unable to own publicly, but did decide to journal about that weekend, dealt with past sexual indiscretions that had left me fearful that Chuck's becoming MIA was punishment.

It was during the mid '60s that I acted out the shadow side of my sexuality, creating a great deal of guilt that would haunted me after Chuck left. While it is very difficult for me to write about my sexual indiscretions of that period, I feel that it is necessary background to understand my state of mind when Chuck became missing. Those were pivotal years for me.

In my early 20s, having worked hard to maintain the figure I'd finally achieved after my first pregnancy, I liked having other fighter jocks find me attractive and desirable at parties, as did Chuck. He had always thought I was a sexy, beautiful woman, but I had attributed his sexual ardor as merely the result of being in love with me. I was quite amazed to find that other men shared his image of me. After a few drinks, I found that I liked being desired by them as well.

There were several couples with whom we socialized most during this period, all young and happily married like us, living on a budget. One of our cheap entertainment evenings was getting together with one couple at a time for some penny ante poker. We were all close in age and all inexperienced sexually—the women probably more so than the men, I think. None of us wives had ever known any partner other than our husbands. The more we drank, the more flirtatious we all became. Soon the ante became an article of clothing. It was all so daring and at the same time innocent in a way. There was a huge thrill to flaunting the puritanical taboos of our upbringing. One evening our strip poker session led to us swapping partners.

I ignored the guilty twinge I felt on the mornings after, rationalizing that we were all consenting adults and there was no harm done. I never discussed my feelings with any of the other involved parties, including Chuck. I find it interesting even now as I acknowledge my shameful behavior (and that *was* how I judged myself when I was sober) that I had my own "rules" about my exploits.

I would never have sex with any of the bachelors in the squadron—and there were plenty of opportunities when I could have. Our brief swinging lifestyle really was a couple's deal we did together. Ours was a very happy marriage. I adored my husband and knew that feeling was mutual. I never felt threatened in any way by any of our "adulterous" actions. Nor did any of the other couples. All continued to stay happily married and be our friends. These encounters just sort of went by the wayside as our life circumstances changed.

In retrospect, I see our sexual exploration as a common thread of the times. There was indeed a sexual revolution happening across this nation, in part due to the availability of the birth control pill. I was unaware of the pill until after my first son was born in 1962. I loved it that Chuck and I could have a sexual life free from any fear of another unplanned pregnancy. We had lucked out that I had not gotten pregnant before we married. Our petting became more and more intense until we finally succumbed to full-fledged intercourse early on in our dating relationship. In fact, it happened on my living room couch one night, knowing that my parents were in their bedroom just behind that west wall. My parents' trust in us both was phenomenal. Funny, Chuck had just assumed that I was not a virgin because I had been so blatantly sexual with him. He was quite surprised when he broke through that hymen! We were both so naive then.

I explored all of this in my journal that weekend, and then, turned my mind back to thinking about Chuck's funeral. After hearing about Jim's funeral, I was becoming clearer about what I wanted from Chuck's. My overall goal was that everyone there would feel as if they really knew Chuck, the kind of person he was, especially his grandchildren who had never met him. To them he was just a photograph on the wall. I wanted a slideshow of family photographs and I wanted a limousine to transport the whole family—sons and grandchildren—together from the church to the DFW National Cemetery. I also wanted the services videotaped.

Of all the times to get yet another unique opportunity—I was asked to pose for a new book about make-up tips for the book *Looking Younger*. I had come to know the author and make-up artist, Robert Jones, through my boss. I felt honored that he would ask me to be a model for a makeover to make me look "as young as I feel." It was quite the fun experience for a Sunday morning. He straightened my hair and gave me a style I was not sure I liked at the time, but I trusted his judgment. My friends and family liked it though. The make-up part was amazing and I definitely left his studio looking younger than when I had arrived!

As I waited to hear from Pleasant Mound's minister, I began to feel anxious that the place for Chuck's service was still in limbo. I decided to visit a funeral home close to me and check out the feel for such an option if the church didn't work out. I quickly discovered that their cost for their services I wanted was prohibitive for the budget I was allowed.

Then I spoke with Chuck's sister Wanda about the still-pending arrangements and she told me that Laurel Oaks, the funeral home where my mother-in-law had worked for years and the cemetery where Chuck's stone was laid next to his parent's double marker, had called to offer their services. It wouldn't hurt to meet with their director to see what they might have to offer.

Why had I not thought about Laurel Oaks to begin with? It was certainly located with easy access to LBJ for the half-hour drive to the DFW National Cemetery and was close to both Charles and Scott's houses. We could have both services on the same day. Chuck's urn and the bone identified as him would be on the altar for his individual service in the morning, just as Brenda had buried Jim's urn in Pampa. And the group burial with a flag-draped casket for the remains not identifiable as either man specifically would share a coffin and group grave at the National Cemetery.

CHAPTER 12

DAVE'S SECOND INTERVIEW

When I next met with Dave, I picked up my story with the events of 1973. President Nixon ordered a halt to the bombing blitz of North Vietnam mid-January. During that time the U.S. lost 34 planes, including 14 B-52s, adding another 12 killed, 23 captured and 74 listed as MIA, to the already heavy losses of the almost nine year war against the communist regime.

In outlining the terms of the Peace Accord, Kissinger declined crediting the bombing efforts with bringing the peace, though he did say the North Vietnamese became more willing to talk afterward. The Peace Accord would be signed on Saturday, January 27th, 1973 in two ceremonies so that North and South Vietnam would not be placed in a position of having to recognize one another.

This was it, I thought! The weekend I would finally know if I was a widow or a wife. Talk about pins and needles—I nearly jumped out of my skin every time the phone rang that Saturday. All day friends were calling asking if I'd gotten any news. Finally about 11 p.m. the phone rang and a male voice identified himself as an Air Force sergeant with the Casualty Office. He read a telegram to me that stated there was no list from Laos, and Chuck would continue to be listed as Missing in Action. I was stunned. I had been prepared for anything but this.

"The major will continue to be listed as missing in action," he said.

It didn't take long for my anger to erupt. I went through the house slamming doors and shouting obscenities until I got to my room where I fell onto my bed and cried tears of fury, frustration, disappointment and disbelief. I wanted to kill Kissinger with my bare hands. I wanted to strangle him for this betrayal. He had promised us he would never agree to anything other than a package deal that would include Laos and Cambodia.

I felt nothing but anger for days afterward, but I only expressed it to my mother and other "sister" wives. When the *Dallas Morning News* reporter Marilyn Schwartz called me, I simply told her, "We're at the same place we were last week before the peace agreement was signed. We have no intention of giving up, but the waiting is so cruel, and now we have no idea how much longer it might be."[21]

Angry as I was, I still could not criticize my government publicly. I could not acknowledge to the world that I felt utterly betrayed. I was delighted that some of my "sister's" husbands would be home soon. But that joyous news was darkened by my own rage. On February 1st, 1973, the Defense Department released a short seven-name list of military POWs held in Laos. "There's nothing that would make me believe there were only seven men surviving out of 311. I can't figure out what they're up to," I told DMN reporter Doug Domeier. He asked if I believed there would be a fuller accounting later. "You bet your boots. I find it difficult to believe [the government] would accept that as any total."[22] Absurdly unbelievable!

The next afternoon produced the most dramatic and life-changing event of my life. I had seethed in anger all week, cursing Kissinger initially, adding Nixon to my list along with my entire government as the days passed. By Friday afternoon I came home before the boys got out of school and went into my bedroom, slamming the door with a vengeance, having reached the breaking point. I raged at God for His betrayal. I fell to my knees and screamed at Him, cursing Him, all the while knowing I was committing an unpardonable sin. But I didn't care. Nothing could be worse than what I was going through right now. I could stand no more. Death was preferable to more years of uncertainty.

"Damn You! Haven't I kept my promise to be the faithful wife and good mother? You sent me that dream telling me he would come home then. What the hell did you mean by a long, long time? What more do you want from me? This is so unfair!" I screeched.

Instead of being struck dead by lightening, as I had truly expected, in an instant all of my anger and frustration was immediately replaced by the most incredible peace, love and light. I knew then that it didn't matter that I had no answer. My happiness or wellbeing was not dependent on an answer. Everything was going to be okay. I felt an incredible embrace of a loving, caring God. Nothing else mattered.

I know now that I was being blessed with "the peace that passeth all understanding" that Paul had promised the Philippians when he told them not to worry or be anxious about anything. I was certainly aware of the concept, but it was no longer just a concept. I felt that peace, and it did indeed surpass any intellectual understanding. I didn't have to earn it by being "good." In fact, it had come in response to me violating what I thought was a cardinal rule. The peace I was feeling defied logic or words, but it was as real as anything I had ever seen or touched. It showed in my face. I was asked more than once about what had happened by friends who had seen me before my outburst.

For two years I had lived with the widow or wife question. Every action had been geared toward finding that answer. Now I knew it ultimately didn't matter. Did that mean I wouldn't continue to seek an answer? No, I just knew I would be okay with or without one. Was I still numb from the shock of betrayal or living in denial? Perhaps. All I knew for sure was that I felt peace rather than fury and right then, that was enough.

Only 555 names appeared on the first POW list handed over with the Peace Accord. Another 55 were identified as having died in captivity. Pentagon representative Jerry Friedhelm acknowledged that the list was incomplete, that they still expected to receive a list from Laos. At least six airmen were known to have been taken alive and another 311 missing in Laos. The National League of Families pointed out the absence of others known to have been captured in North Vietnam as well.

By the time the release of the first 140 POWs was announced, the North Vietnamese named 562 U.S. servicemen held captive, leaving 1,328 still missing. Of that number identified as alive, 456 were in North Vietnam, 99 in South Vietnam and seven in Laos. In addition, the communists listed 27 American civilians captured in South

Vietnam. Only seven men of the 600 missing in Laos had survived? I didn't believe that for a moment. It was impossible! I remained hopeful that Chuck and others were still alive somewhere for future bargaining.

By February 5th, 1973, U.S. officials announced that the first POWs held in the jungles of South Vietnam would be released in the An Loc area, 60 miles north of Saigon and 10 miles from the nearest point on the Cambodian border. The Sunday morning paper five days later announced that Operation Homecoming would bring the first 115 POWs home from Hanoi that evening. Sure enough, three of our Dallas-area men were among the first to be released. These were only a fourth of the total from the lists turned over at the signing of the Peace Accord. The remainder of those 562 identified as alive at that time would be released in three more increments, the last one by March 29th, 1973, Charles Jr.'s 11th birthday.

Watching the televised return of our POWs was bittersweet. I was glued to the news, not wanting to miss anything. Tears of joy flowed freely for both these men and their families who I had come to know, as I watched those first valiant soldiers silently boarding that C-141 bound for Clark Air Force Base in the Philippines. It would be six more days before our Texas contingent arrived at Sheppard Air Force Base.

February 18th, my 12th wedding anniversary, one of my "sister" wives, Shirley, was pictured on the front page of the *Dallas Morning News* greeting her husband after his more than seven years in captivity. And Major Warren Lilly, another Dallasite, bore a huge smile as he gave the hook 'em horns sign to the cameras. I felt tremendous pride seeing these men in their Air Force uniforms, home at last. But there were pangs of longing as well since Chuck was not among them.

I had no time to dwell on those feeling though. Dallas Cares was having the Freedom Tree Dedication that afternoon at the Hall of State building at Fair Park. The program was titled "Spirit of Concern for All the Prisoners of War and Men Missing in Action in Southeast Asia." Not only was it happening on my anniversary, but at the very site where Chuck had proposed to me. The missing man formation flyover was particularly poignant for me that afternoon.

The Dallas Cares office was swamped with calls from people wanting to know what to do with their POW bracelets, and we told them to wear them "until the prisoner whose name was on the bracelet is home or until the missing man is accounted for" over and over again. There was no plan as of yet for the bracelets. Melting them down and making a sculpture dedicated to the men was one possibility. My arm continued to be green from the copper of Chuck's bracelet. With more than 1,300 still MIA, there were going to be lots of bracelets still worn and sold. Our work wasn't done with the return of these few.

Communities all across America reveled in welcoming their resident POWs through the winter and into the spring. There were massive crowds at the home of returning Army Major Art Elliot for a party organized by Dallas Cares. His wife Wanda had given me a copy of a poem that had become a mantra for me, entitled "Wait For Me," written by a Russian war correspondent to his fiancée during World War II. I clung to the words of that poem, refusing to harbor any notion that Chuck was dead without some sort of proof. My dream was still so vivid, so real.

Dallas hosted the only national homecoming celebration for those heroes as part of a huge Memorial Day undertaking to honor all our veterans from every war, especially those who served in Vietnam. Invitations were extended to all 50 states to send delegations for this Dallas Salutes event.

Ten states sent representatives and they, along with some 415 of the returned POWs flew in Friday afternoon in time for a parade through downtown Dallas to begin the weekend festivities. All three major television networks bore witness to an enthusiastic crowd of some 35,000 as they stood cheering and applauding each group of former POWs and their wives.

I was honored to represent our MIAs. Governor Dolph Briscoe, former governor John Connally, Bob Hope and numerous other dignitaries and celebrities participated in a grand two-hour extravaganza. Jets from Sheppard Air Force Base provided a missing man flyover followed by an evening filled with patriotic pageantry and entertainment that closed with a glorious fireworks display and the singing of "God Bless America." It was truly a memorable celebration in Texas style.

That Cotton Bowl Stadium bonanza kicked off a pretty exciting summer for my family. Apollo 15's Astronaut Jim Irwin's High Flight religious foundation invited us to participate in one of five POW and

MIA Family Renewal Retreats at the YMCA's 3,000-acre Snow Mountain Ranch in early July.

Bill Rittenhouse, vice president and executive director of High Flight, knew firsthand of the trauma of readjustment facing our families from his own experience as a POW in Romania during World War II. Jim Irwin was a Baptist layman who had traveled all over the world sharing how he'd felt God's presence when he walked on the moon. He showed us the film of that famous walk.

I could feel God's presence as well watching that amazing event. I found the testimonies of all the leaders there quite inspirational. Former Miss America and celebrated vocalist Anita Bryant was part of that leadership. It was a delight to meet her and listen to her sing. My father always thought I looked like her. In fact, he once overheard a woman asking in the airport if I wasn't Anita Bryant when they had just sent me off for a flight. We wore similar hairstyles then, and I thought fondly of Daddy telling that story when I met her.

Stephen was barely six then, and it was the first airplane ride he could remember. He was in utero for his first flight when my father died during my seventh month of pregnancy, and we flew back to Dallas for the funeral.

I felt blessed beyond measure after that incredible week and still have my treasured autographed copy of *The Highest Flight*, their special illustrated edition of *The Living New Testament*. I took special note of in the text of my favorite scripture at the time after Jim's testimony: "And we know that all that happens to us is working for our good if we love God and are fitting into his plan" (Romans 8:28).

I had no idea how often I would look to that verse again after we got back to Dallas. Five days after we returned from this wonderful retreat, Chuck's father Eurcil died suddenly and most unexpectedly in his backyard. My boys were really saddened to lose yet another beloved "papa" figure in their lives. Now there was only my brother and Wanda's ex-husband to fill that gap in terms of family. He'd worked his postal route that morning, come home and was resting out under the trees with his granddaughter in his lap watching his grandson mow the lawn.

Lori and Norman were living with Jean and Eurcil at the time after Wanda and her husband Tommy divorced. He had complained of indigestion and had taken some Tums. I remember him doing that often. Apparently he'd had heart problems for a long while, but it had gone undiagnosed. He just dropped dead instantly with no warning whatsoever.

By the end of July, Hanoi agreed to let the United States recover the remains of 23 American prisoners of war who died in captivity and were buried just outside of Hanoi. The chief of our Joint Casualty Resolution Center gave a Pentagon news briefing during which he disputed the belief held by a number of organizations that some of the 1,300 missing might still be alive, a belief I held as well. He insisted he had no indication that there were any Americans who were still alive or escapees in Southeast Asia. However, he was hopeful about expanding his casualty forces soon, from government-held areas of South Vietnam, to areas held by the Viet Cong, to North Vietnam, as well as to communist territory in Laos and Cambodia.

Stephen started first grade in September, so now all three of the boys were in public school together—Scott in the fourth grade, and Charles in the sixth grade—which made my life easier in terms of transportation for at least a year. It also gave me more time for my volunteer activities. My associate pastor approached me about expanding my role with the Children's Division of my church. I had been serving as coordinator of the Children's Sunday School Department and director of our Vacation Church School.

He asked me to consider going to the United Methodist Educational Assistant Seminar at Perkins School of Theology, a four-year summer program that could lead to a paid position with the church in the future. I could begin next July, and the church would cover the cost of the program. It was certainly becoming obvious that I needed to start planning for our future, as the resolution of Chuck's status was not looking promising. I agreed that it would be a good move and liked the idea that I might eventually have more input regarding our curriculum.

My relationship to the church had certainly strengthened over the past three years and this church family had been an invaluable support system for us. I had begun regular attendance in large part for the boys, wanting to provide them the background I'd not had as a child, and with Chuck flying combat missions in Southeast Asia, I had felt a strong need for more than just my individual prayers for his safe return.

I continued to seek avenues for public awareness to put pressure on our government to not just sweep our guys under the rug, with the idea of more involvement in my church in the future. By November an appeal was made to Texas Governor Dolph Briscoe for his support. He announced that he had sent telegrams to the president and congressional leaders voicing concern about the lack of an accounting to date. Dallas Cares still had funds from bracelet sales and agreed to honor the families' preference to use those for one more big campaign on behalf of an accounting as opposed to scholarship funds for the children of these men.

The holidays were rapidly approaching. In lieu of Christmas cards, I drafted a form letter update to mail out to the almost 500 bracelet wearers who had corresponded with me, along with family and friends, personalizing it a bit with a photograph of the boys and me and each of our written signatures. It seemed an excellent way for me to do my part in public awareness, for every letter to a person with a connection to Chuck and me could in turn generate support from their circle of friends. It certainly helped me to feel that I was at least doing something to help resolve this limbo..

December 11, 1973

There have been no major changes for our family this past year. We have had no further word about Chuck. I've kept busy as ever with my church, my Cub Scouts, and "Dallas Cares." I bowl on a league and keep house in my spare time. The boys are all in school this year, Stephen, in the 1st grade, Scott—4th, and Charles—6th. They're well adjusted, normal, happy boys, characters and hams, and like all other little boys, eagerly awaiting Christmas Day.

I know you've all been wondering about the status of the man's bracelet (I hope) you're still wearing, so I'll bring you up to date. There are still 1,233 Americans missing in action in Southeast Asia, our major being one of them. (He was promoted six months after he became MIA.) There are 55 men still listed as POWs who have not returned, nor been accounted for. (These are men our government had tangible evidence to indicate they were captured.) Less than 100 status changes have been made as a result of the debriefing of our returned POWs. Not a single body of the 55 that North Vietnam admitted died in captivity has been returned.

The United States has honored the January Cease Fire Agreement. We halted the bombing, pulled out our troops, and removed the mines from Haiphong Harbor. Hanoi returned some 600 POWs, but other than that has blatantly violated that agreement. Only 10 of 320 returned who were captured in Laos, and they had been held in North Vietnam. Laos had signed their ceasefire in February, and on September 14th the protocol to set up their coalition government was signed. Any remaining POWs were to be identified, and a list of those who died in captivity was to be released within 15-30 days of that date. Nothing has been released yet.

Our government is making every effort to find out what happened to these men. In Thailand we have teams of experts ready to go at a moment's notice to investigate crash sites and exhume remains. Inquiries are constantly being made on the diplomatic front. But Hanoi continues to block these efforts. And we no longer have leverage to force her to abide by the agreement she signed.

I don't know if any Americans remain alive in Southeast Asia, and I feel it's irrelevant. We know Hanoi and her allies can give a better accounting than they are doing. The National League of Families is preparing to launch a nationwide campaign in which every American will be asked to help. I know I can count on you.

Let me take this opportunity to thank all of you for your support and your prayers. We are most grateful. And I want you to know that I have complete faith and trust in God. I thank Him even for this experience, for through it, He has taught me many things, brought me closer to Him, and given me a peace I've never known before. There is true joy in my life in spite of the difficulties. I no longer worry about the future, for it's in His hands where it belongs.

Merry Christmas and God Bless.

CHAPTER 13

TIRED OF FIGHTING

When the anniversary of the Vietnam Peace Accord rolled around, the National League of Families asked Americans to send telegrams to Hanoi expressing strong concern over the lack of accounting or returned remains in the year since they signed an agreement to do so. They also sent representatives before the Senate Foreign Relations Committee complaining that this nation had forgotten our loved ones and demanded that they put new pressures on Hanoi to account for the more than 1,100 still missing and return the bodies of those deceased. Maureen Dunn, wife of a Navy pilot shot down nearly six years before, accused the senators of failing to live up to their obligation to serve the country and defend its citizens.

"Gentlemen, how can you allow hundreds of men like Comdr. Joe Dunn to be written off by their government as unverified statistics of the Vietnam conflict? I am beginning to feel, as do most family members...that our problem has been Watergated, Agnewed, Richardsoned, energy Crised and Mid-Easted practically out of existence,"[23] she told them.

Administration spokesmen said that continuous efforts to gain information and search for gravesites had been rebuffed by both North Vietnam and the Viet Cong. "It is clear that they are continuing to use the suffering of the families of the missing to achieve political gains," she continued. They welcomed suggestions for a worldwide awareness campaign to arouse public opinion on the issue. One of the MIA fathers added a ban on reconstruction aid to North Vietnam and a denial of trade concessions to encourage Soviet intervention for that idea.

By February, some 60 congressmen urged President Nixon to meet with the families who were becoming increasingly disgruntled. Dallas Cares was back at the drawing board developing another campaign for an accounting because the League had withdrawn their support from the first one submitted. On the home front, I was still quite active with my Cub Scout pack. The leadership wanted a returning POW to be the guest speaker for our annual Blue & Gold Banquet to be held that last weekend of the month. Everyone wanted to meet one of these valiant heroes from Vietnam and hear something about how he had survived his ordeal. Major Robert Jeffrey consented to join us that evening. His own son Billy was of Cub Scout age. I was thrilled to have some time with this man who had been my inspiration to hold out hope that Chuck had survived since he had been such a miracle survivor himself.

In mid-April the North Texas MIA families sent a telegram to Secretary of State Kissinger urging that he seek an accounting of our men from the newly formed Laotian coalition government. The prevailing atmosphere now was desperation for the accounting to be completed. My optimism was certainly fading. Within a month I joined my Dallas MIA families in asking Sen. John Tower to co-sponsor legislation denying "most favored nation" trade privileges from countries failing to express official outrage over the failure of governments in Southeast Asia to cooperate with the United States in getting an accounting of our MIAs. We wanted action, not words. We wanted to know what had happened to our loved ones.

July proved a very busy time for me. In addition to Vacation Church School and my first Educational Assistant seminar, Dallas Cares launched their new campaign, "We Think It's Important." We asked the people of Dallas to send a few grains of soil to North Vietnam, believing that American soil is a natural vehicle—warm, genuine, easily obtainable, definitely American—and even the North Vietnamese revere their homeland. We wanted to emphasize that Americans cared and wanted our men back on their own soil. By September, the National League of Families endorsed the project and made it a nationwide effort to pressure Hanoi for answers.

While I was walking on forked paths that summer, one toward a future with the United Methodist Church, and the other still connected to the activism of the League of MIA Families, our nation was staggering in the throes of the culmination of the Watergate fiasco. President Richard Nixon announced his resignation before a live television audience of millions worldwide on August 8th, effective the following morning. Vice President Gerald Ford was sworn in on August 9th , becoming the only president of the United States who was elected neither president nor vice president, yet served as both. "Our long national nightmare is over," he announced, and proceeded toward the goal of healing our truly wounded nation.

Within a month he granted a complete unconditional pardon to the former president, and a week later announced a conditional amnesty program for Vietnam War deserters and draft evaders. The conditions? They must pledge allegiance to the United States and serve two years of public service. These highly controversial acts of forgiveness and compassion cost him any hopes of remaining in this high office. He had chosen to follow his conscience rather than political aspirations. What a pivotal summer it was, for both America in general and me very personally.

Our Dallas mayor Wes Wise declared September 9[tht]-16th the "We Think It's Important Week" with Sunday the 13th being a citywide day of prayer for the missing servicemen and their families. On the 11th, Dallas Cares set up a Soil Mailing booth at the Northtown Mall Shopping Center, and enlisted the support of PTAs and civic organizations and churches throughout the city. The *Dallas Morning News* continued to support our efforts and printed a detailed article describing exactly how and where to mail a few grains of soil. "MIA families still hope,"[24] the headline read. "You can adjust to anything, any condition, but you can't live with uncertainty," I told the reporter. "We *need* to know before we can get on with the business of living." Lion Country Safari gave 75-cent discounts for every envelope of soil properly sealed and stamped on the 21st and 22nd of the September. Two envelopes were needed for this project—one for the soil itself, sealed and securely taped inside a larger envelope, also sealed and securely taped, and addressed to the Ministry of Foreign Affairs, Democratic Republic of Vietnam (DRV) Hanoi, North Vietnam. Postage required was 26 cents per ounce.

We spent the rest of the year then flooding Hanoi with good old

American soil, hoping to give our government the needed leverage to negotiate for our MIAs. By November the United Nations Assembly took an unprecedented step in appealing for help in accounting for the dead and missing from "armed conflicts" (Vietnam was never a declared war) regardless of their character or location. And in December, Dallas dedicated its official Christmas tree to the 1,300 Americans who remain POWs or MIAs from Vietnam, giving yet another platform to remind people that resolution to the problem was still lacking.

By mid-December, the U.S. House committee report concluded that all our MIAs (751 by their count) were dead. Needless to say, that stirred angry rebuttals from the Dallas area families, and accusations that the report was incomplete and very premature. I told Doug Domeier, the very reporter who had done the first story of my family back in 1971, "I think we all realize the possibility of no one being alive, but an accounting is still needed....but in all reality, I don't think it's going to happen...it's unrealistic to continue leaving the status of these men open. I can't see how it helps the situation at all."[25] I knew my remarks would not be welcomed by many of my fellow MIA families opposed to the government just rubber stamping a write off of our men with no attempt to account for them. And those words were more indicative of my own loss of hope that an accounting was even possible.

In fact, five primary next of kin (PNOK) in New York had filed a class action suit against the secretaries of all branches of the Armed Services, challenging sections of military law allowing for status changes of MIAs to KIAs. They were successful; the suit had halted the process of those determinations until new protocols could be developed (*McDonald vs. McLucas*).

On Christmas Day, a homey picture of me and my sons decorating our Christmas tree, with Chuck looking on from his portrait in the background, graced the front page of the C section of the DMN. The photographer sent me several other photographs he took for the story that day of the boys and Rainbow, their beloved cat, outside with the crèche that decorated our front yard. The article, "MIA Family Waits, Watches, Hopes at Christmas," actually found my hopes for getting an answer about Chuck's fate waning. It was our fifth Christmas now without him and I was finding it difficult to remember what a Christmas *with* him was like.

I expressed to the writer of that story, Laura Allen, my concern about the priority our country seemed to be setting with regard to the MIA issue, and how it would affect future conflicts. "I expect my sons to serve [in the military]. What do I tell them if we just shove this under the rug? I won't be able to let this issue go until I feel that every human effort has been made to account for our men." When she asked if I had any New Year's resolutions, I told her that even though I still didn't feel like Chuck was dead, that I would not spend another Christmas as an MIA wife. "I will not be an MIA wife forever. I feel if we don't get some answers in the next few months, we won't ever get them. I'm taking...the avenue of how we're going to live the rest of our lives."[26]

Another two years had passed since the psychological deadline I had set for myself back in 1971 for the proverbial light at the end of the tunnel, and we were still no closer to a resolution of Chuck's MIA status. January 1st, 1975 the jury brought in a guilty verdict for Nixon's three top advisors, Attorney General John Mitchell and White House aides Bob Haldeman and John Ehrlichman, on all counts of the Watergate cover-up. And on that same New Year's Day, Communist troops launched an offensive that collapsed the Khmer Republic in 117 days of the hardest fighting of the war.

March 10th the North Vietnamese Army began their final offensive as 25,000 troops attacked the South Vietnamese town of Buôn Ma Thuột, in the central highlands. By the 25th, Hue was lost and Da Nang was endangered. The U.S. ordered a refugee airlift to remove those in danger. The South Vietnamese army was in full retreat. Two days later the Pathet Lao launched an attack against Hmong defenders in Laos, as the North Vietnamese forces continued pushing toward Saigon. On Apr 4th, a U.S. Air Force C-5A transport plane evacuating Vietnamese orphans as part of Operation Babylift crashed shortly after takeoff from Saigon, killing 144 adults and 76 babies. There were over 170 survivors. On April 17th, the U.S.-backed Lon Nol government of Cambodia surrendered to the Khmer Rouge.

On April 21st, Nguyễn Văn Thiệu resigned after 10 years in office, and handed the presidency to Hương. In his address to his people, this last South Vietnamese president accused the U.S. of breaking its promises of support and military aid. On April 28th, 1975, after one week as president, Trần Văn Hương resigned and handed power over to Military General Dương Văn Minh, who presided over the surrender of the government two days later.

April 29th, U.S. forces pulled out of Vietnam. The U.S. embassy in Vietnam was evacuated as North Vietnamese forces fought their way into Saigon. Conditions deteriorated further as South Vietnamese civilians looted the air base. President Ford ordered Operation Frequent Wind, the helicopter evacuation of 7,000 Americans and South Vietnamese from Saigon. At Tan Son Nhut AFB, frantic civilians began swarming the helicopters. The evacuation was then shifted to the walled-in American embassy, which was secured by U.S. Marines in full combat gear. But the scene there also deteriorated, as thousands of civilians attempt to get into the compound.

Three U.S. aircraft carriers stood by off the coast of Vietnam to handle incoming Americans and South Vietnamese refugees. Many South Vietnamese pilots also landed on the carriers, flying American-made helicopters that were then pushed overboard to make room for more arrivals. From our living room television, we watched the horror of these events as they unfolded. It was a sickening sight to behold and one I will never forget. Even Stephen, who had just turned eight, still remembers those images vividly. The last four Americans killed in action in Vietnam died that day—one was another Texas pilot.

On April 30th the city of Saigon fell to communist North Vietnamese and National Liberation Front forces. At 8:35 a.m. the last Americans, ten Marines from the embassy, departed as North Vietnamese troops poured into Saigon, encountering little resistance. By 11 a.m. the Viet Cong flag flew from the presidential palace. President Minh broadcast a message of unconditional surrender. Graham Martin, the U.S. ambassador to South Vietnam, made a hasty departure. The city was renamed Ho Chi Minh City. Closing a very costly chapter of U.S. history, President Ford called upon Americans "to avoid recriminations about the past, to look ahead to the many goals we share." On May 7th, our President formally declared an end to "the Vietnam era."

That spring marked the end of my era as an activist MIA wife. What was the point? Watching Saigon fall evoked a healthy anger that prompted a new resolve within me. Disillusioned about the efficacy of yet more letters or speeches, I decided to back away from the

League and Dallas Cares completely. I was tired of fighting an impossible battle. It seemed to me that staying angry, no matter how justified, only fueled more anger and potential bitterness. I questioned whether perhaps my sons felt neglected because most of my energies were always focused on Chuck.

The Vietnam War had cost me my husband. I'd be damned if it would destroy my family too. That's when I made a conscious decision to accept that I would never know if Chuck had survived that crash or not. I knew clearly that God was with me, that all would be okay somehow, and that would have to be enough. I also knew that if Chuck were alive somewhere he would know that I still loved him and was not abandoning him, rather simply turning him over to God, in whose loving embrace he had always been anyway.

July brought my second Educational Assistant seminar at Perkins. Those two-week courses were filled with both lectures and then individual group work associated with the theme of the training focus. In thinking about stewardship responsibilities, my group was assigned to interview Rev. Fred Gealy about the ethics of spending so much money on the Space Program when there were so many social issues in need of funding, and people still starving to death on this planet. At some point during his responses in favor of continuing our space exploration, he said to us that phrase I mentioned before, "Under God we are obligated to know what we can know."

Those words went straight into my gut like a flaming spear thrown with great force, igniting a fire to know more. I knew instantly that I had to return to college. I no longer wanted to be just an Educational Assistant. I wanted to be the Director of Education. I was filled with excitement, yet fearful at the same time. I was thirty-three years old and had been out of school for fifteen years. Could I really do this? I talked to a dear friend from the class about it and he was most encouraging, saying, "Of course you can do it. Go for it!" Despite my trepidation, I felt as though I really had no choice. This was clearly a calling that refused to be denied.

CHAPTER 14

IVORY TOWER AWAKENING

I discovered that I could get basic credits from Eastfield Community College. It was less expensive and closer to home than Southern Methodist University. There would be other students there who, like me, were returning to college later in life, in addition to the eighteen-year old high school graduates. I could structure my classes during the times the boys were also in school and be home for them in the afternoons. For years I had known that I could use Chuck's VA benefits to get a degree. Never had I been the least bit interested in doing so—until now. So by August I was enrolled and officially a student at Eastfield.

My fears and doubts dissipated quickly that first semester as I became totally enamored with learning. *Every* class was meaningful on some personal level, a veritable crucible for self-awareness. My thirst was unquenchable. Returning to college as an adult with more life experience was far more rewarding than it had been back in 1960. I had been in the nursing program at the University of Texas for only one semester after I graduated from high school. I had none of this same kind of drive that consumed me this time around when I was at UT in 1960.

Seeds of feminism were sown that first semester, most unexpectedly in the mandatory math class that had given me much angst. When we were given a list of mathematicians from which to choose for a final paper for the course, I asked the professor if there were any women mathematicians throughout history, as none were on that list. He didn't know the answer to that but said it would be a perfect thing for me to research. Lo and behold, in the library I found a book published just the year before by MIT Press entitled *Women in Mathematics.*

I began my report with this paragraph: "Lynn Olsen quoted from Lewis Carroll's *Through the Looking Glass,* where the red queen says to Alice, "It takes all the running you can do to keep in the same place. If you want to get somewhere else, you must run at least twice as fast as that" (p. 1189), claiming it an applicable metaphor for women in mathematics. (That was pretty much the message I got from my own mother regarding my desire to become a doctor.) Yet despite the prejudice against intellectual women through almost all ages, there have always been those with the courage and determination to make their gifts their own. Ms. Olsen wrote the stories of right remarkable women, Hypatia (370-415) being the first notable female mathematician."

I told the essence of each woman's contribution in my report, but focused primarily on Russian Sonya Kovalevsky (1850-1892), the only woman in the field of mathematics to have been honored with a postage stamp. And I presented my professor with that postage stamp for his collection. He was impressed and I felt exhilarated to be a woman.

In an American literature class I did a paper for extra credit titled "A More Powerful Female Realism with Kate Chopin." Though she viewed New World feminists as unrealistic, she strongly felt that women had the same drives as men and therefore should have his "rights" also. She thought the many problems confronting her sex far too complex for any easy solutions. She was well acquainted with the female psyche and had a compelling urge to write openly about its various aspects. Women's spiritual emancipation was a major theme for her.

The critics, who at the same time condemned it on moral grounds, called her novel *The Awakening,* published in April of 1899, a brilliant piece of writing. Her heroine, Edna Pontellier, is awakened in full to an imperative craving for sex, independence, clarity and self-knowledge and accepted her animalism, feeling neither shame nor remorse. Neither does she blame the rake with whom she'd had an affair that summer. Such was Chopin's "female realism." She was shunned by friends and the literary world and was crushed that others could not see her truth. She soon ceased to ever write again and died practically forgotten.

I wanted to be like Edna in terms of her embracing her sexuality without shame or guilt. She was a 28-year-old wife of a wealthy businessman who traveled much of the time, leaving her to tend to their sons and run the household. I very much related to Edna's journey toward her own independence and sexual identity.

Chopin was clearly way ahead of her time. But *The Awakening* was resurrected in 1969 and began to receive the acclaim it had been denied for some seventy years. I was a little shocked by the ending of the book though. I felt really saddened by Edna's suicide and her inability to live with her newly found freedom. I suppose it would have been much more difficult for her in 1899 to maintain that freedom, given the culture of the time.

Being back in school really expanded my thinking. I was a compulsive student, which left me little spare time outside of my studies. I gave up my Cub Scout den and any PTA duties beyond just being a member. I was still active in my church, but had resigned my position as the Assistant Director of Education. I was becoming far more liberal in my Christianity than our current pastor and found myself attending Sunday school to make sure that my sons were getting the benefit of Methodist teachings in the curriculum we were using at the time. But then I would leave before the church service and go home to watch the Rev. Barry Bailey's service at the Ft. Worth United Methodist Church on the television. I always felt renewed after his services.

I did attend an old fashioned revival that year where a hell fire and brimstone guest preacher was brought in. As I listened to his message shouted with great urgency, I took what seemed valuable to heart and let the rest flow through and back out into the cosmos. Stephen brought me back to the reality of what I was doing as we walked out of the sanctuary that evening. He was very disturbed and muttered something about how he must be really bad because God was punishing him. When I stopped and asked him what in the world he was talking about, he told me that he must have done something really bad because God hadn't answered his prayers about his daddy.

I was stunned and of course told him that was not true. I assured him not getting his daddy back had nothing to do with anything he or any of us had done that was bad. Talk about an eye opener. I had to really face my own crisis of faith in Christian theology and the more fundamentalist path my church was taking. The leadership who had inspired me to take on the education role in the church had been reassigned elsewhere. Suffice it to say, I no longer took for granted that I could subject my sons to sermons I disagreed with, assuming they could take away only the good and leave the garbage.

My spring semester American Literature class introduced me to Flannery O'Connor, the writer my professor suggested I read because of my religious studies major. Reading *Wise Blood* was probably *the* most difficult novel I have ever read. I could stomach only a chapter at a time and was grateful that all those chapters were short. Hers was considered a Southern Gothic style relying heavily upon regional settings and grotesque characters. Grotesque? Understatement! Ms. O'Connor was a devout Catholic who claimed she saw from the standpoint of Christian Orthodoxy.

Her protagonist, Hazel Motes, a twenty-two-year-old recently discharged from service in WWII and surviving on a government pension for unspecified war wounds, returns to his family home in Tennessee to find it abandoned. The grandson of a traveling preacher, Motes grew up struggling with doubts regarding salvation and original sin. His war experiences led him to become an avowed atheist who intends to spread a gospel of anti-religion, and he founds The Church of God Without Christ.

Hazel boards a train for Taulkinham where he befriends a profane, manic, eighteen-year-old zookeeper who introduces him to the concept of "wise blood," an idea that he has innate, worldly knowledge of what direction to take in life, and requires no spiritual or emotional guidance.

During an extended period of living as an ascetic at the boarding house, he begins walking around with barbed wire wrapped around his torso and sharp rocks and pebbles in his shoes, and after paying for his room and board, he throws away any remaining money from his military pension. Although at first he rejects conventional religion, he is obsessed with salvation, and eventually blinds himself in an act of atonement.

Flannery O'Connor's first novel certainly prompted me to re-examine religious dogma. I did not enjoy reading *Wise Blood*, but I was grateful for that professor's insight to suggest I do so. It was definitely thought-provoking.

It wasn't until the fall semester of 1976 that I had a class in my actual major: Religion in American Culture. I was in heaven as we studied the spectrum of denominations that have competed for the faith of Americans since the founding of this great nation. I did a paper for our second test on liberal/conservative Protestantism and it really helped me clarify my own position and understand the reasons why I definitely fell under the liberal label.

Our professor took us on a field trip to visit various churches in the city at the end of the course. What I remember from that day was the extreme contrast between this ornate Greek Orthodox church and a poor Baptist church in West Dallas. The first was a work of art with all the mosaic tiles with real gold. It gushed wealth. Yet the smaller simple frame church in West Dallas also housed a children's day care center. Every square inch of their space was in use for the community. They desperately needed more space, indeed, more of everything. But their ministry was far more impressive to me and called forth that same line of questioning I'd had about the space program that had landed me back in school in the first place.

I was also most fortunate that semester to have chosen an art appreciation course that was team-taught with a philosophy professor. It was an experimental class, one never done before. We would be looking at art phenomenologically, experiencing art works themselves rather than just studying them historically. We were given a formula to use as we looked at each art piece, with the goal of the process to get to the essence of the work, i.e. evoke an aesthetic experience with the art piece itself.

It all sounded interesting as the professors described the nature of the course, but I was not at all convinced there was such a thing as this so-called "aesthetic experience," let alone that it might be possible to achieve one. For the class, we were to journal in *The Nothing Book*, a cleverly designed blank hardback book "for poets, travelers, writers, doodlers...and all of us who've every wanted to do a book." I thought the H. L. Mencken quote on the back inside flap seemed appropriate for what we were doing: "Nothing can come out of the artist that in not in the man."

We attended lots of art exhibits during that course, two especially impressive ones: an Edvard Munch exhibit at the Dallas Museum of Fine Arts and one on Fauvism at the Kimball in Ft. Worth. With each show we were to pick one particular piece to study, spend time with it, use the formula we'd been given, and then write about it in our journal and say whether or not we had felt its essence and had an aesthetic experience. A daunting assignment for sure! I was not a woman greatly in touch with her feelings then. I lived primarily in my head.

Well, the field trip to the Kimball would change that. It was, without a doubt, *the* most awesome experience of my educational endeavors yet. Upon entering the exhibit, I felt assaulted by two enormous canvasses of Andre Derain's: *The Dance* (73"x90") and *Turning Road L'Estaque* (51"x776 3/4"). Screaming at me in vivid primary colors that literally took my breath away, I gasped in horror. My heart literally beginning to race. Panic grabbed me. *Oh my God, I'm gonna have to engage with one of these!* I thought. "Fauves," as the critics of 1905 had dubbed these artists, means literally (and perhaps appropriately) "wild beasts."

I steeled myself, took a deep breath and continued following the line into the exhibit. I wandered through the entire show a couple times, trying to find a more subdued work of this movement that I felt somewhat drawn to. I finally settled on one, another Derain in fact: *The River Seine at Chatou* (27 1/4" x 43 5/8"). It felt quite tame in comparison to the others, though the smaller size may have contributed to that notion.

I stood a safe distance away from the canvas and began with my formula, first describing it in as great a detail as I could, looking at the technique, the working form, the color, and my reactions. Then I began to subtract all preconceptions on our list of all the ideas we tend to project onto an image, to see what emerged from the piece itself. I don't know how long I stood there looking at this one canvas, waiting, staring intently. But suddenly I found myself pulled into that scene by those enticing branches, down toward the river, into the church and there was this incredible feeling, no—a *knowing*—that I was one with this painting. There were no longer any boundaries separating us. We were one. Talk about an *a-ha* moment! I truly felt that, indeed, all is one. I felt totally alive, joyously excited.

I left the exhibit and went into the older classical wing of the museum, looked at the paintings I would have appreciated before this experience, and found them dull and boring. I couldn't wait to get back to the Fauve pieces. They were alive. All those colors that I had described as unreal felt now the most real. With every walk through that exhibit I saw more works I actually liked. I felt that perhaps I could actually deal with the two at the entrance now, but our time was over. We were called to board the bus again for home. I was revved up all the way back to Dallas, images racing through my mind. Surely this must have been what my professors had talked about. I had achieved an aesthetic experience with a Fauve work of art.

I went back to the Kimball the following weekend and spent another three hours with the Fauves, loving every minute. To this day *The Turning Road* is one of my favorite paintings. I went to New York years later to see it again. And I have seen it in Houston where it is a part of their permanent collection. I discovered later that *River Seine at Chatou* is part of the Kimball's permanent collection. My perception of art was transformed forever through Derain's Fauve works and a philosophy called phenomenology. I was opened up to my feelings as never before. I was somehow transformed too through this very personal encounter with Derain.

I learned at the end of that semester that I would have to transfer into SMU for the spring term. It seems the 19 credits from my 1960 UT transcript all counted toward my degree plan. I could take only more three hours at a community college level for credit. I had assumed I could stay at Eastfield for two full years so this news really unnerved me, rekindled some of that fear I'd first felt at Perkins. I didn't feel ready for the "big league" yet. But ready or not, I had to transfer. At least it meant I would finally get into my major. While hungry for more religious studies hours, I felt resistant to the change. I was just becoming comfortable as a returning student at this community college.

It had been a rewarding year in so many ways. I loved being back in school. I felt as though I could easily stay a full-time student forever. While my studies demanded a very tight schedule with precious little down time, it was not energy draining like the battleground of my MIA activities after the Peace Accord. The expansion of my world in the academic setting was invigorating, yet unsettling too, as I became aware of how I would not want to give it up if Chuck did by some miracle turn up alive.

I had turned my back on the League, but doing so didn't take away the twinges of uncertainty that lurked in the shadows. Even worse, I began to notice how appealing some of my professors were. And there were a couple of men in my Educational Assistant summer group I felt attracted to. Of course, they were both married; but so was I. In fact, there was a degree of safety in that fact. The occasional fantasy was assured of remaining only that. It was a new phenomenon for me though. I had never been attracted to other men before. Sure, I'd flirted. But no one was ever as handsome to me or as desirable as Chuck was in my eyes.

America celebrated her bicentennial that year and elected a Democrat, Jimmy Carter, as president, sweeping the Vietnam and Watergate era out for a start fresh. Personally I was looking at what needed to be swept out of my internal state of the union, like my future at Pleasant Mound United Methodist Church. We did have a new minister that I really liked, but his "good news" Methodism was not the direction my theology was taking me. I was in a very transitional space that was anything but clear as 1976 came to an end. All the holiday festivities and preparations made it easy to stuff those feelings down and focus on just being the mother of three terrific sons, enjoying our winter break together.

I entered SMU that spring semester of 1977 with lots of feelings rumbling beneath the surface. It was a bigger challenge being further from home, driving 16 miles versus 6—more preparation in terms of meals and snacks for the boys until I got home from classes. I would prepare casseroles and meals that they could start to heat in the oven or microwave. I was now in classes predominately filled with 18- to 20-year-olds, though eventually I would encounter a couple of older women returning to school. The grandson of Fred Gealy was in one of my religious studies classes during my semesters there and I told him how his grandfather had been the initiating spark for my returning to college.

I was really thrilled at finally being able to take all religious studies courses. The available menu was amazing. I was in heaven. Well, not without a little hell first. My courses that first semester included Highlights of the Old Testament, Great Religious Leaders, The Psychology of Religion, and Woman, Myth and Society. Dr. Thomas Moore, who would go on to write the best-selling book *Care of the Soul* and become my therapist, was my professor for those last two courses. C. G. Jung's *Religion and Psychology* was a primary text for the first one and my introduction to archetypes. We also read Robert Ornstein's *The Nature of Human Consciousness,* Sam Keen's *Beginnings Without End,* Peter Shaffer's *Equus,* and essays by James Hillman.

The Woman, Myth and Society course introduced me to the goddesses and many of the "occult" arts–astrology, I-Ching, and the Tarot. Erich Neumann's *Amor and Psyche* was our text, supplemented with handed-out essays. In one of our first class session, Dr. Moore told the Greek tale of Demeter and Persephone, prefacing it with how myth is sacred story, a way of imagining archetypal issues that shape every human life.

Hearing about how Hades had abducted Persephone as she was merrily plucking flowers in the meadow, whisking her away to the underworld in his fiery chariot, was like another almost mystical experience. Intuitively I knew it was a myth I was living, and somehow that gave meaning to the chaos I was feeling, though I was not sure exactly why. The understanding wasn't as important in the moment as recognizing that I wasn't crazy, just simply in the midst of some archetypal realm. In fact, the depths this particular myth held for me continued to unfold for years. Suffice it to say here that I knew what Dr. Moore was saying was Truth as I had never envisioned it before.

My first thoughts about why that myth resonated so with my soul had to do with Chuck's becoming MIA. It probably triggered a body memory of that morning I got the news. It certainly felt then like I was sucked into the underworld against my will as Persephone had been. By December of 1970 I had begun to let down and enjoy life, feeling that my foreboding about Chuck's Vietnam tour was unfounded. I was merrily picking the lovely flowers of the meadow as I greeted a new year, 1971, the year Chuck would come home.

As I reflected more, I realized that since then I had tended to almost dread going into the holidays. I had always loved the Christmas season—the decorating, the celebration of Advent, Santa Claus with the boys, all of the joys of the season. I had never associated that dread with depression connected to becoming an MIA wife, not wanting to relive that morning. I figured my intense reaction in class that afternoon was connected to being thrust into SMU ahead of my expected schedule and facing another "unknown" scenario as I had been in 1971.

My introduction to the archetypal psychology of C. G. Jung and the power of myth was the beginning of a whole new world for me. Seeds were planted that would take root in the next year, and lead me to double major in psychology. I also learned the importance of paying attention to my dreams in that class, and I began keeping a dream journal. There was one holiday weekend that spring when SMU chose not to close. Dr. Moore was aware of how few students would probably actually attend that Friday, so rather than have a structured class, he just told us to bring our dream journals and we would work on some personal dreams that day. Of course, I was the only student to make an appearance. So we went to his office and worked a dream I had recorded earlier in the week.

I was astounded at how that dream reflected what was going on in my life after we began talking about associations with particular images. What had seemed to have no relevance to my everyday world was on target with the feelings about my "real" world. The dream was some sort of war drama with Germans and Japanese characters that included a foreign word that had been spoken to me. Dr. Moore asked me if I had looked it up to see if it was a real word. Well, of course not. That thought never occurred to me.

I left his office for the library and lo and behold, it was a real word that meant butterfly—the symbol for psyche and transformation. I was totally blown away by that hour we spent looking at a dream that had made no sense to me when I struggled to write it down. I didn't even believe I dreamed before taking that course. It was only after following Dr. Moore's instructions to keep a pad and pencil by the bed and record whatever image I could remember upon waking that had brought me to this place of actually remembering an entire dream scenario.

The Demeter/Persephone myth continued to churn underground throughout the semester. Persephone is the archetype of the young daughter still unaware of who she is apart from her mother and in my case, also apart from my identity as Chuck's wife or Charles, Scott, and Stephen's mother. She is a victim of her circumstance. In the myth it is Zeus, Persephone's father, who sanctioned her abduction by his brother. Zeus betrayed his daughter. Zeus was my government and "father" God. Psychologically I was still living the role of daughter, sharing my mother's home after Chuck left.

Discovering the power of my dreams and of myth, I wanted to

leave my role as waiting wife, to be the "innocent" young maiden again. I was starting to notice and be attracted to men, feel the rumblings of desire for contact with the opposite sex. I knew that dating was out of the question as long as I was still married. The military was beginning their push to change the statuses of all MIAs to KIA. Was I ready to take that action myself? Was that part of all the rumblings I had felt at the beginning of the semester?

Being an MIA wife was like trying to walk balanced on a tight rope up in the air with neither foot firmly planted on the ground beneath me. Every major decision that came up would hinge on the question of whether or not Chuck would ever come home again. Politically nothing seemed to forecast any resolution to the MIA accounting any time soon. The military would most certainly have him declared dead before much longer with no evidence to prove otherwise. What if I requested a status review, took that step myself to have him presumed dead? I didn't want to marry again, but I did want to be able to express my sexuality and date again.

When the semester was over I sat down with my sons and asked them how they would feel if I requested a status review for their dad to have him presumed dead. We could have a memorial service then to honor him. They had nothing much to say about that idea except that they were okay with whatever I wanted to do. Charles had just turned fifteen in March, Scott remained twelve until September, and Stephen was ten in April.

Then I had that same conversation with Jean, my mother-in-law. She too said she was supportive of whatever I wanted to do. So I sent a letter of request for a status review to the Casualty Office at Randolph AFB. I listed a narrow range of dates I was available to make it happen. I had my last Educational Assistant summer session at Perkins, plus our two-week annual vacation with Mother to work around. Col. Gratch scheduled the hearing for June 8th.

I took Jean and my sons with me to San Antonio so they would hear everything I did during that review of all the known facts of Chuck's case. That car ride was memorable for sure—and I think it may have been the first time in my life I'd wished I had told a lie. Jean began to ask me about my studies for this religious studies degree. She was shocked that I was studying anything other than the Christian Bible.

The revelation that I did not believe in a literal translation of her sacred scripture was a devastating blow to her. I made the mistake of referring to some story as a myth, and all attempts to soothe her by explaining the truth of the story as I saw it metaphorically were to no avail. She finally asked me point blank if I believed that Jesus died for our sins. When I said no, her tears turned to hysteria.

I know she was genuinely concerned for my salvation. She was afraid I was going to hell and taking her grandsons with me. Hard as it was in the moment, however, it felt great to be honest and own the questioning of many old religious beliefs. I continued to feel the certainty that I was loved just as I was from that incredible moment God had held me in that glowing peace back in 1973. But the boys looked as though they just wanted to fade away into the upholstery of that back seat. They were not about to open their mouths and say a word. That last hour of the trip was made in silence.

We had to resume polite conversation by the time we were getting checked into our motel. Needless to say we did not talk about religion again. Cordiality would prevail the rest of the weekend. We all needed to get some rest because our appointment with the Colonel was early the next morning. I felt worn out after upsetting Jean so badly, like the driving wasn't tiring enough.

I was amazed at the astute questions the boys all had after listening to the presentation outlining that last mission Chuck flew. Col. Gratch was pretty astounded too. Gratch described Chuck's mission that night—to take out a truck storage site where supplies were being brought from the North into the South, and how his F-4 had crashed with a huge fireball explosion very close to the target area. One of the boys stated proudly, "Then he accomplished his mission, didn't he?"

The officer stammered a moment before his words, "I guess you're right, son," finally uttered from his dropped jaw. After everyone had all the time they needed to ask whatever questions had arisen during that briefing, we were sent on our way for lunch. Col. Gratch would call me when they had the paperwork ready for me to sign.

By early afternoon, he had called and I drove back alone to sign the paperwork. However, upon reading them there in his office, I saw that they wanted to me to sign off saying Chuck was KIA as of January 3, 1971. *No, No, No!* I firmly told the Colonel. I would accept a presumptive finding of death as of this day, but not this backdated KIA.

"Oh but, Mrs. Stratton, it's all the same—your benefits will all be the same," he assured me.

"It may be the same to you. It's *not* the same to me. A PFOD is an acknowledgment on your part that you really don't know for sure what happened. No one has gotten into that crash site you say you have the co-ordinates for. No! I will sign only for a presumptive finding of death, nothing else."

Begrudgingly, he took the papers back to rewrite them. He was definitely not a happy camper. I, on the other hand was, because I had stood my ground. It was a grand first step for this Persephone woman who no longer cared whether or not she "pleased" the military. During all those years of my activism and constant exposure to the media as I spoke out for our POW/MIAs, I had always been most careful about any comments regarding the Air Force and government policy, given them the benefit of the doubt, so to speak. After all, I was still being supported by Chuck's salary. I should be grateful, right?

No longer was that my primary concern. Chuck had been willing to give his life so that his family would be cared for. I was determined now to make sure they had to admit they couldn't tell me with any certainty that he had died.

I received word from San Antonio then that Chuck was presumed dead officially on July 8th, 1977 and I arranged for a memorial service at Carswell AFB in Ft. Worth on August 20th. My minister at Pleasant Mound officiated in the very orthodox service. For me it was just a formality. I knew from my Christian education training that funerals were a necessary ritual after death to assist loved ones in the healing process.

The only emotional part of that memorial ritual for me was the missing man flyover which always evokes the tears. I felt no real grief at the time beyond that moment when "his" plane shot upward out of the formation, symbolizing Chuck's loss. I was merely complying with what I thought appropriate, the next step toward a new future.

My lack of feelings was not a reflection of the service. It was carried out with the utmost love and sincerity. I believe however, it meant much more to Jean than to me. My proactive move to bring about this declaration of death was not because of any feeling that

Chuck was dead. I just knew that he was dead to me in that I had done everything I had known to do to solicit an answer, but to no avail. It was necessary for me to cut that cord to Chuck if I were to ever be able to date again. The legality would let me know what my financial situation would be without him as well. As long as Chuck was MIA I continued to draw his salary. That would no longer be the case if he was declared dead. I had no idea what my benefits would be then as a widow.

Much to my surprise, it accomplished much more than that. After we returned home that afternoon, I was walking through the hall to my bedroom and I overheard one of the older boys, Scott as I recall, telling his friend about his dad, apparently showing him the model they had of an F-4. "This is the plane my daddy flew!" he exclaimed excitedly.

In that moment I realized that we'd not talked much about Chuck over the past couple of years. He really had been absent from our household. Sure, his portrait still hung in the living room, a beautiful oil painting my dear friend Wendy had painted from the last photograph we had of Chuck in his black "party" flying suit at Korat. (Wendy was the only one I had ever told about my fear when Chuck got those first orders for Vietnam at Oxnard in 1968.) But the reality was he was an invisible presence, there on the wall, but not here in our world. He was missing in action from our family. But no longer would that be the case.

August 20th, 1977 marked the day Chuck rejoined our family. We were free to talk about him again, share the stories we had buried in our memories. When someone has been gone for seven years, to speak of him as if he were still alive doesn't feel real, yet to speak of him in the past tense felt as though you were killing him off. Chuck had a place now. There was no body, but there was a stone at Laurel Oaks next to his dad matching the double marker open for his mother when she died.

As we talked openly now, I discovered that Charles had long ago responded to any questions about his dad that he was dead. He found it too painful to go into the whole MIA story. Any doubts I ever had about the decision to settle the open-ended uncertainty of an MIA status vanished that day.

Chuck's memorial service had a really huge effect on Stephen. Two to three weeks after that Saturday, Stephen came to my room wanting to talk about something bothering him. As we sat down on the bed, he began to confess about yet another time he had felt guilty about his dad. On Thanksgiving when he was pulling on the turkey wishbone with his brother, he wished for a little piglet of his very own.

No sooner had the bone snapped and left him with the winning short leg guaranteed to fulfill his wish, he suddenly felt this guilty pang. *I should have wished for my daddy to come home*, he said to himself. He'd been too ashamed to ever tell that to another soul before then. One more layer for his ball of guilt that began with him unlocking the doors back when Chuck left in 1971, then at the revival just four years later when he felt like a bad person because God didn't answer his prayers to bring his daddy home.

I had no idea that any twinge of guilt was left deep inside him. I thought I had convinced him then that he was not in any way to blame for his father's loss. Apparently all these memories had come back to revisit him since that day at Carswell AFB. While I was questioning my own parenting skills for being so oblivious to him still holding onto any such notions, I also felt incredibly grateful that he felt free to confide in me now. We talked a good long while. And the next morning we all slept in and watched Barry Bailey on the television, still in our pj's, for our Sunday worship.

It was definitely an act of God that we did. Of all mornings, Barry's sermon was about a young girl who was made to feel guilty about the premature death of her liberal theologian father by someone who had rejected her dad's interpretaton of the scriptures, and had written to say his death had been God's will because of his faulty theology. Barry totally dispelled that misspoken letter. It was like his message had been written especially for Stephen. We both looked at each other dumbfounded. Stephen's prayer had been answered at last, in a way neither of us ever expected. That sermon hit Stephen in his core and he finally really got it that his dad's death was in no way his fault or God's punishment.

We decided we needed to write to Rev. Bailey and thank him. His message was like a miracle. It was no happenstance affair that we were home listening that particular morning. We watched again the following week and the dear reverend acknowledged Stephen's letter in his remarks. I will be forever grateful for Barry Bailey whose theology had brought my entire family so much peace.

CHAPTER 15

BEYOND THE DEATH OF GOD

The fall semester was a lot calmer after the events of the summer. I signed up for the class called Religions of China and Japan, eager to learn more about Taoism. I took the two classes—Jesus' Life and Teachings and New Testament Origins—classes my mother-in-law would have been very happy about had we ever discussed what I was studying again. Beyond the Death of God was my fourth choice. I had so many questions about traditional Christianity and hoped that particular course would help me find some answers. In our second exam I wrote that it had done that, but at the same time raised new ones even as old ones were answered.

"The options presented were more than I ever imagined. And I can see the validity of each, though, obviously I do not agree totally with any... I have never thought of the word 'God' as any ultimate reality. The whole notion of transcendence, as noun, verb, active, passive is extremely helpful. And prayer defined as talking to myself in the presence of God—it's so simple, yet I've never thought of it that way. I had questions about prayer. I've experienced its power—but as my whole notion of God has changed, I can not help but question its validity.

"This course has enlarged my scope, put some 'scattered' thoughts and views into perspective, confirmed my searching—'the truth really does set you free'...now I am so much more comfortable with not having 'the answers'—The more I learn, the more I'm impressed with how little I know and understand.

"I am committed to life lived and experienced in *this* world—active participation with God. That's an exciting thought! The justification for life is in the living. And it may well be all fiction—but that doesn't bother me either. At the beginning of class it might have. I plan to pursue thoughts on process theology. A definite goal for me is to find the symbolic language to communicate with people of all persuasions, for only in so doing, through affirmative action can the world be turned around and thought patterns changed."

The spring semester of 1978 continued with more amazing courses of study: The Psychology of Women; Myth, Dreams and Self; Hinduism and Buddhism, plus a Yoga physical education class. All were rich with new knowledge, new ways of seeing. My interest in my dreams was further nourished in Dr. Moore's class and at some point I asked him what he would charge for some private sessions with me to further explore my dream images and personal myth. Apparently he hadn't done that kind of dreamwork with clients before, but said he'd think about it. He finally agreed to try a few session and see how it went.

Buddhism brought another amazing insight regarding my MIA experience. I was writing a paper on the koan—basically a riddle or unanswerable question a master gives his student to promote enlightenment (satori). The student then exhausts his every human effort to find the answer. At the point of crying "uncle," satori happens. Suddenly I realized that I had been given such a koan with the question *Am I a widow or a wife?*—one for which there was no definitive answer. I spent two years engaged in activities I thought would lead to me toward that answer. Then when I raged at God for not rewarding me for all my efforts, in that sudden flash—I knew the answer didn't matter. That was my satori experience. Now I had another way of understanding that powerful experience, previously associated with Paul's blinding flash on the road to Damascus. It was clearly archetypal, encompassing both Eastern and Western cultures, the result of finally surrendering the ego.

My Hinduism class brought me a really joyous experience that was totally unexpected. Our final exam was a take home. One look at the instructions sent me into a panic.

"Let us say that you are (for all practices and purposes) an omnipotent genie who has set for himself the somewhat amusing task of converting the USA to Hinduism. Outline (with copious illustrative detail, please) (a) your message—the sort(s) of Hindu teachings you'd select, and (b) your path—the sort(s) of Hindu practices you'd encourage. Be sure to indicate the position you'd take—one way or another—on the teachings of the major Upanishads, the teachings of the Gita, devotionalism, tantra, and the guru. You may consider the question of "tactics," but the "bottom line" must be the truth of the Hindu viewpoint, nothing less.

Advice from your "friendly local prof": (1) assume the reader's ignorance, (2) originality earns blue chip karma—do not follow class notes slavishly, (3) remember that the Banaras-Good-News has many sections, justify your emphases, (4) feel free to be intelligently critical of the Hindu tradition."

Sound a bit daunting? Surely did to me. But something happened as I began to ponder the idea and before I knew it, I became this genie on this magnificent mission to convert Americans to my beloved Hinduism.

I wrote, "I hear much in this country about 'liberation' and 'freedom.' That it appears so widely sought attests to its importance. True liberation, however, can come in this life only when one breaks the chains of ignorance and sees the universe as it really is. If you are not presently enjoying such a state of mind, but would like to, then perhaps Hinduism has good news for you, for within this ancient tradition is a path which virtually assures this kind of radical transformation within yourself." And off I went to make my case, continuing, "The hard truth is precisely this: There is One Ultimate Reality, the very nature of which is diversity. You would call it God. In India there have been many names throughout history. The tradition from which I come would prefers Shiva. Indian mythology provides an imaginative way of understanding the ineffable. Shiva is pure consciousness, the unity of the cosmos. His activating principle is the feminine Shakti. She is the energy, that constantly moving potentiality of everyday existence. Through her, one regresses as it were, back to Shiva and pure unity, and in turn progresses through the introspection process from that Divine Source to activity in this world."

The paper flowed as if this genie Professor Alper invoked was indeed at the helm. I actually had fun writing that paper. Always before, the fun came when an assignment was completed. But this one proved fun in the process. Seeing that A+ for my efforts was pretty gratifying as well!

I believe that pleasure was due to the fact that the polytheistic religion of the Greeks that I had come to value as operative archetypes within my soul, was meshing with the monotheism of the Christianity in which I had been raised in a way that provided some consistency within my ever-evolving credo. Articulating my understanding of Hinduism began to reconcile the aspects of Taoism and Buddhism, all the Eastern philosophies in which I had recognized great Truths, with those of my own Western civilization.

Heading into the summer of 1978 with that grand finale experience, I decided the whole family needed a really special fun vacation after the past few very trying years. All of Chuck's life insurance claims had been paid and I had the cash available to me. I had dreamed of meeting Chuck for R&R to celebrate our 10th wedding anniversary in February of 1971. Mother had always wanted to see Hawaii. My sons loved the ocean. So I set up a Royal Orchid two-week, four-island tour with a travel agency departing Dallas on July 29th. I had another year before graduating SMU and had no idea what my employment situation would be after that. The only thing I was clear about was that I wouldn't be content working within the confines of the institutional church.

While the boys liked the idea of flying to the Hawaiian Islands, they were none too keen of the very long flight part, especially Stephen. The entire flight to Colorado in '73, he was sick to his stomach. However, they all still wanted to go. They were the envy of all their friends. Hawaii—land of orchids and "the Aloha Spirit."

We spent two glorious weeks island hopping, soaking in the beauty, basking in the sun and surf, rejuvenating in the laid-back demeanor of the natives, partaking of their aloha spirit. My sons, then sixteen, almost fourteen and eleven, were impressed with the "shaka" sign greeting—extending their thumb and pinky finger while keeping the three middle fingers curled, waving at friend and stranger alike to gesture "Hang Loose."

It reminded them somewhat of our hook 'em horns greeting in Texas and they had fun using that sign to greet everyone. I preferred "aloha"—the very sound conveyed warmth and love with its melodious syllables. In the Hawaiian language, aloha translates to affection, love, peace, compassion and mercy. Westerners use it widely for both hello and goodbye. Like "shalom" in the Jewish tradition, or "namaste" in India, it carries the spiritual significance of a blessing, an awareness of the divinity in each of us.

And we experienced it daily, from our arrival in Hilo and the presentation of the first of many lovely orchid leis, to the sacred City of Refuge on the Big Island, to the black sand beach of Maui, to Pearl Harbor and the Byodo-In Temple on Oahu, to the magnificent lush fern grotto of Kauai—we did indeed inhale the very breath of the place.

The fall of '78 heralded my last year at SMU. Most of my courses were in psychology to fulfill the requirements for my second degree. While all were interesting, none captured my enthusiasm the way my religious studies classes had. I did have one more treat from my primary major, however, to add some spice to the more mundane curriculum—a class called Religion as Story. It was my second with Professor Kliever who was the head of the Religious Studies Department. (The first, Beyond the Death of God, had been a great preparation, as my understanding of religion was broadened to include all forms of transcendence.)

The syllabus we were given that first class period began with the precis that we would be exploring an interpretation of religion as a story-making and story-meaning process. Special attention would be given to the narrative forms of myth and autobiography as modern religious discernment as well as means of religious communication. "The course will seek to involve you in a process of story reading and story making as ways of discovering and assessing your own religious commitments."

Our texts were *Ancient Myth and Modern Man* and *The Autobiography of Malcolm X*. I was profoundly moved with Alex Haley's rendering of this militant black religious leader and activist of the early '60s. It was the first time I had ever been forced to stop reading because I was crying so hard. I knew very little about this man beyond his association with hatred and violence prior to reading his story.

His trip to Mecca was the crowning event of his life, one that broadened his image of Islam to see the message of world brotherhood. He was murdered by the perverted Muslim leadership he had devoted the last twelve years of his life to serving, precisely because he would have been more powerful than they with his new vision.

Malcolm X described racism as the inability of God's creatures to live as one, and called it the most explosive and pernicious evil on earth. I agreed with that assessment and saw parallels with sexism that had discriminated against women through widespread tokenism and stereotyping. Once again, lessons I derived from all my studies found their way into my psyche in very personal ways.

Dr. Kliever gave us autobiographical exercises to bring home quite personally the value of looking back at our own story to see how we have come to the religious identity we now hold. I've kept those and to this day am amazed at the revelations from those pages. It was the first time I had ever reflected on my life history as a whole. Thank goodness I had my mother around to help me with details like where all we lived when I was a child, and to help jog my memory of childhood events that were pretty scant. It was part two of the exercises that went into a more self-reflective mode. The very first question was about what my names meant to me and, whether or not I liked them, would I change them if I could.

"Sallie was my paternal grandmother. Mae came from Daddy's sister, Ethel Mae, an aspiring actress who died quite young, a victim of the flu epidemic of 1920 in New York. Her portrait had hung in my bedroom growing up. She was so very beautiful. My entire name conveyed my roots in a particular Hodges clan.

"Stratton is deemed my most important identification, deliberately chosen, binding me to the man I loved, the father of my sons. I liked the fact that Sallie was not so common, especially spelled with an ie. I went by simply Sallie Stratton, but had changed my signature in the past few years, at least in the way I signed my 'S's—a move I'm sure is associated with my search for identity and acceptance of the title as me," I wrote. As the little German guy used to say on "Laugh In" (Chuck's and my very favorite television show from its inception in 1968): "Veeerrry eeenter-resting."

Our final exam was a three-pronged take-home assignment.

Against the background of the semester's work, we were to (1) write a story that expressed our own fundamental religious outlook, lifestyle, worldview; (2) an essay or creed explaining the story; (3) then comment on the differences and difficulties we found in attempting to give an account of our life's final meaning and purpose in these two ways. My story was titled "Reflections" was inspired by my receiving a Christmas card from a dear old Air Force wife whose address I had lost.

In my reverie my attention was drawn to my bookshelf where a favorite story and verse collection my mother had read to me as a child caught my eye. Pulling it from the shelf and thumbing through the index, my eyes were drawn to the section "Roads to Anywhere."[27] I spun my story from that metaphor.

'The road I had found most significant to date had been that of the great dark cave of Psyche within which were indeed great treasures. This road has brought me home to my center within, giving not only depth to my life, but meaning to mythic traditions heretofore literalized unto death," I wrote.

"Depth psychology with its goal of 'soul-making' is for me a path to Truth," I continued in the credo. "Doctrinally I find more Truth in Buddhist philosophy—concepts like that of dependent co-origination, desire and clinging as the source of suffering, mindfulness, emptiness, the emphasis on right attitude and action (here I see Jesus as a parallel), the letting go of ego, the Buddha within, personal responsibility."

I concluded that both my story and creed expressed where I currently found myself along my particular road of life so far. The difference was that the story came to me, while the creed took more conscious effort, and I was aware of more discomfort with sharing the creed. Story seems the more communicative of the two forms. It opens up room for exploring meaning beyond the words themselves, offers more opportunity for comparing one's own journey to mine, seems more conducive to stirring one's own imagination. It could be read by persons of very differing religious outlooks and still speak to them. Anyone who has no Buddhist background or experience of depth psychology would not understand my creed. (It would seem that Dr. Kleiver planted the seed for this memoir way back in December 1978.)

The highlight of my last semester at SMU was Abnormal Psychology taught by none other than Dr. Jack Strange, who actually wrote our text for the course. He knew of my interest in Jungian Psychology, so had me actually plan and teach the session on C. G. Jung. I became his teaching assistant, a delightful and challenging experience. He autographed my copy of his book: "For Sallie Mae, Excellent TA, Phi Beta Kappa and Jungian 'extraordinaire.'" I have kept that treasured book, outdated though it is, having been published in 1965.

I graduated SMU Summa Cum Laude in 1979 with a BA in Religious Studies and a BS in Psychology. I was then faced with another decision about my future. I had two more years of VA benefits available to me. I had reached that place of knowing I would not fit in the institutional church any more and was more interested in the psychology of women at that point.

I applied for the Social Psychology program at SMU because they pretty much guaranteed employment at the end of that program, and I was accepted. My head knew it would be a better option career-wise, but my heart leaned more toward continuing my studies in archetypal psychology at the University of Dallas. Even though I saw no job potential as a result, I finally chose to follow my heart, trusting it would lead me to where I needed to go. And it did—but again, in a way I could never have imagined.

My undergraduate education had given me far more than diplomas to hang on the wall. It provided me with invaluable tools for understanding myself, for developing my own identity as I examined and clarified my deepest values through all I had learned from my studies of religion and psychology. I wanted to take advantage of the opportunity to soak in even more at a graduate level while the opportunity was there for me.

The overarching theme of the '70s for me was education. When Chuck became missing, the doors to the political realm and history of Vietnam and our involvement were opened wide. And it was through my desire to understand the backdrop of the POW/MIA situation that I was given a glimpse of the war from the Vietnamese Taoist perspective as well as the perspective of my own government. The lessons gleaned from my experience with the National League of Families were eye-opening in many ways and laid the foundation for my spiritual quest that sent me back to school for a more formal education.

In retrospect, I find it interesting to note that all my seeking during that very transformative decade was initiated by events to which I was reacting as opposed to conscious decisions I had come to on my own. In the beginning I followed the lead of the Dallas area POW/MIA wives. With no idea of what was next for me when Chuck was continued as MIA after the Peace Accord, I followed my associate pastor's vision for me. During my experience during that second summer seminar, I felt the first claim from an inner directing, Divine Higher Self. But answering that call did not feel voluntary at all. It did not initially feel like a real choice I was making on my own.

Deciding to have Chuck's status changed was the first time I was very clear about choosing to act on my own behalf without outside influence from friends. It felt very important that I take that action myself rather than wait on the government to make the decision for me. Financially it would have been more beneficial because I would have continued to draw his full salary for another year, but not emotionally or for my own self-esteem. It was a very empowering decision, which taught me at a heartfelt level the value of choice as a lifestyle. Choosing to end the limbo of those MIA years in order to focus on the future without Chuck proved to be very therapeutic.

Movies were also therapeutic agents, particularly *Coming Home*, released in 1978 with Jane Fonda in the leading female role. Still seen as "Hanoi Jane," due to her Vietnam war protests and actually posing for photographs with the North Vietnamese on their anti-aircraft gun that shot down some of our pilots now in the Hanoi Hilton, her films were being boycotted by the military community. Animosity toward her was high. I decided to break away from that mindset and see this film. Mother actually joined me.

I was really moved and in fact identified a lot with Fonda's character, Sally, who was a loyal and conservative military wife when her husband left for Vietnam, but essentially became her own person in his absence. The movie was nominated for six Academy Awards, including Best Picture, and Jane Fonda did win Best Actress for her performance. I was definitely rooting for her that year. I'd come admire the fact that she was willing to risk her career to stand up for her political beliefs against the war. That took a lot of courage. I shared the letter I had written to her telling her that with Dave that afternoon.

The Deer Hunter was the winning competitor for Best Picture then in 1979. Charles and Scott both wanted to see that film when it came out, so Mother and I took them. Stephen didn't go. I felt twelve was still a little too young for this "R" rated film. It was a powerful and thought-provoking film for sure.

This three-hour epic portrays the profound effects of the war upon the lives of Mike, Steven and Nick, steelworker friends from Claritin, PA. who enjoyed deer hunting on their off-weekends. They went to war together in '67 and became POWs in a camp where the guard entertained themselves by forcing the prisoners to play Russian roulette.

Steven breaks down and refused to participate and was cast into a pit filled with rats and dead bodies. Mike leads a revolt to rescue his friends and they make it out of the camp, but Steven is wounded and ultimately loses his legs. Nick, the youngest, is most severely damaged by the roulette torture, and goes AWOL in Saigon after leaving the hospital there. He makes money playing Russian roulette to send home to Steve. When Mike finds out, he goes back for Nick.

Mike finds him in a game and joins to play against Nick, hoping to jog his memory and persuade him to come home, but Nick's mind is gone from his drug use. At the last minute, Mike reminds him of their hunting trips together. You see a glimmer of recognition then in Nick's eyes and he smiles, puts the gun to his head and fires. Mike brings his dead body back home for burial.

I remember Charles commenting in the car as we left the theater, *"That* really was an Academy Award movie." He and I had often argued about what performances or movies were really of award-winning caliber. He understood what I had told him many times before after seeing this movie. He was right. The acting was great, but the intensity I could never watch again, though I have watched *Coming Home* many times.

Very few movies had been made about Vietnam at this time. John Wayne's *The Green Berets* from 1968 was a typical gung ho war drama prompted by the growing anti-war atmosphere. It was an anti-communist, pro-Saigon film that came out the same year as the Tet Offensive.

Both *Coming Home* and *The Deer Hunter* reflected a shift in national consciousness that was ready to look at the insanity created by that war. Both reminded me of the healing still needed for me personally as well as the rest of the nation. I let go of any anger toward Jane Fonda that year, but I am well aware that I am part of a very small minority of military families who had done so by then.

I still hate the fact that she let herself be used by the North Vietnamese with those propaganda photos. In May of 1969 the North Vietnamese invited her to come to Hanoi. She wanted to photograph proof of the bombing damage to the dikes she'd been hearing about. Her husband, Tom Hayden, felt strongly she should accept. By July 8th she was on a plane for Hanoi with letter she'd picked up from the Committee of Liaison with Famailies of Prisoners Detained in Vietnam.

She was shown lots of ruins and damage from our extensive bombing. On one such excursion, her guide had the driver pull off the road quickly because of an approaching raid and they hid in manholes for safety. When it was safe and they came out, she could see plumes of smoke in the distance. She began to cry and apologize to her guide. "You shouldn't cry for us. We know why we are fighting. The sadness should be for you country, your soldiers. They don't know why they are fighting us"[28]

On her last full day there, she was taken to a military installation and was required to wear a helmet, despite having made clear that she was not interested in such a visit. She admits she should have known something was up when she saw all the photographers and journalists there when they arrived. The soldiers sang "Uncle Ho" to her, then asked her to sing a song for them.

She had memorized one, "Day Ma Di," written by the students in South Vietnam which she sang. All applauded and laughed. While that joyous laughter and applause were going on, she was led toward the anti-aircraft gun and seated there. Lights flashed then from photographers. She realized pretty quickly the implication being recorded—that she would appear to be shooting down U.S. planes. She pleaded with them to not publish those photos.

I do believe it was her naiveté that was exploited that day. While I think she made it possible to be used for propaganda, I still admire the fact that she was willing to risk her career to stand up for her political beliefs against the war. That took a lot of courage.[29]

CHAPTER 16

THE MIRROR OF PENELOPE

By the time I finally applied for admission to the University of Dallas, it was too late enter the psychology program, but I could register that fall for an interdisciplinary humanities program that required studies in three different disciplines. Psychology, literature and civic leadership were my study choices. I learned that the University was steeped in phenomenology, that particular philosophy I had encountered in my Art Appreciation class at Eastfield, as well as archetypal psychology. It felt as though I had entered a very different world than that which I had experienced at SMU. But it was a stimulating new adventure to be sure.

My first semester that fall of 1979 brought an amazing intuitive insight like a bolt out of the blue. In a class about Freud called Psychoanalytically Speaking, Dr. Robert Romanyshyn introduced the term paper assignment with a premise of J. H. van den Berg's which stated that any shift in man's consciousness would be reflected across the board culturally—in art, architecture, literature, etc. We were to take whatever area we wanted to explore and show that shift Freud heard in the scream of the hysteric. Instantly I knew Fauvism must be that moment in art. I had certainly heard that hysteric's scream upon entry to the Kimball exhibit that afternoon four years ago. I felt excited about researching the art world to see if that intuitive hit could be validated.

However, with the heavier workload in the Master's program, I was unable to complete the assignment that year. I did take the oral final exam, but took an incomplete for the course until I could finish writing the term paper itself. In fact, I wound up passing the two-year deadline for incompletes and had to request that the professor accept it in 1984 so that I could finally get my degree from UD. I knew there was no time limit for completion of the humanities degree and had assumed that included course incompletes. I was most fortunate that the professor was willing to accommodate my request.

That same semester I took Greek Epic to satisfy the literature requirement. I discovered another mythic figure I related to very personally as we read *The Odyssey*. Penelope, as I've discussed before, was the wife of Odysseus, who had waited another decade after the return of the survivors from the Trojan War for her beloved husband to return. Suitors from Ithaca and the surrounding states converged upon Odysseus's household in hopes of getting Penelope to choose one of them to replace her husband as ruler of his kingdom. She had shrewdly kept them at bay for three years with the weaving and unweaving of her father-in-law's shroud as they grossly wasted Odysseus' wealth. When our professor spoke of Penelope as less than the admirable character I felt her to be, I took issue and heartedly defended her, sounding something like this.

"Was not Penelope's epithet circumspect? She knew Odysseus' renowned resourcefulness would enable him to survive and overcome whatever obstacles he might have encountered after leaving Troy. And there was the prophecy of Ithaca's soothsayer, Halitherses: that after much suffering Odysseus would come home in the nineteenth year. How could she ever give up hope or not be subject to tears of sorrow and longing during her years of waiting? Penelope was as cunning as Odysseus in her resolve not to be forced to choose another mate who could not possibly measure up to her undisputed hero husband. Penelope was not a weak or wishy-washy woman as you have implied."

Even as I railed that afternoon in class, I knew from my studies in psychology that the intensity of my reaction pointed to something unfinished within me that could use further examination. I was clearly identifying with her ambivalence to give up on her husband's return and being forced to choose another mate who could not possibly measure up to the renowned hero Odysseus.

Apparently having Chuck's status changed hadn't rid my psyche of the Penelope within me. Burning his letters hadn't either—though at the time it seemed a necessary step in my process to get on with my life. I don't remember exactly when I became aware that re-reading Chuck's letters every night was not helping me move forward without him. Certainly the fall of Saigon in '75 made me acutely aware of the possibility I would never know what happened to him and needed to make a decision about how I wanted to proceed. Those letters were sacred to me though and if I were to let them go, it needed to be through some ritual to acknowledge my reasons for doing so. There have been times I regretted it, but I still believe it was necessary at that time.

A young woman who had witnessed my intense reaction to the denigration of Penelope introduced herself to me after the class, and I shared with her a little of my history. Through her I met other students with whom I would become friends outside the classroom. At SMU I didn't fraternize much with any of my classmates. Most were so much younger that we had little in common. But at UD these students I met had more life experience and their primary interest was psychology. My social life expanded as I was included in their after-class discussion forums over a glass of wine.

I was particularly drawn to a woman named Nancy who impressed me with her quick wit and knowledge. We were both airy Geminis who thrived on academia, but polar opposites when it came to feelings. I was still very reserved at the time, and not only did I not talk about my feelings, I often didn't even recognize them. Nancy's feelings were always right there on the surface, and she spoke readily of them. She challenged me to become more open and aware of my feelings as our friendship deepened.

Nancy and I both took James Hillman's Alchemy class in the spring of 1980. I had another intuitive hit there for my term paper. We were to find a vessel through which we could describe a psychological process alchemically, based upon all we learned during the course. It reminded me in spirit a little of that Hindu assignment at SMU where I had to pretend to be a guru and try to convert a Westerner to my form of Hinduism based on our understanding by the end of the course.

The question of whether or not Hawthorne's *The Scarlet Letter* fit into the patterns of alchemy popped into my head quite spontaneously as Professor Hillman described the assignment. I had not read the book before, so it was quite surprising to have that image evoked in class that day. It didn't take much reading to recognize how beautifully this novel lent itself to an alchemical interpretation.

I based my premise on the 17th century English theologian and alchemist John Pordage's instruction to "look with earnestness to the union of your own Mars and Venus…. then the Virgin Venus will bring forth her pearl, her water spirit, in you, to soften the fiery spirit of Mars." The title of my paper was "From the Pearl of Love, Gold and Silver." On page two I wrote, "Hawthorne unfolds this psychological drama with such apparent understanding of the necessary process outlined by Pordage, one would suspect that he himself was an alchemist. Whether or not his knowledge of the art was extensive is irrelevant. In fact, it is doubtful that the novel was deliberately so designed. It lends itself too naturally to alchemical interpretation to have been contrived."

That paper was a real labor of love for me, quite evident by its excessive thirty-six page length of which Hillman noted, "Too long for this course, but that's excusable." The distillation of all that material instilled a real appreciation for understanding the psyche through the language of alchemy. Dr. Hillman offered lots of questions in his comments of my work, and pointed out many areas where I needed to delve deeper into the nuances of images I saw as important to that process. "What's the difference between Hester's and Arthur's process, so that she 'succeeds' and he doesn't? Why does the sun not like Venus? What does the child do in 'imitating the letter'? What is the difference between the green and red letter?"

These unanswered questions would continue to cook within my psyche. What also cooked were his suggestions that it would be better if I could free myself from reductive tendencies, and speak to the images of the elements and metals and substances and planets working through the personalities of the figures in the story, rather than stock-casting them into Mars or the feminine. "This is your strength: seeing parallels, making things fit, finding the apt reference…but I miss the moments of dwelling longer on a single psychological place with possibilities for more insights—but for this you would have to forego your own 'sunlight.'"

It was clear to me that my own psychological opus was somehow like that of Hester Prynne's. Her process wasn't as focused on in the novel, as was the male minister's. After his death on the scaffold, Hester disappeared, thought to have sailed back to her European origins with Pearl. She returned years later to Boston and her little cottage by the sea, where of her own free will, she donned once again the scarlet letter, a wounded healer-therapist amongst the people who had played such a heavy role in her evolution. I too used my wounds and experience to relate to the women I counseled, and to bring the importance of having their choices and experiences be compatible with their religious values when they were in the clinic.

By my second year at UD, Nancy and I were part of a little group who met pretty regularly at a little bar over on Oak Lawn after classes to unwind and process all our new insights. We had our own "salon" going, like in the 18th century Age of Enlightenment. I always enjoyed these gatherings even though I felt not quite up to par with their levels of understanding much of the time.

One afternoon Nancy asked to come home with me instead, preferring not to be social with everyone. She had something troubling she wanted to discuss with me. She told me she'd just discovered she was pregnant, but the medications she took probably made the chance of a viable fetus pretty slim. Nancy had lived with a diagnosis of schizophrenia most of her life. She knew she was not capable of taking care of a baby right now. Just taking care of herself, especially when she was in the throes of a psychotic episode, was more than enough challenge.

She didn't really want to have a baby with this man and saw no future for the two of them together. In fact, she had been trying to put a stop to the whole relationship. Yet she was still in turmoil over the thought of having an abortion. She told me she'd had a couple of abortions when she was married and it was quite traumatic for her.

With all these circumstances that would be seen by most as justifiable reasons for choosing termination of the pregnancy, she still questioned whether abortion was murder. I was having a difficult time understanding why she was so distraught. But the more she talked and the more I just listened, a light bulb suddenly popped on inside my head. I got it. I related to her dilemma. I too had felt like I was a murderer in a way when I asked to have Chuck declared dead. I asked Nancy, "Is all killing murder?"

"No," she replied.

"Then when is it not considered murder?"

"When it's in self–defense or to protect someone you love."

Now we were getting to the crux of it. Murder carries a malevolent intent by definition. Killing to protect oneself does not. And in this case, the killing of an already potentially non-viable fetus was not a choice made from ill intent. In fact, it was being made out of love—for herself and for this still very tiny pregnancy she feared had been harmed by her medications.

The more we talked, the more comfortable she seemed to be with her choice for abortion. I told her I'd accompany her to her appointment. I drove her to the clinic and saw picketers as we entered the parking area. Everyone in the abortion facility was very nice. Counseling was pretty short.

Nancy had been told that because of her medications and history, the doctor was afraid to use any kind of anesthetic, even a local. Did she think she could handle the cramping? She actually felt relieved. She too was afraid of the way her body reacted to drugs of all sorts. She was more comfortable with the idea of none being used beyond an antibiotic afterward. She told them she'd be fine. Actually, with her history of dissociating from her body this would be one time that defense reaction might work in her favor.

The procedure didn't take long. They called me back into recovery to be with her right afterward. I was very impressed that the doctor himself came in to check on her. He was very caring and wanted to make sure she had done okay without the local. We drove back to my house to stay the night. Actually, she felt very relieved and knew she'd made a wise choice.

I was glad I could be there for her. Knowing it was right didn't make it any easier. She and I talked about it, but kept it between the two of us. There was no need to advertise the event. I don't think she ever told the man involved. They were no longer seeing one another. Now she could get back to concentrating on her studies.

Going through this experience with Nancy made me remember a story I had heard from someone in the family once, probably my Auntie Merle, about my grandmother trying to self-abort a pregnancy with a knitting needle, her sixth one I thought, which would have been my father. Her attempt had been unsuccessful and she'd had to spend the last months of her pregnancy in bed, wondering if she had damaged her unborn child.

However, when I asked my mother about it, she denied any such story. There was no one else to ask, as all the Hodges were dead by then. Either my mother really didn't know the story or it was one of those she refused to admit and talk about. When I got old enough to put two and two together, I realized that if I were born in May weighing over seven pounds and she and my dad hadn't married until the November before, she must have already been pregnant. But when I asked her about it she hastily said that was absurd and ended the conversation by walking out of the room. I knew then that some things were just taboo subjects to discuss with her.

The fall semester that year brought another very dramatic experience evoked during a course on Memory and Imagination. Our prima materia for the class was to record and share "distinctive imaginal events" (DIEs) from our lives to see if and/or how they were still operative within our psyche, and not just past history. While several traumatic events surfaced as I recorded my DIEs, it was the story of that fateful morning I was informed that Chuck was MIA which consumed me, demanding an audience, despite my resistance to relive it complete with all the emotion it evoked.

After I read that DIE to the class, my professor thought Chuck was the companion of the heart for whom it was intended. I disagreed with him at the time. Perhaps it was I who needed to "hear" it. Keeping the memory private had been a way of forgetting, of avoiding still the proximity of death, the risk of true relationship to others. That life-changing event was deepened for me by virtue of putting it back into the community.

Even though I had spoken about my experience during my activities with the League and Dallas Cares in the early '70s, I had never related my story emotionally. I had only told it detached from feelings, resistant to tears, not wanting anyone's pity, but their action instead to help bring him home. This time, the memory of that morning claimed me so totally that it violently stripped away all my defenses. And it was great relief I felt after writing the words that had come so suddenly and out of the blue. I knew they were right and that I wanted to share them, even if it meant doing so tearfully or risking my fear of sentimentality.

Later that week I shared the DIE with my two closest friends and the result was almost overwhelming. With each telling some new detail would reflect another facet for me to look at. It was almost like unpacking a dream image, revealing deeper levels of meaning and understanding about myself with each telling. It certainly opened up different relationships to all my other classmates. Once again I was in awe of this inner force that had broken through and dictated an action from me that I had not consciously intended.

After my sharing that night, I was approached by two of the men in the class, one wanting to pursue a relationship, the other to share with me that he had been one of those opposed to our involvement in Vietnam and that I was the first person he'd met from the military side of that war for whom he felt genuine respect. His confession opened the door to further dialogue about the politics of that war. I could easily have confessed to him that he was the first "hippie" I had met that I was willing to debate with. Both of these men initiated a new era for me in terms of relationships with the opposite sex.

I did not take the other young man's flirtations seriously at first—not because I didn't find him desirable. He was that for sure. But he was so much younger than I, nine years to be exact. However, my fear about the age difference melted away by the end of the semester. After a few too many glasses of wine at a party with my UD friends before our break for the holidays, I became quite flirtatious with George myself, letting him know that I was available if he were serious. And so began the on-again, off-again dating relationship I discussed in an earlier chapter that would continue for several years.

My undergraduate studies had been all about scholastics and coming to know myself through my studies and dream therapy. My graduate level studies were especially enlightening in terms of the more shadowy aspects of my psyche. I was drawn to explore the darker necessities—like the place of violence and fear in the achievement of a sense of wholeness.

My appreciation for art and literature as valuable tools for self-discovery was enhanced even more during my two years at UD. I returned to the grotesque style of the very Southern Flannery O'Connor's work in my Comedy Class with *The Violent Bear It Away*. I became enamored by the enigmatic character of Hamlet and saw this Shakespeare play as a tragedy of transition, calling for a shift of perspective from an Apollonic to a Hades mode of seeing.

Both of these works are clearly religious dramas that built upon and deepened the foundations laid by Professor Kliever's class at SMU. Added to that was the amazing novel *Jane Eyre* that we read for the Psychology of Emotion course, through which I wrote about horror as a particularly intense and repulsive form of fear.

The thread of connection to all these revelations hinged on the recognition of demon and daemon being one, part and parcel of the same spectrum, as is fear to anger, the blue to red spectrum of the emotions. The work I did through all the papers I wrote at UD were seeds of understanding that I recognized intellectually, but had yet to fully integrate. They were/are like the DIEs we wrote about from our memories—still active and operative within my psyche—the gifts that just kept on giving.

I had been called to return to school by a daemon for which I had no name, only the feeling of its fire and the intensity of its command. After six years of the hard work and joy within the ivory towers of academia, I knew I could trust this daemon to point me in a new direction.

Equally influential to this renewed sense of trust in my inner promptings was my friendship with Nancy. It was in acting on my intuitions with her, despite my fears that I would somehow do more harm than good, that my willingness to trust my own inner voice shifted. On several occasions I witnessed Nancy's inner daemon leading her out of harm's way. And in working with her when she was psychotic, we both came to see how the demon voices brought positive messages too. We just have to see them metaphorically or symbolically rather than literally.

It had been a long time since I had had a really close woman friend. My mother had served in that role since my return to Dallas in 1970. In Nancy I found someone much more like me. In fact, she was like a mirror image in many ways. She was a seeker like myself, with an inquisitive, astute mind and the ability to talk to death on any new train of thought. Her appreciation for the study of psychology, particularly the archetypal arena of Jung and Hillman, equaled my own.

Nancy's openness softened my reserve (one of the ways I *was* like my mother) and opened me up more, helping me find more balanced sharing in my relationships. And she has remained one of those lifetime friends with whom I can pick up right where we left off, no matter how much time has lapsed since we last spoke or saw each other.

CHAPTER 17

WEAVING A NEW TAPESTRY

I finished the class work for that Master's in Humanities in the spring of 1981 with not a clue as to what I was going to do with those three degrees. All that knowledge I had so eagerly devoured was now swimming in my brain with no real focus toward any practical use. I decided that my first agenda must be to have a tubal ligation that summer before beginning any kind of job search. I was becoming more sexually active by then and was very clear that I never wanted more children. Nor did I ever want to find myself in need of choosing an abortion. So I set up the surgery with my OB/GYN early that summer.

I'll never forget my shock when the nurse came into the hospital room with her consent forms and told me she'd need my husband's consent when she saw I was married. I fired back at her that it was fine with me but she'd have to find him first.

I had reconnected with my old high school flame a short time before this elective surgery. His reaction was amusing. He asked why I was doing it, as he'd had a vasectomy. I guess it hadn't occurred to him that I might want to have sex with anyone but him in the future. What if I were raped? My action was for me to have control of my own body and be protected from another pregnancy ever again.

After my recovery and our usual two-week family vacation, I was sitting in my bed with the want ads one Sunday morning and boom—there it was. One ad caught my eye—indeed, it seemed to be so large it was all I saw on the entire page—for an abortion counselor. I had never consciously thought about doing anything like that. Yet in that instant I knew that was what I was being called to do next. I remembered that day with Nancy at the abortion clinic.

I recognized that I had actually done my first abortion counseling with her and felt good about the results. I knew clearly how I could relate to women in need of those services even though I'd never experienced an abortion myself. As the memory of that day flooded back into my mind, I knew I could do this. I was being called to serve in the abortion arena.

I got busy drafting a resume to submit with the job application. Imagine the challenge in writing an enticing resume when you have no job history beyond baby- sitting and odd sales jobs from high school? I considered listing my employment as a domestic engineer with twenty years of experience managing a household. My better judgment convinced me to use my volunteer work in a way that would demonstrate skills for the job. I didn't get that particular counseling position from the ad, but took my resume and applied to every abortion clinic in Dallas.

During this same time period I received a mailing from the Texas Abortion Rights Action League (TARAL) about a meeting in Austin. I noticed that Dallas' Charlotte Taft from Routh Street Women's Clinic was conducting a workshop. I sent in my reservation with the sole intention of meeting her and asking what I needed to study in order to do abortion counseling. She sent me to Majors Books for a copy of *Contraceptive Technology* and told me to send her a resume so she could send me an application. They weren't hiring at the time, but she would keep me in the files for future reference. Of course, I followed her every instruction.

By the end of October I had finished reading that overwhelmingly comprehensive volume of information and wrote a note to Charlotte with my resume and an invitation to take her to lunch some afternoon to learn about any other suggestions she might have for me. She sent me an application that was almost as extensive as *Contraceptive Technology* had been. It took me three pages, type written, to field the subjective questions:

What is your interest in working in abortion? What would you like to contribute to the clinic by working here, and what would you like to get out of it for yourself? How would you respond to the argument that abortion is murder? Write a little about how you feel about the following: 1. Abortion as a method of birth control. 2. Women who have more than one abortion. 3. Teenagers having sexual activity. What do you think of abortion as a political issue?

Who would have ever suspected that the job application itself would offer such a great opportunity to clarify and articulate that intuitive knowing I had experienced that Sunday morning as I searched the want ads?

I did get a part time counseling job at another abortion clinic and had worked there for three months before Charlotte called me to set up an interview if I was still interested. She began the conversation acknowledging her reservations about calling me because she had heard I was employed at another clinic. However, she felt it was important to honor her promise to me back in the summer to let me know if a counseling position opened up at Routh Street. I went in for an interview and realized it was everything I had dreamed it would be. I quickly saw that no one would question my decision to return a patient's money and not do an abortion until she had done some "homework."

I had only encountered that situation once at my current place of employment, but I clearly got the message it was not a popular decision. I frequently felt rushed at times in a counseling session where I needed to explore more feelings and values before I felt comfortable signing my name on the consent form. I gave my two-week notice at the clinic where I was working immediately after that interview, knowing Charlotte would never limit my counseling session or question my assessment that she might need homework to do. And I felt excited at those prospects.

Routh Street Women's Clinic was, the beginning of a remarkable thirteen-year vocation, albeit in another war zone as controversial as Vietnam had been. I would never have been able to survive the stress had I not known I was called to use my experience and religious studies background to help women make choices that were congruent with their beliefs. It wasn't always abortion either. Sometimes adoption was their best option. There were times I refused to provide services because I chose not to participate if they believed abortion was murder.

As I moved from my mother and student roles into that of a career woman, I thought I'd put Vietnam behind me. However, the ramifications of those MIA years lingered in more subtle ways to be uncovered more slowly and painfully through therapy and twelve-step work. I became involved with a man recently out of prison with three children to support. It culminated in two years of abuse and craziness that left me broken in every way physically, emotionally and financially.

A weekend spent writing my fourth step moral inventory and needed amends in September of 1986 proved most enlightening. I realized then that the entangled relationship that had brought me into therapy was an attempt to work through every piece of unfinished business in my life.

For years I had dreamed of welcoming my POW husband home and helping him reintegrate back into the family. I had tried to do that for this man I thought I'd fallen in love with. What's more, he had two small children the ages of my brother and me when my mother left my alcoholic father after a physical fight.

I left this man after a replay of that event from my childhood. But still I grieved this man, as I had never really done with Chuck. And I was confronted by my own abandoning of both his children and mine to maintain peace in the relationship, something I had been very critical of my mother as an adult.

In retrospect, I was eventually able to see the gifts in the trauma of those two years, and my role in creating and sustaining it. Jung was right about the value of facing and owning my own shadow. It was ultimately a healing and necessary integration in moving toward a sense of wholeness.

1990 brought me to the Goddess through my bioenergetic therapist and retreat workshops to identify where I was in my own femininity—the maiden, the mother, or the crone. The theme of the nineties was about getting in touch with my body, bringing my energy down from my head into my heart and a more grounded position. The Maiden, Mother, and Crone retreats added the spiritual dimension. It was a timely process considering I was entering menopause at the time, and taking hormone replacement therapy.

During the course of the second retreat I came to see my major block as the fear of a broken heart and journaled about it. "I think that pain goes back to the crib—no—in utero—when I was conceived out of wedlock. I was told the story of being loved—but didn't believe it—Knowing that my mother stayed in a marriage to an alcoholic 'for us kids'—Then Chuck was the first dramatic event of losing the love of my life—not the death of my father. I did not grieve for months because of fear that the pain wouldn't let me continue my pregnancy and have a healthy child— 'for the sake of the kid' and my mother—taking care of everyone else—But Chuck— I had forsaken my parents—left my home—forsaken college and career to spend my life with him—And I did not believe I could live without him—I gave my power to the POW/MIA movement and was 'screwed' by God and Government—I continued to give my power to the Church—to a point—It was hard to let it go—Now here I go again with the clinic— I have shielded my heart forever it seems—That's what I need to place on the altar!

"My fear of the pain of a broken heart is like: stifling; having no imagination; the scarlet letter—A—burning from the inside out; having no fire; drowning or suffocating; being in quicksand; a bird with no song; the little mermaid without her voice pursuing her lover."

Like bioenergetics, these exercises shared within the sacred circle of women tapped into body memory in a way that bypassed the mind and its stories. And like my therapy, the retreat provided a safe container to process. However, after leaving this space, my return to the routines of home and work, this awareness of placing my heart on the altar of the Divine faded into the shadows again.

During the third retreat in November, I did place a symbolic heart on the altar in response to the message from the last retreat. When describing "this phase of my life" that first evening, I wrote that it has become increasingly clear to me that something has to change—"my passion is missing, My bioenergetic work and dreams indicate I am pregnant, approaching some new birth. It feels like the winter of my life—like being in a dark cave, sheltered and protected but unable to see what's out there."

During one of the exercises I felt a block between my heart and throat chakra I described as—"like I have no voice. And this no voice, no passion is like being in limbo. I am coming to believe it may be about past lives as well as this one. An image of a gate came up during a guided imagery meditation—one that reminded me of the one in *Four Daughters*, an old John Garfield movie I loved as a young girl. That gate for me is about unconditional love and acceptance of my own inner child and her needs."

By spring of 1991, after some 18 months of grounding and bioenergetic work, I was aware of being in another major transitional place. I cut my hair short again. Perhaps it was a sign of my current commitment about being faithful to myself. Long hair had always been the preference of the men I was involved with. I was certainly forming a new relationship with myself that was affecting all my other relationships.

Then the last week of June I received a call from Jo who had introduced me to the Maiden, Mother, Crone Retreats, about this Indian Devi known as Ammachi who was here offering Darshan. She urged me to go see her. Because I trusted Jo implicitly, I went one evening after work to see this woman she raved about. We were given a pamphlet upon entry to the large auditorium that gave us the appropriate guidelines for the Darshan. Mata Amritanandamayi (Ammachi), is looked upon by many who have net her as an embodiment of love, a mystic having come to the full knowledge of the one unique Spirit—the source and support of all things, I read. Darshan is the time when Amma individually receives those who wish to come to Her for Her blessing. The Darshan Hall should be treated as a temple, and a reverential attitude should be maintained.

As I joined the end of the very long and growing line waiting to be presented to Amma on the stage, I had plenty of time to ready the rules of etiquette for being in the presence of a guru and to "reflect on the inner attitude with which I was coming to Amma." When my turn finally came, I walked up and knelt before her. At her gesture I lay my head in her lap and immediately tears began streaming down my face as this incredible love flooded over me. The feeling was indescribable. Really. There were no words, though I think she may have uttered a prayer in Sanskrit before I left her presence. It was an awesome experience that I did not understand. I felt as though I were falling apart, that I was about to have a total breakdown. And that feeling grew stronger in the week that followed.

I finally sat down with Charlotte and told her I needed some time off. She helped me with a plan for a six-week sabbatical. While I knew in my heart it was what I needed at the time, I still felt terrified. The clinic had been so supportive of me when I had the broken arm. I had no physical injury this time, but I felt every bit as vulnerable and broken as then. What if six weeks wasn't enough to pull myself back together? To get the six weeks I was going to three-quarter time and using all the vacation I had accrued for the year. What if the clinic decided in my absence that they didn't need me anymore? Would I be okay with the pay cut? And there was that sermon I had agreed to do in August. Would I be able to write that? So many worries. I felt angry that my process was so hard, that at forty-nine I still didn't know who I was. It became pretty obvious I needed to work the twelve-steps with this deal. I was definitely powerless over this emotional collapse and decided to turn it over to Goddess and trust all would work out for the best.

It took a couple of weeks to pave the way for my absence for such as extended time. Just knowing that it was in the near future made those days tolerable. Tuesday, July 23rd was my last day to work until September. I woke to a terrible dream image of this young man—boy? who "they" beheaded as I screamed *Noooooo!* The feeling was that he'd done nothing wrong to be punished for—and the sense of a head versus the heart struggle. I was glad I had dream group that night.

At the clinic I received well wishes from many of the staff who said they would miss me but supported me taking care of myself right now. Saying goodbye to my flow administrators was very emotional. Victoria was the one whose presence always evoked any tears rumbling beneath the surface that I was unaware I was holding in. That day I was very aware of them and made no attempt to hold them back. She presented me with this special lavender mug for me with astrological symbols on it and the words "explorer of darkness" in gold. The gratitude I felt for her and Charlotte was overwhelming. I would miss seeing them every day. But I looked forward to being a lady of leisure for a while.

I felt such relief that next morning as I took my morning tea out to the pool. The peace and quiet was soothing. "Explorer of darkness"—I loved it. My new mug had both the sun and three clouds dropping golden rain. The crescent moon was on the handle. I could feel Victoria's loving support with every sip. I enjoyed listening to the birds and trying to see which voice belonged to which kind of bird.

I found it interesting that Charlotte chose to name this "time off" for me as a sabbatical, not a vacation. Reflecting on that word, sabbatical, a term used most often to denote a leave of absence for university professors approximately every seventh year. Seven years ago I was feeling heartbroken, totally devastated, no hope in sight with regards to the whole situation with the abusive man I was living with. I moved away from him into my own space again to regroup then. Stephen was more dependent upon me then, so I couldn't totally fall apart. The term sabbatical also relates to Sabbath, hence has a religious dimension. My breakdown this time definitely had a sacred dimension. It was precipitated by my physical contact with the Great Mother Herself, through Ammachi. Yes, it was definitely a sabbatical, a desperately needed one, albeit a short one.

I did have one pressing concern that troubled me though. I had been doing some public speaking about the religious component of a woman's abortion decision and had been asked to actually preach a sermon at the Unitarian Church.

I certainly knew the material I wanted to convey, but how to make it a sermon was troubling—the format I might use. One morning after sitting at the pool with my tea listening to the birds and journaling, I headed back into the house and was stopped in my tracks by this cardinal on the power line by the backdoor just chirping away at me—like really carrying on a conversation with me. He seemed to be urgently trying to convey a message. I said to him, "So that's your voice. It's so nice to recognize which song is yours." We conversed that way for several minutes before I finally went in for a shower, still amused at his beauty and his song.

Then as I showered, suddenly, out of the blue I saw exactly how to structure the sermon. I would create an altar and place objects on it that represented aspects I wanted to discuss about a woman's abortion choice. I titled the sermon, "Honor and Remember Her."

That altar was dedicated to the women who'd chosen to abort an impossible love, honoring them for their strength and their courage to follow an inner wisdom. I also honored those women who suffered for their decisions to abort and became WEBAs (women exploited by abortion). That sermon was a true labor of love and was very well received. I bought some cardinals for my own altar at home in gratitude for his inspiration.

New Years of 1992 began on a dramatic note. I had a session with my Jungian analyst around the anniversary of Chuck's becoming MIA. For some reason I was feeling that old depression again. It had not surfaced much for a couple years so it came as a surprise. For the first time ever in therapy, I told Tess my dream of Chuck that had given me so much hope and comfort during those early years.

When I got to the part of him communicating with me through his eyes that we would be together again, but it would be a long, long time, I heard my words of explanation—because *he was across the river*—I stopped in total astonishment.

Oh my God, he was across the river—it was the River Styx of the Greek Hades that separates the living from the dead. Chuck came to me after he died. Needless to say the tears gushed in the deepest grief I had ever experienced.

Tess didn't have to say a word. For the first time in 21 years, I knew in my heart Chuck had died that night of January 3rd, 1971. Obviously, I had never been ready to know that before. God truly works in very mysterious ways!

Then on February 25th, 1993 I experienced the same rage toward the military that I had felt toward my government at the Cease Fire in 1973. The "even keel" I'd begun to enjoy was rocked to the core on the February 25th when the mail delivered a copy of my husband's military file that was being turned over to the Library of Congress and no longer considered classified. What I read in that file that was new information to me were reports of American POWs captured in Laos around the time and within 60 miles of where Chuck's plane crashed, POWs who met his description.

One report even stated that the Vietnamese source of the information identified Chuck from photographs of missing personnel in Southeast Asia as the POW he saw in May of 1971. Upon reading that, uncontrollable tears of sadness, anger and fear gushed forth. The feelings were as intense as if the news was current.

Reading on, the government evaluations of these reported sightings were not valued as reliable. However, I felt that I should have been given them at the time. This report thrust me back into that terrible limbo of questioning everything I thought I knew and had resolved already.

I went to bed that night feeling terribly confused. I had to leave work early the next day because I couldn't stop crying. This news of information the government had concealed all these years had put me right back into the limbo I'd felt in 1971. I found it surprising because of my experience the year before with Tess and seeing my dream as a death dream. What was I to make of this current reaction to those military reports?

The good news, however, was that I didn't repress my feelings as I had in 1971. I went to an ACA meeting where I was able to vent the anger I felt toward the military for withholding this report.

The next day I shared my experience with the clinic staff in a letter so they would know what was going on with me. After having fallen apart and left on sabbatical some six months before, I felt they needed an explanation for my behavior.

I concluded that letter with: "I still don't know what to make of all this. It's not like it changes anything or means I have any regrets about my decisions during these years. What I did yesterday was honor my feelings by just letting them be (which is certainly different from 1971 and many years thereafter). But I have to say, I *hate* this part and I know why I have defended against having feelings for so many years. This is definitely not being fun. I want healing to mean the hurt goes away; I don't like feeling the wound again so intensely. I don't like knowing that it will never be over and there will always be doubt and I don't get to live with the definitive certainty I think I want."

I wrote another more detailed letter I addressed to Haley, my oldest grand-daughter. I never delivered that one. Perhaps it was just my ears that needed to hear it. Haley was only seven at the time, far too young to comprehend what I was telling her. That letter ended with my receiving the call after the Cease Fire and the rage I felt at being utterly betrayed by my country and God. My trust was renewed as I realized that once again, I was given information only when I was able to process it. But I do wonder what it would have been like if I'd been given that report when it happened.

My immediate feeling response was most encouraging, though, a sign that my therapy was really working. While it was anything but pleasant, it was definitely a healthier way to deal with trauma. That anger was defused, as I was able to own my feelings and admit that the whole experience sucked. I was reminded once again that I was powerless to change anything except my attitude toward it.

In early '95 I turned in my resignation at the clinic. I felt parched from so many years of doing crisis counseling and bombarded by negative, hateful anti-abortion foes day in and day out.

I moved my life to Castle Matrix in Rathkeale, Ireland to re-green my soul, I told Dave, but that's another long story. I had been back stateside a year when I learned that Chuck's crash site was due for excavation in November of 1999.

Once again Dave and I had spent three hours talking, and still were not finished.

Dave commented that afternoon that I processed organically, a term I had never heard before. "What do you mean by that?" I asked.

"Simply that one stage of your life naturally grew out of another. Your becoming a widow and single led to you becoming a student. Then your studies widened to include psychology, in part due to your own experiences, and that led to a counseling career. It seems like a lot of your interests just naturally grow out of interests you already have," he explained. I had never quite framed my experiences over the years in that way, but could see how it seemed true.

Initially my personal interest in my husband's fate led me the League of Families and a phase of activism around the POW/MIA issue. My interest in the church's educational programs ultimately led to me returning to school. Then at Routh Street my work with women in crisis over an abortion decision led to me seeing the ideal of choice as much more encompassing than just one's reproduction rights. It's a way of life that is empowering.

As we set up another visit, I was beginning to wonder just how "in depth" his story was going to be. He asked if he could take all my scrapbooks and letters to look over before we met again. By that time I trusted him so much I said yes without hesitation. He'd not been out the door long before I felt a momentary panic about my hasty action. But the fear subsided pretty quickly and I knew those precious papers were safe with him. I could resume my pursuit of where to have Chuck's service with no worries.

I called and set up an appointment with Jonathan at Laurel Oaks. He was far more helpful than the first funeral home I had visited. He asked me about the Patriot Guard, so was well aware of their services and how to contact them. He also told me they would not charge for their services, only the rental of the chapel the day of the service.

They were well-equipped to do the slide show and play the music I wanted as well as print a program of my design, capabilities I was not sure the church would have. He also knew of a man who did videos of services that he could contact.

After my visit with him I felt very optimistic that everything I wanted was definitely possible. He knew my budget and felt he could work with it. I really liked Jonathan and had no doubt I would work with him to create everything I wanted for Chuck's homecoming. My only reservation was the size of the chapel. Would it be large enough? The church sanctuary was much larger. I told him I needed to connect with the PMUMC minister before making a final decision.

The reverend called me early the next week. This school that met daily at the church included some 300 students who ate lunch on a staggered schedule. That meant the kitchen and fellowship hall would not be available to me until 2:30 in the afternoon. How hectic would it feel trying to have a memorial service with that many children milling about? That was the real clincher in my decision to go with Laurel Oaks. Chuck's service had to be morning if we were to have the group burial that afternoon. Though I was a little disappointed, the greater feeling was one of relief to have made a choice. Trying to make Pleasant Mound work had begun to feel like trying to fit a square peg into a round hole.

When I spoke with Jonathan again to tell him I wanted him to handle the service, he had already contacted the video guy who was willing to film both services for a reduced fee. I couldn't believe his generosity and was moved to tears at the way it was all beginning to come together so beautifully, without me having to borrow money to do so.

I had four weeks left before flying to Hawaii to escort Chuck's remains home. I needed all the details ironed out by then so I could be totally present to that experience. With Jonathan's help, I could pull together the photographs for the slide presentation and ones I wanted in the program. He would implement production of the finished products. I could concentrate on connecting with old military friends whose addresses I had not kept up with to invite them to the service. The Casualty office in San Antonio could assist me there.

What did I want in the way of music? The service I imagined was not traditional in terms of any funeral I have ever been to. How could it be? Thirty-six years had passed since Chuck disappeared from our lives. I wanted something more akin to what I thought a wake must be—a welcoming home and birthday celebration that would bring his essence into that chapel.

The music became the most challenging and last component of the entire service to finally come together. Stephen was the one who suggested the two songs that seemed best to me the fit. "Home" by Michael Buble I'd never heard before and had to buy the CD to listen to it. "Somewhere Over the Rainbow" I knew and had heard the version he was referring to from the movie *50 First Dates*.

It was actually a medley that combined "What a Wonderful World" sung by Hawaiian Izzy Kamakawiwo Ole. I searched for a CD that would have that particular rendition to make sure it was available. As I played those CDs I knew they were perfect! I would use Izzy's song for the slide show of Chuck's life in photographs and "Home" would be good between the shared memories of family and friends and mine. As the program continued to take shape in my head, I shifted my focus to making the calls and connections to old friends now that I had a definite date and place.

The Strines were among the first on my list. Dick already knew about Chuck's identification from their aviation Cadet Class, 61-03 website. I learned that they had had three daughters and now had a granddaughter. I was aware of two girls, but must have lost touch before the third one arrived. Dick had retired in Florida and they were really enjoying their community there. Aris emailed me photos later. And within two days Dick emailed me to say they were coming and he would be happy to say a few words at the service. I felt elated at that news! Two of Chuck's oldest military friends would speak along with a bracelet wearer. I wanted a family member or someone from his younger years to give us a glimpse of Chuck before his Air Force career.

I thought about Don, Chuck's uncle who was only a few years older than he and had been more like a brother. He had written me the most eloquent letter after Chuck had become missing that I treasured. Because he'd always been so quiet at family gatherings, I had no idea if he would be receptive to the idea. He was out of town when I called but I spoke with his wife and gave her my number and asked her to relay my message. A week later he called me back and sounded genuinely pleased that I had asked him to participate. He would be very happy to speak at the service.

During my next meeting with Jonathan at Laurel Oaks, we talked about possibilities for lunch for the family in between the two services. He suggested calling a deli to deliver sandwiches and drinks, and then showed me the room he had in mind for everyone to gather afterward. It sounded perfect. I actually checked out the chapel that visit and saw where the screen would be for the slide show. He would be able to scan any photographs I sent him and make the DVD for that slide presentation. That was going to make my work there ever so much easier. I would have a long walnut finish table at my disposal for the altar. I thought about Jean's beautiful lace tablecloth we'd used every Christmas and hoped Wanda still had it. Choosing to use Laurel Oaks was undoubtedly the best decision I could ever have made for this service.

We talked more about the program I was envisioning. I had finally chosen Josh Groban's song "To Where You Are" to be played between my sharing and the Reverend Joy Cox's message that she was calling a "Celebration of Life." I wanted the cover of the program to be the photograph Stephen had taken of Chuck's flight boots at the Vietnam Memorial Wall below the panel where his name was located. Could we use the etching of his name we made that day as well? Jonathan thought it would work fine to do that. I also wanted that last photograph ever taken of him there at Korat AFB to appear somewhere in the program along with the poem, "High Flight," by Royal Canadian Air Force Officer and pilot John Gillespie Magee Jr.

I hoped we could we have an insert for favorite family photos from over the years. I also had a great color picture Chuck had taken from an F-4 climbing into the sky at sunset. Maybe we could print the words of the Air Force song with it? We needed a little bio somewhere and of course the order of the service itself. Jonathan saw no problem at all with creating a two-page fold-over program that would include all these components. I just needed to get it all to him and he would figure out how to include it all.

He also reminded me that we'd need a guest book and showed me their options to choose from. He told me about a nearby florist that I visited when I left the funeral home. I asked about orchids for the altar table arrangement, but due to the expense, went with fall flowers that would include some red roses in a copper vase instead. I was rapidly hitting my budget limit.

By the time I met with Dave again I was feeling very pleased with the way the pieces were falling into place so nicely for the memorial. And of course, as promised, he brought back all my scrapbooks as we sought to fill in the remaining events the new millennium had initiated.

BOOK III

EXCAVATION OF SITE AND SOUL

"How do you suddenly revise images and understandings you've carried in the cells of your body for thirty-three years?"

Sue Monk Kidd, *The Mermaid Chair*[30]

CHAPTER 18

RENEWED HOPE

After three amazing and adventurous years in Ireland that did indeed re-green my soul, I returned stateside December 11th, 1998 to spend Christmas with my family in Dallas. Charles and his wife Diana let me stay with them for a while and Scott loaned me his truck. I didn't even buy a proper journal until January. My pocket calendar was my lifeline for those first couple of weeks. Stephen flew in for the holiday, so we had a wonderful family Christmas all together again even though Scott and his wife Dawn were separated at the time. My brother drove up the day after Christmas and we had a good visit.

That's when I found out he'd been bitten by a rattlesnake while hunting in West Texas over the Labor Day weekend and almost died. They transported him on an Air Care flight to San Antonio when he had an allergic reaction to the anti-venom. I questioned him about the time and realized it was that weekend I had gone to the funeral in Rathkeale for the husband of a friend of mine and suddenly seen Olin's face in the coffin. The next morning I awoke to a dream image of a little girl asking me what was wrong with my arm. It was all bandaged up. It was my left arm and hand—it was his left hand where he was bitten. My left hand was itching badly and no amount of rubbing it or scratching it seemed to help. Olin said he itched like crazy when he had that allergic reaction to the anti-venom. The hair stood up on my arm and the back of my neck as he told the story. Later when I checked my journal and the time I had written about it, it was the exact time all this was happening in Texas.

No wonder I had begun to feel like it was time to return to the states. Almost losing my brother, Charles developing high blood pressure, Scott and Dawn separating—all that happened late summer and fall of 1998. I asked Olin if he kept the rattle from that snake, which of course he killed after it bit him. "No, but my boss does," he told me. His hunting buddies had gone back after they had connected with the 911 ambulance to transport him to the local hospital, and they cut it from the snake. When they asked if he wanted it after he was finally home and recovering he told them, "No, I think I've had about all of that snake I want, thank you very much."

When I told him I wanted it, he assured me he would get it for me. We laughed about how we'd terrified Mother with our snakes as children and marveled again at how we'd never gotten bitten then. I've always felt we'd been blessed with good snake medicine. His survival would confirm that I believe. However, he would certainly never let himself be distracted again and take his eye off his kill before reaching down to pick it up. That careless mistake almost cost him his life, but didn't deter him from hunting.

I remained a nomad for all of 1999, living for months with a friend of Stephen's who wanted the company, and then in Houston with my dearest friend Risa, with whom I'd grown up from the age of nine in Pleasant Grove. For years she had raved to me about Dialogue Racism and wanted me to attend the series at The Center for the Healing of Racism. It was in November then that I got a mailing from the Department of Defense about a Family Update Meeting not far from Risa's house. I decided I would check it out. I had certainly lost all contact with the military over the POW/MIA issue over the past few years.

It was there that I discovered Chuck's crash site was on the top of the list for excavation in Laos. Not a lot had changed in terms of the families I discovered. There was a lot of frustration expressed. Some still believed we had men alive over there, some felt animosity toward those who weren't helping the cause. Ann Mills Griffith was still the head of the League. Yes, there was a lot of pain still there amongst the families and I found that disturbing.

I stayed with Risa to help her paint the kitchen and attend her

Christmas party before returning to Dallas on the 13th. I based myself at my mother-in-law's home this time, as Haley was with Charles, giving them a full house there. Jean was comfortable having me stay on with her then until I left for Ireland again.

With the whole Y2K scare at the time, she wanted the company. The media hype predicted all sorts of problems due to computer glitches and failures when the systems tried to shift into the year 2000. Just in case, we stocked up on candles and oil lamps, canned foods and water. We spent a quiet New Year's Eve watching television until the Times Square ball dropped, signaling the arrival of the new millennium. None of the predicted catastrophes manifested at that moment. It was a HAPPY NEW YEAR indeed.

The end of January of 2000, I went back to Ireland with my good friend, Jo, for a Peace Conference in conjunction with the Feille Bhride or Festival of Bridget in Kildare. I stayed the rest of the month to visit with all my Irish family and friends for a few weeks after Jo returned to Dallas. I experienced a resurgence of the enchantment of Castle Matrix I'd lost by the time I left in '98.

I returned stateside via New York to visit with my son Stephen, and reconnect with old neighbors in Rome when we were at Griffiss. I flew to Kalamazoo to connect with a dear friend I'd met through my ACA work in the late '80s en route back to Dallas to live with my mother-in-law until I could decide what was next for me.

Learning about the pending excavation of Chuck's crash site had sparked this desire to reconnect with my past. In June I flew into Washington D.C. for the 31st annual meeting of the National League of Families of American Prisoners and Missing in Southeast Asia with my son, Scott. It was his first such meeting ever.

Stephen took a train down from New York and met us. I wanted them to know about all the efforts being made to resolve the MIA cases, and to be able to review their father's military records. That record review turned out to be full of surprises. There was information in that file I had never seen before.

Our trip to the Vietnam War Memorial Wall together was a very moving experience for me. I felt such sadness that Chuck had missed out on watching our boys grow up and at the same time those tears were for the pride I felt in the fine young men they'd become. We left Chuck's flight boots at base of Panel 5W, along with all our nametags from the League meeting plus one we made for Charles, stuffed into the tops of them. Stephen captured the moment for us all with his dad's very own camera.

By March of 2001, the Joint Field Activity Team was led to a crash site in the Savannakhet province of Laos that correlated with the approximate date and time of Chuck's loss. They found there a 16-meter diameter crater that had a portion of a landing gear strut protruding from it.

In surveying the area, the team retrieved survival vest and flight suit material, boot heels and a turbine blade. The field notes read, "Life support equipment and boot soles suggest at least one individual was in the aircraft at the time of impact. The items photographed and left in place correlate to an F-4 aircraft. Further analysis is required upon return."

In April, a helicopter carrying part of a JFA crew crashed and the next search mission was cancelled. That news brought up for me the question of whether those JTF missions were worth the risk of losing more lives for remains that might not be recoverable. Granted, this had been the first loss experienced in the ten years the task force had been in operation. Nevertheless, that crash was a stark reminder of the risk those teams were taking to bring our guys home. My heart broke for the families of all on that helicopter, Vietnamese and American. I sent notes to them through the Commander of the JTF in Honolulu.

September 11th, 2001 happened, and shifted my focus. Like the rest of America, I was reminded that today, this very moment is all I have, so what do I want for myself right now? I began to think about working again and getting a place of my own. I wanted to get my belongings out of storage where they'd been for the six years while I was in Ireland and being a nomad.

I started work as Dr. Blumer's office manager in October and moved into my new apartment the first weekend in December. During that period another JFA team recovered numerous life support fragments and a data plate from a rocket ejection seat which they deemed sufficient evidence to correlate this crash site to Chuck's F-4.

It was August and September of 2002 before the next JFA continued excavation, but monsoons again hampered their efforts.

The Explosive Ordinance Disposal technician did remove some unexploded ordinance and moved it to a holding area before they had to leave the site. And the team recovered one portion of the emergency oxygen valve assembly, indicating again the likelihood of at least one individual being onboard at the time of impact. This JFA was suspended early due to the flooding of the site and the team went to another site that was accessible.

Since the teams went into Laos quarterly, I assumed that next JFA would have been in December, so I could expect the report in early 2003. When I did not get one I called my casualty officer to inquire about the next expected visit. It seemed that they were going to have to wait until they met with the Laotian officials in May to request permission to go back to Chuck's site because they had left it early and gone to another excavation site south of that location.

The guidelines established by the Laos government would not allow the teams to backtrack to an old site. My immediate thought was *you gotta be kidding–if it's not the weather it's some stupid rules to slow down this process.* I did a lot of internal self-talk about the folly of getting upset over things I was powerless to change.

Current events of the day no doubt contributed to my frustration that any resolution regarding Chuck's fate was not going to manifest just yet. I was afraid we were about to get into another Vietnam situation in Iraq. President Bush was setting the stage for the United States taking action against Saddam Hussein if the United Nations failed to get compliance from him to voluntarily disarm Iraq's stockpile of weapons of mass destruction from the past twelve years. Secretary of State Colin Powell would present the case to the UN Security Council on February 5th that Iraq posed a threat to our national security and to international peace.

There was much disagreement world-wide about whether an attack without clear support from the UN Security Council was advisable. Several close allies opposed military intervention, thinking it would increase terrorist attacks rather than decrease their risk. NATO, Britain and other members of the EU supported the U.S. position. Opinion polls showed the general population was against military action without UN sanction. By mid-February millions of people in the major cities of Europe, and hundreds of thousands in major cities of North America were participating in peace demonstrations.

On March 15th, I joined a group of forty-two plus Dallas-area women to express our objection to military intervention in Iraq, calling for peace instead through a Bare Witness demonstration. The organizer had been motivated by such an event in Big Bend. I had also heard of that one through my friend Nancy in Seattle. A very good friend of hers was the photographer for it. After I had agreed to participate, I learned it was already an international phenomenon, brainchild of a California artist and political activist, Donna Sheehan.

The idea had begun with a dream she'd had of people creating shapes with their bodies. Her inspiration for how that might take place came from a story about how 600 Nigerian women had threatened using their nakedness to force Chevron to listen to their families' needs. The image of those women occupying that oil terminal willing to shame those men into conceding to their demands led to Donna envisioning the word PEACE formed from women's naked bodies.

She put her vision to the test and on November 12th, 2002, some fifty women showed up at Pt. Reyes Station in California to disrobe in protest of a pending war with Iraq. More came willing to help in other ways. As their PEACE photograph hit the news and the Internet, the idea spread like wildfire around the globe. And thus was born a new peace movement called Bare Witness.

It maintains a website showing photographs of such demonstrations around the world. Having missed out on the peace demonstrations of the '60s, I was more than ready to participate in this one. At my heaviest weight ever, I knew baring my body naked to the world would be a real stretch for me, but it felt so right for me to be a part of this local demonstration.

Our instructions were to gather at Peace Point on Lake Lavon with a pink sheet to lie down on for protection from the field of tall sun-parched grasses and weeds that would be prickly for sure. I called my friend Cynthia, the woman I had lived with back in '99. I felt sure she would find participation in this event as appealing as I did. Sure enough, she agreed and recruited another friend. We three formed the top of the "P" that afternoon.

As I lay there preparing to take my clothes off when the helicopter was approaching for the photo, I thought about how my mother was probably turning over in her grave at that moment. This location was merely a stone's throw from where her dad, my

Pawpaw, had lived. Mother was so very reserved and would never have participated in this kind of action, though she had often surprised me by supporting my activism for the most part.

Bearing (and baring) witness that day, totally vulnerable in my nakedness, was transforming in a way I had never imagined. It was like an initiation of sorts. There were women of all ages present, some with their very young daughters, all seemingly comfortable with their bodies, seeing them as sacred, powerful vehicles for focusing attention toward peace and oneness.

Being with them shifted the way I saw my own body and reconnected me with my spirituality in a new way. I'd spent my whole life never being thin enough or having that 36"-24"-36" figure I wanted. I came away from the lake that afternoon with a new appreciation for my body, excess weight and all.

Bare Witness had been an unexpected, liberating and empowering experience on another level as well. I had also never taken part in a public demonstration against my own government's potential military posture. During Vietnam I had thought the anti-war protestors detrimental to our efforts in Vietnam. Granted, this was a little different in that we weren't at war with Iraq yet, only threatening to take such action. Even so, as a military dependent, I felt it was an action the military community would frown upon, not to mention possibly embarrass my sons.

Yes, it was a huge statement for me—this *is* who I am. I no longer blindly trusted that my government knew best or was being honest with me. I believed it would be a mistake to enter into a war with Iraq, especially without the sanction of the rest of the global community.

Wednesday evening, four days after our plea for peace at Lake Lavon, President Bush announced to the nation, "On my orders, coalition forces have begun striking selected targets of military importance to undermine Saddam Hussein's ability to wage war."[31] The president promised it would not be a campaign of half measures. An Air Force targeting expert told the reporter, "The war might be a few days, it might be longer, and it might be months...I think there's going to be a wide variety of different reactions by the Iraqi people and the Iraqi military."[32]

In less than two weeks we watched television coverage of Iraqis and U.S. Forces toppling the huge statue of Saddam Hussein in central Baghdad after we had stormed the city. This historic image didn't mean the war was over, the White House added. "With hundreds of thousands of troops in the region, the United States has lost 101, with 11 missing and 7 captured," according to the Pentagon. Great Britain had lost 30 troops.[33]

In 1982, veteran John Devitt had attended the dedication of the Vietnam Veteran's Memorial and felt the positive power of "The Wall." He left D.C. vowing to share that experience with those who didn't have the opportunity to get to Washington. He and several other veterans built the Moving Wall, a half-size replica that went on display for the first time in Tyler Texas, in October of 1984. Two versions of the Moving Wall now travel the USA from April through November, spending about a week at each site.

The Moving Wall came to Allen, a little town twenty miles north of Dallas, on Saturday, May 24th, 2003 in honor of Memorial Day. My former daughter-in-law, Dawn, had taken my youngest grandchildren there the Saturday before. Eight-and-a-half-year-old Brittany was making an etching of Chuck's name when Brandon spotted a silver POW/MIA bracelet on the ground close by, and like any curious seven-year-old boy picked it up only to discover it bore the name of his grand-daddy Chuck. Dawn burst into tears when she saw his name. The kids, of course, wanted to take the bracelet home. Dawn told them she didn't know if that was possible. They needed to check with the people who brought the Wall.

Sure enough, they were told all memorabilia left at the Moving Wall was stored in California (like those left at the D.C. Memorial are maintained in a special storage warehouse there). The officials had no way of knowing who had left the bracelet to ask if it was okay to give it to a family member. As luck would have it, a witness to this amazing discovery did know who had left it and went to telephone his friend. By the time David arrived Brittany was wearing the bracelet. "I want the little girl to have this bracelet," he told them. "She can hold it or pass that down, or give it to her family in 31 years. But as long as it keeps part of him alive, I want her to have it."[34] Needless to say, Brandon felt left out. He wanted a bracelet too. I gave him Jean's bracelet on Sunday.

Monday morning I was moved to put on my old copper bracelet again myself as I dialogued with my beloved husband in my journal.

Oh Chuck—I miss you so. I do wonder what my life would be like today if you'd come back from the war. But it's hard to imagine. It's as if I was re-born from that experience of you being missing. There's no doubt that you were part of my sacred contract—I loved you so very much–still do—you're a hard act to follow Mr. Stratton! Also hard to imagine you being 62—know you would have been handsome and not looked your age. You have quite the legacy now—five grandchildren. Your sons are wonderful young men. Charles actually looks the most like you I think–though Stephen has your build and many of your mannerisms. I wonder how they would have been if you'd come back. They all suffered without you—though I believe you've been our guardian angel all these years...

I am thankful for the sacrifice you made for me... I really grew up during those years—had experiences I'd never have had otherwise... I still feel this pride in the Air Force—yet also have an animosity toward the military and my government—maybe animosity isn't the right word—certainly distrust....

I still have the cranberry scoop from Cape Cod... the jewelry box you sent me... Most important—I have years of wonderful memories—which no one can take away.

Scott and I took the kids back to that Moving Wall later that week to meet David and his family. It was always such a pleasure to actually meet people who had worn Chuck's bracelet in the '70s. There's this incredible bond that comes from that shared energy. I was thrilled to be able tell him that excavation had begun at Chuck's crash site. I promised to keep him posted about the progress there. We had exchanged emails on the telephone earlier.

Since a 1979 Congressional Resolution, there has been an annual National POW/MIA Recognition Day observed in September. This year the New York Stock Exchange invited Jerry Jennings, deputy assistant secretary of defense for POW/Missing Personnel Affairs, to be the second to ever ring the closing bell in honor of our POW/MIAs.

The year before the Casualty Office personnel from Randolph AFB conducting a Family Update meeting in New York had learned that a POW/MIA flag hung over the trading floor. They contacted a public affairs manager for the NYSE about visiting and having their picture made under that flag. The woman who made the arrangements had worn a POW/MIA bracelet for over thirty years.

They brought her a picture of the man whose bracelet she had worn along with the news that his remains had been recently repatriated. They were asked to ring the closing bell that day.

My casualty officer called to ask if Stephen would be willing to represent the families on the podium with Jennings on the 19th. Never one who liked the publicity he'd grown up with during my active years with the League and Dallas Cares, he was not excited at the prospect, but agreed nonetheless to be there. He juggled his work schedule around to participate. Though he had lived in New York, he'd never been inside the Stock Exchange and knew it would be an interesting experience to actually be there on the floor.

With tremendous pride, I watched the television coverage to get a brief glimpse of my youngest son there to honor his dad and all those still missing. What had begun as a happenstance prompted this coordinated event to highlight the POW/MIA issue on this special day. Stephen learned from his contact who had arranged the Stock Exchange event that the JFA team was scheduled to be back at his dad's site in January. That was certainly welcome news. There had been no excavations of Chuck's site all year, and I'd not heard if the Laotian officials had given permission for the teams to return after they'd met in May.

By mid-December, U.S. troops found Saddam Hussein hiding in a hole outside his hometown of Tikrit. He surrendered without a fight. However, the infamous weapons of mass destruction still eluded discovery.

CHAPTER 19

35th ANNUAL MEETING OF THE LEAGUE OF FAMILIES

While there were no more excavations of Chuck's crash site in 2003, a fruitful excavation was going on within my own psyche. I had been reading Caroline Myss' book *Sacred Contracts* in which she articulated the concept that we each contract with twelve particular energy principles or archetypes when we incarnate. While there are countless archetypes we might experience in our lifetime, these twelve will be our primary guides toward the evolution of our own souls. Everyone has the child, victim, prostitute and saboteur. In addition we each have eight very personal patterns. I began the process of identifying those eight for myself, seeking to view the major events of my life from an archetypal perspective. Would it provide a helpful framework for writing my story, I wondered?

On January 3, 2004 I began my journal:

> *33 years ago today my life changed forever—Chuck became missing in action—Wonder if the teams are at his crash site now? I need to email Barney... I am a very different woman now—not so naive—but have I really changed so much? I'm back to not watching the news—not feeling very political—really wondering if Bush is doing the right thing in Iraq.*

I didn't keep up with the news about the Vietnam War before Chuck left for Southeast Asia. I did, however, when he became missing—at least for a while.

Then during the Gulf War I couldn't watch the news either. One morning while driving to work the radio announced that a fighter plane had been shot down and I burst into tears. My heart went immediately to the poor wife somewhere getting the news that her husband was missing. At times I judged myself rather harshly, seeing my aversion to news and politics as being apathetic. Now I think it is simply an avoidance of pain that kept me distanced from too much news.

When March rolled around and I still had no report, I emailed Barney in the Casualty Office at Randolph asking what was going on. He didn't respond for a couple of weeks because he was on vacation. By the time he returned, the 83rd JFA was back in Laos again and indeed at Chuck's site this time through the end of March. He assured me that I would receive a report when they had time to process that trip. Apparently they had been at another site in January. I prayed they would at least find some evidence this time that would give a positive correlation that it was indeed his crash site, like maybe a dog tag. Time would tell.

While I waited, I picked up a copy of *In Love and War: The Story of a Family's Ordeal and Sacrifice During the Vietnam Years*, co-written by Sybil and Jim Stockdale. It seemed very appropriate reading for the time. Sybil had started the League and was still on the board when I became a member. When the book had come out in 1984, I had put Vietnam out of my mind and was focusing on a career. The excavation process and trying to write about my own experience had certainly renewed my interest in the other stories that had been published. It began with Jim's telling of the lie of the Gulf of Tonkin incident that was used to get us into that war. I couldn't help but compare the weapons of mass destruction hype that got us into Iraq. I was most curious to see what he thought after his eight years as a POW.

In early May 2004, I received the report from the JFA. They did recover some fragmentary osseous remains along with unremarkable aircraft wreckage fragments and aircrew related artifacts. The recovery efforts were curtailed by the grounding of air-transport assets after only two weeks. Life support material evidence indicated that at least one individual was in the aircraft at the time of the incident. Further excavation was recommended before the wet season, which villagers said started during the sixth month and could run into October.

Shortly after this report arrived, I got a mailing from the National League announcing their 35th annual meeting scheduled for June 24th and 25th. I decided it was time to renew my membership and attend this one. I had only attended the military briefings at my last two visits to D.C. with my sons and then with Brenda and Allison. It was time to go back and actually participate in the League business meetings. I knew I could attend a Family Update in San Antonio and get current records from Chuck's file, but returning to an actual League meeting felt like coming back full circle somehow and that appealed to me. I wanted to reconnect with that year I had served on the League board. My airfare would be covered with COIN Assist travel. Undoubtedly reading Sybil's account had been the impetus for my renewed interest.

Then May 19th, an episode called "Leave No Man Behind" aired on *60 Minutes* about the Joint Task Force accounting efforts. That program raised the question: What is it about the American psyche that continues to pursue the finding of remains after 35 years? Actually I believe that the League was in large part responsible. Never before had our government been so pressured by military families for an accounting. When will it be enough? The reality is that all will never be accounted for—they can't possibly be. But until we reach that day when we have exhausted every possible avenue, the search will continue.

I was reminded during that hour special that it could take months to examine artifacts after they came back from the excavation sites. I wondered if the Vietnamese continued to wonder about the fate of their loved ones who never returned home. Perhaps their Taoist perspective helped them accept the uncertainty easier than the American psyche. Actually I had found that acceptance was easier to maintain than hope. I hated feeling in limbo again with the excavation potential dangling that hope before me again. I was thrust back into wanting an answer again, even though I also feared how that answer would affect my life now.

When I told Stephen I was going the League meeting in D.C., he wanted to train down to do some research at the Library of Congress.

He would stay with me and not have hotel costs. It was no more for me to stay at the Hilton than for the two of us. Crystal City was an easy subway ride to the Library. We could have some time together in the evenings. Barney also called after I had made my reservations and asked me to sit with him at the head table during the Air Force Luncheon. I learned that Shirley and Sam Johnson would be coming to the big League dinner, so I made arrangements to meet up with them one evening. I hadn't seen Shirley in years. She had been my first League contact and mentor until Sam came home. He was now a Congressman and they lived in Crystal City. How I looked forward to reconnecting with her!

When I arrived at the airport headed for D.C., I encountered Barbara Lewis at my gate. Her husband had been missing in Laos since 1965. His crash site had been excavated several times now so she too was awaiting a final answer regarding his fate. Apparently he had been sighted alive after the crash. She told me he had been the next-to-last declared dead from the Vietnam era back in 1980. We had a lovely visit as we awaited departure. She'd never remarried either.

Thursday was a full day of meetings starting at 8 a.m. I found myself getting irritated at times during the meetings, as well as getting sleepy. I was not used to sitting all day. I felt such a mixture of feelings as I listened to all the presentations—pride in my country and the Air Force at times coupled with the feelings that I no longer fit in this group. There were very few wives there, mostly brothers, sisters, sons and daughters. I was struck by a couple of comments made though. One man spoke of the accounting being our "sacred obligation"; then the Cambodian ambassador remarked—"we do it because it's the right thing to do."

I ordered some red POW/MIA bracelets from one of the vendors for all the grandkids. The most exciting part of the day was my contact with a family member whose wife had come with him to offer her services free of charge to any family member who was interested. She did some sort of healing, intuitive work. I took her number so I could set up an appointment with her. I was always open to any new mode of bodywork. Her ad in the program was titled "Spiritflite, integrative and preventative medical therapies." I was intrigued. I made it back to my room in time to clean up and change into more formal attire for the big dinner.

Except for the gushing accolades honoring President Reagan, I enjoyed the evening celebration. I had not been a fan of his policies and refused to give a standing ovation for him now. He was the one who cut Social Security benefits for Stephen while he was in college, which added a financial burden on us at that time. I sat next to probably the only other Democrat in the room who shared my opinion, so we rebelled together when everyone stood to applaud after the presentation by remaining in our seats. Bare Witness had unleashed my rebel archetype for sure.

Friday's agenda was filled with all the POW/MIA accounting operations. At the Air Force Luncheon I sat next to our Chairman of the Board, Jo Ann Shirley and former POW David Gray, also one of our Board of Directors. He told me he had been with Bob Jeffrey in Hanoi. I also discovered that he was the vendor who sold all the patches and pins and military items. Jo Ann told me about the Purcell's book, *Love and Duty* which I definitely wanted to read. I returned to my room briefly before the afternoon session to freshen up a bit and found that I had a message from Shirley asking if they could pick me up for an early dinner together. We had not had any time to visit at the dinner the night before. I was thrilled.

We had a wonderful evening together. I felt honored that they made time to see me. Sam told me that there had been weapons of mass destruction in Iraq that were moved to Syria. And he spoke of how Kissinger had sold us out. Twelve POWs were left in Laos and shot, as were some thirty in Cambodia. I found that upsetting of course, and wondered if Chuck could have been one of them. It was obvious our politics were very different. Nonetheless, I had the greatest admiration for Sam and the sacrifice he had made for this country. I really liked him and trusted him, despite my skepticism.

Saturday was the day set aside for individual file reviews in the morning and the League business session in the afternoon. At breakfast in the hotel restaurant, I had met a couple of other MIA wives. One of them remembered me from 1971-72. Both of their husbands had gone down in Laos in 1969 and those sites were also being excavated now. I imagined that was probably where the team had been to in 2002. We exchanged emails and I asked that they contact me if they got resolution to their cases. One of them told me his wedding band had been found, so she expected it was just a matter of time now before the completion of her husband's case.

I learned while reviewing Chuck's files that the teams were going back to the site the following week. That was most welcome news. Perhaps that meant his site would be their primary Laos pursuit this year. I had set my appointment for a session with the Spiritflite therapist following this review. I had no idea what to expect, but looked forward to learning her approach to heart-healing therapy.

My session with her turned out to be amazing. Deborah told me the process she practiced was called RoHun, a spiritual therapy designed to remove unconscious blocks and alter faulty perceptions or beliefs. She had just finished her certification at Delphi University and believed MIA families could benefit from the process to help heal our very old wounds. From what emerged during my process, she told me that it was my emotions that I had imprisoned. I was cut-off across my pelvic area. I knew from my bioenergetics work that my pelvis was frozen. She spoke of how critically I judged myself.

She asked me where I left my body. The throat chakra popped into my mind. We talked about that. I shared with her that past life regression experience where I felt myself on a blazing pyre. She said it made sense that if I were tied to something, I would have cut off low from the pain and I probably left my body from behind my neck because the hurt in my throat was so intense. Perhaps that was the connection to finding my voice again. When I told her I wanted to do more with RoHun when I got back to Texas she assured me that if I did, my life would be changed forever.

I left her room feeling very sleepy. That was a typical response from my body after doing any intense emotional work. I went back to my room and actually took an hour nap as the session continued to process within my psyche.

It was most interesting being in an actual League business meeting again after so many years. I had an opportunity to ask about the current rift I was seeing between the League and DPMO (the Defense Prisoner of War/Missing Personnel Office). Obviously I had missed out on all the politics of the League over the years since the accounting had begun.

That night Stephen and I connected for dinner in Chinatown. After our wonderful meal, we walked to the WWII Memorial, then on the Vietnam Wall. Half the wall was covered now, being cleaned. However Chuck's panel was not; nor was the one that had the names of the husbands of the women I had met at breakfast. By the time we were walking back to the subway, my left toes were killing me. I did not regret the walk, however. After days of meetings and sitting, it felt refreshing.

Stephen's train was departing earlier than my flight on Sunday. We ate breakfast at the hotel before checking out. Then we left our bags at the hotel and caught the subway to Arlington National Cemetery. With all my trips to D.C. over the years, this was the first time I had even been there. It was a perfect finale for this trip. We skimmed the surface of the Military Women's Museum, eager to take in the Tomb of the Unknown Soldier and see some of the well-known gravesites like John F. Kennedy's eternal flame, Audie Murphy's, and the Challenger and Columbia memorials. Quite unexpectedly we passed the grave of General Chappie James whom I'd met at a League meeting back in 1972. He had died in 1978. I had really admired Chappie. He was quite the speaker and a true patriot. He was the Deputy Assistant Secretary of Defense (Public Affairs) when I was on the board, and was very suited to the job.

Stephen rode with me to the airport before heading back to Union Station to catch his train. Linda was at the airport to pick me up and take me to dinner. I was eager to tell her about this new RoHun therapy I had experienced. Had she ever heard of it? I wanted to do more and planned to check out resources in the Dallas area for a therapist. I had reflected on that powerful hour throughout my flight. Deborah had asked me what I saw as the gain for getting a definitive answer about Chuck's fate. Would it give me closure I don't have now? It was a good question and one I couldn't answer. Why *was* it so important to know how or when he died?

As soon as I returned to Dallas I made a trip to Half Price Books in search of a copy of the Purcell's *Love and Duty* or Sam Johnson's *Captive Warriors*. They had neither, but I did run across *M.I.A. Mythmaking in America* that intrigued me enough to purchase it. Reading it really shook up all the perceptions of what I thought I knew. I found the author H. Bruce Franklin's supposition that President Nixon and his administration had used the MIA issue to extend the war and our presence in South Vietnam very disconcerting. He pointed out that extending the MIA status of our men kept hope alive for families. It did that for sure.

I also began to look for RoHun therapists in my area. I found the name of a woman in Bedford, but she was not actually practicing and gave me the contact information for a woman in Austin named Linda Yeats. I emailed her requesting information and giving some background as to how I had become interested in RoHun. I needed to know an approximate cost and the process for doing more of this work. It would have to be budgeted for, both money and time-wise. I had some dental work coming up that had to take priority.

Linda emailed me back that it would be best to wait until after the dental work before beginning any RoHun. I called her then to talk about what the specific process would be then when I was ready to schedule. She recommended a full weekend for the Purification Process to be followed in six weeks by the Shadow Process. She shared with me how the process had worked for her. I was convinced after our conversation I wanted to make this commitment. We settled on mid-September and Rosh Hashanah to begin. The Jewish New Year felt like an auspicious time for purification. As I gleaned from my reading about this holiday, it beckons one to prepare for a new reality. Purification, cleansing each chakra of all faulty perceptions, certainly felt like the first step toward transformation.

Knowing this timeframe allowed me to work out all the logistics. My friend Cynthia had relocated to Austin. Perhaps she would be willing to give me a room for that weekend. That would be a huge help in terms of the financial commitment. In the interim I continued reading Franklin's *M.I.A.*

By the time I finished the book my inner dialogue rebutted: *In reality—what difference would it make if Nixon did use the MIA issue to prolong the war? It doesn't change anything now. How does this information relate to the way I feel now about Iraq or the League? Strange, I actually feel grateful for the whole experience. Does the why it all came about really matter anymore?* Once again I was referred back to Myss' "rules to live by"— release the need to know why. Accept the gifts—the initiation—all the lessons from that experience.

As I continued my own internal excavation process with these RoHun sessions throughout 2004, JPAC got serious with the physical excavation of Chuck's crash site and worked his site four times that year.

The team removed all soil and associated artifacts from within the crater feature project area and screened approximately fifty percent of the total soil matrix during their 84th June/July JFA.

Fragmentary osseous remains, aircrew-related life support material and clothing, and very small unremarkable aircraft wreckage fragments were recovered from within that area.

The report from that 85th JFA arrived in November. Twenty-one of those piles of artifact-bearing sediment that were excavated the previous July, each corresponding to a two meter square excavation unit, were wet-screened. Fragmentary possible biological remains, a possible personal effect, numerous possible aircrew life support-related items that were potentially diagnostic, and non-diagnostic fragmentary wreckage representing a McDonnell F-4 Phantom II aircraft carrying a rotary canon were recovered.

A possible personal item—that grabbed my attention. It turned out to be a U.S. penny dated 1968, which meant this aircraft was lost no earlier than that year. Wouldn't that narrow down the possibilities for positively identifying this crash site? I read further. Yes it did. Based upon the location relative to that reported for case number 1688, the witness testimony regarding the time and season of the incident, the characteristics of the recovered evidence including this penny led to them concluding that it was most likely the one associated with #1688. The recommendation was to return in October/November to screen the eight remaining piles of soil and address the crater's interior along with the surface area around it. The site might require at least two additional JFAS to close out.

Obviously the final reports wouldn't be available until the following year, but 2004 was ending on a very positive note. And on a very personal and spiritual level, I had been introduced to the powerful process of RoHun that had brought not only an inner peace but a sense of expansiveness that led me to actually share what I had written thus far in "my book" with my sons and two dear friends. I felt very optimistic about the coming new year and far less restlessness that I had felt since the beginning of the excavation process.

CHAPTER 20

CLOSING THE CRASH SITE

I received a letter from my Casualty Officer in mid-January of 2005 with several copies of the 86th JFA to share with my sons. It summarized the essence of all the preceding JFAS and stated that the crater was two-thirds filled with water at the beginning of this excavation on October 19th—that water had to be pumped out to examine the floor sediment. All the structures constructed during the 84th and 85th JFAS were intact and reused during the 86th. Only a few fragments of flight suit material and aircrew-related items were recovered this visit.

The Recovery Leader/anthropologist concluded, "All evidence recovered was consistent with that found during previous JFAS. The excavated crater was produced by the impact of a USAF F-4 carrying a 20mm canon and BLU-26 submunitions, which was consumed by a high-order explosion as a result of impact. Both crewmembers were on board at the time of impact. Additional excavation of the internal margin of the crater is still necessary, particularly to the north and east of the excavated area and may require only one more JFA."

That statement—*both* crewmembers—never registered upon the first reading. I think I had become so accustomed to skimming those reports because of their length and detail that I glossed right over that. What I remembered was that field analysis still had not established an exclusive correlation to Chuck's F-4E. "Further analysis will be conducted at the JPAC CIL." I went back to that report from the 85th JFA which had concluded, based on JPAC's database of F-4 losses in the area carrying such ordinance, plus witness testimony regarding the time and season of the incident, that it was most likely case #1688. Were they ever going to be able to say for sure it was Chuck and Jim's aircraft? When was the 87th JFA scheduled? Could they be at the site even now?

These questions stirred the unrest again. One of our clients at work had so many airline miles that she offered to get me a ticket to Ireland with some of them this year. Now I questioned whether or not I should leave the states with this possibility of some definitive answer coming at last from the JFA investigations. Realistically, I knew even if they were at the site now I'd never see a report before March.

I finally came to the conclusion that I had waited thirty-four years now with no answer, so if I was out of the country when one finally came they could wait on me this time. I was not going to put this wonderful opportunity on hold for some illusive answer now. I decided to go full speed ahead with my plans. I also had been trying to schedule that second RoHun shadow process to augment the work I had completed with the purification sessions. We finally set the weekend of February 24th. She referred to this process as "Caged Energy" work. It's about finding Trickster and seeing his many guises for stealing my power and, like those first sessions, would process through each chakra.

In the interim, I received lots of very positive feedback from both Charles and Stephen about the writing I had shared with them talking about my life with their dad over the years of his career prior to Thailand. Both felt it all needed to be included in the memoir because all was relevant to creating the person I had become.

"The events are the journey," Stephen wrote, "and you're taking us along with you. The reader will understand and probably get things you don't even realize you're telling. You just tell the tale and I suspect a style will emerge without you realizing it. Describing the memories and thoughts is far more important than any analysis of why it's important."

By mid-April I learned that the 87th JFA had been at the site from January 14th-21st. The Recovery Leader/anthropologist felt no further excavation was needed now and the site was officially closed. No more suspected remains, personal effects, ID media, or diagnostic aircraft debris had been recovered from the last two areas they searched during that JFA.

Given the total artifacts found during the seven visits to this site, field analysis showed it was definitely an F-4E Phantom II with a rotary canon lost no earlier than 1968, almost completely destroyed by a high order explosion following impact with the ground. Life support artifact evidence supported the presence of two crewmembers at the recovery site and the incident was deemed non-survivable. Items recovered supported a time frame of 1971; the flight suit, boots, anti-gravity suit, torso harness and ejection seat artifacts would have been worn or used by 1971 U.S. Air Force crews.

It certainly looked like my prayers had been answered. Both Chuck and Jim were in that plane when it crashed. My biggest fear had always been that the remains of only one would be found and I might still never know Chuck's fate. Knowing for sure he was in that plane was a huge relief. No more doubts. No more MIA.

I assumed I would be getting a call from Mortuary soon. Would we be looking at a group grave situation, or was it possible to identify them through those "osseous remains" that had been recovered? How long would the final analysis take of all the materials recovered now that the site was closed?

On April 28th, I boarded my flight into Boston where I would transfer to Aer Lingus for Shannon—all first class. What a different experience that was as opposed to my usual economy fare travel. I was offered champagne while other passengers were still filing onto the plane. The food was amazing and I had the luxury of a movie on my very own screen there at my spacious and comfortable seat. I knew one could sure get used to this kind of special treatment. I was grateful for this incredible gift from Jill. My prayer that morning was that I remain open to whatever the Castle had in store for me this visit.

The only snafu in my entire trip was that my bag did not arrive with me. There had been a failure to mark it first class. I found clothing items I had left still in the chest beneath my Brittany bed to wear until it arrived the following day. Debra took me into town to get a small gas-burning stove for heating tea water in the mornings.

Liz had been using the fireplace in the dining hall for any cooking she might do. And there were friends around who were willing to let us come and shower when we needed to. We had no hot water of course without electricity. I'm sure it was very like how the Desmond's had lived when they built Matrix in the fifteenth century, a true adventure. I found that the Castle still felt absolutely magical.

In the evenings, after full days of taking in my favorite sites in the Republic, I finished reading Sue Monk Kidd's novel *The Secret Life of Bees*. I was moved by a Eudora Welty quote in that book: "People give pain...but *place* heals the hurt, soothes the outrage, fills the terrible vacuum that human beings make." And by one of the discussion questions in the back of the book: "Have you ever had to leave home to find home?" It was the perfect finale for what had been a fabulous vacation. Both of those statements felt applicable to my experience of Ireland.

I flew back by way of New York and stopped off for a couple of days to visit with Stephen. For an early birthday celebration, he took me to the most amazing art installation at the Nomadic Museum on Pier 54, "Ashes and Snow," featuring some 200 large-scale fantastic photographs of elephants. He bought me three of the leather-bound booklets of my favorite pieces as my gift to take home with me. Both my flights back were very pleasant and my bags were among the first on the conveyor belts at the airports. I made sure they had displayed the appropriate tags. What an incredible treat it had been to fly first class! I was one lucky woman.

There was no new correspondence waiting for me upon my return to Dallas however. And I was so very busy the rest of May catching up on paperwork at the office that I procrastinated in calling Casualty to inquire about the status of Chuck's case at this point. At the end of July, I received a newsletter from the National League of Families. On the first page, under "Accounting Results," the sixth name of the nine listed was Colonel Gregg Hartness.

Tears welled up in my eyes for Paula and her children. Paula had been one of the very active local wives when Chuck became MIA. She lived in Ft. Worth, but was an avid Dallas Cares supporter. She had been one of the four North Texas POW/MIA wives who'd gone to Paris in 1969 seeking information on their husbands. I wanted to contact her and tell her how happy I was for her and her family and to share that perhaps I would be getting this same kind of good news in the near future.

I called my casualty officer and asked for a contact number and/or address for Paula. Of course, Barney had to get her permission to share that information with me, but he said he'd get back to me. I also asked him to check on Chuck's current status since the site had been closed down with the last excavation in January.

"Is the case now closed?" I asked.

"No—it won't be closed unless there is some concrete identification made. All the artifacts excavated from the site are being sent to the Life Science Equipment Laboratory at Brooks AFB in San Antonio," he told me.

"Would it be possible for me to see them?" I asked.

"Let me check with the lab to see if they've received them yet," he replied.

Initiating the search for Paula produced a wealth of information I had no idea was in the works at the time. My mind was reeling at that point. I was eager to see what Paula had to say about this recovery process as she had experienced it. And the idea of being able to actually see what had been brought back from the site, all those items of life support equipment that had been meticulously listed in all those reports, was exciting.

When Barney called me back, he gave me the option of coming down to the lab the end of August or the end of September. They had received the artifacts and had begun to work them already. Of course I chose the earliest possible time. I couldn't help but think Chuck was actually guiding me during this time period. I had dreamed about him just before I got the League newsletter, then again as I waited for answers from Barney. In fact, I had dreamed about Chuck more during this entire excavation process than I had in years. He was definitely present within me again during this period.

I called Paula before I drove down to Randolph AFB. She had remarried and now lived in the Northwest not far from Seattle. Gregg's reconnaissance Cessna had been shot down over Laos on November 26th, 1968. His co-pilot bailed out and was rescued, but Gregg was MIA. She had finally stopped fighting his status change in 1980 and he was declared legally dead at that time. Excavation of his crash site had just begun in January. His identification had come from dental remains. Their son would go to Hawaii to bring his dad home and Gregg would be interred in Arlington National Cemetery on September 14th.

Gregg's dad was deceased. I had actually seen Wally when I was at the League meeting with Scott and Stephen. He was in a wheelchair then. Paula extended an invitation for me to come and see her sometime when I was in Seattle visiting another friend there. I assured her I would take her up on it. Paula told me that Barbara Lewis' husband had also been identified. I had not made that connection when I saw his name in the newsletter. I mentioned wishing I could contact Bonnie too. Paula said she was still in Dallas and would send me her address. It was wonderful connecting with Paula again. Just like in 1971, it felt comforting to speak with someone in your same situation, someone who knew well what I was feeling now with the prospect of bringing Chuck home too.

CHAPTER 21

SEEING IS BELIEVING

On Wednesday, August 31ˢᵗ, I was in my car driving south for San Antonio. I had no idea what to expect once I got there, but prayed to remain open to receive whatever that was. Barney had made reservations at the old Visiting Officer's Quarters there at Randolph and told me he would drive me to the lab the next morning at Brooks AFB. He'd sent me directions and told me to have them call him at the gate when I arrived. Talk about service! The quarters were absolutely amazing.

Randolph has to be one of the prettiest bases I've ever seen. The buildings are all Spanish white stucco with the red tile roofs. Hibiscus, palm trees and tropical vegetation abound. The VOQs have large veranda porches with big wooden rockers to sit outside and enjoy the view. And each suite is spacious, beautifully furnished complete with a small kitchen, microwave, sink and refrigerator stocked with juices and beverages. It's like a luxury hotel with all the amenities. I knew I was going to be *very* comfortable here.

I arrived around 3:30 in the afternoon, so I had time after getting settled to check out the base exchange. I went to the Officer's Club for dinner. This was the first time I'd been on an Air Force Base in such a long time. It was foreign and familiar at the same time. I loved hearing the jets taking off and landing. While exploring the base, I heard the National Anthem and saw the cars stopping for retreat as the base flag was being lowered. I too stopped, got out of my car and saluted in the direction I observed others doing. It was a proud, moving experience, one I'd not had in the civilian world since 1970. Hearing Taps as I prepared for bed was another nostalgic moment, reminding me of military protocols I had long since forgotten.

I slept restlessly that night, waking several times, my mind racing, feeling a little anxious about the lab visit the next morning, wondering what was in store. I woke before 6:00 and was drinking my tea when I heard Reveille, a very pleasant way to greet the morning, a rousing reminder that I was in a military community. Barney picked me up at 0830 on the dot. It was a good forty minute drive to Brooks City Base with the morning traffic. I was glad I wasn't driving. Our sharing of stories made the time seem to fly by, however. We were meeting Barney's son-in-law for lunch after the lab.

Upon arrival, we went straight to the area where the artifacts were being worked. I met Senior Analyst John Goines there. He had just finished photographing a life vest piece. As I entered this cubicle of space, I noticed an ejection seat and a manikin dressed in flight gear to my right. Straight ahead was a long table with about a dozen plastic shoeboxes of materials. Another table was in the center of the space and had the life vest and pieces from the crash site that they had just completed. John explained that the ejection seat and manikin were exactly like the one Chuck would have been in, all the gear exactly like what he would have been wearing. It's their base line for comparing the pieces recovered in the crash site for identification.

Everything from the crash site was neatly sorted in those plastic shoebox bins according to what part of their gear it was. They had already photographed and identified some 58 pieces of flight suit material in one box, and 32 pieces of survival boot material in another. John brought over those two boxes to that center table for me to see as he explained what they had determined from them.

Of the flight suit material he showed me two good sized pieces, and laid them out onto a flight suit identical to one like Chuck would have worn. Both were right leg pencil pockets. Since there is only one such pocket on those flight suits, it was clear that both men were onboard the F-4 at impact. It was amazing to see how the fragments, discolored from both the fire and the clay of Laos, fit so perfectly on the pencil pocket of that intact flight suit. The stitching was identical; clearly they were exact matches.

The same with the boot material—two different treads, two different boots. I told John I felt like the single heelpiece he showed me was Chuck's flight boot. Wasn't it the newer model of jungle boot? It made sense to me that Jim would have had his old ones from his previous tour. John reminded me that they would have been issued whatever was available in their size, not based on a newer issue.

I asked if he could tell the size of the boots based on the pieces they had. He said the toe pieces were probably about a size 11; that heelpiece was from a smaller boot. "See, it is Chuck's. His boot size was an 8/1/2 to 9," I said. John just smiled and let me think whatever I wanted to think. Actually, I had known it intuitively, though by logic even my intuition made sense. It also made sense to me that less of Chuck's boot would have survived the crash. Being in the back seat I felt like he would have experienced more of the fire. Jim's feet would have been more protected because they were buried in the ground as the nose doze into the earth.

What are the odds? Two different kinds of jungle boots were issued during that era and Jim just happened to be wearing one type, Chuck the other. I stood there feeling totally blown away by the luck of having such clear evidence that both Chuck and Jim were inside that plane when it crashed. I felt absolutely elated in the presence of this physical evidence, holding in my very own hands the fabric and hardened rubber that had been on Chuck and Jim's bodies when they left this earth. I was in total awe of the efforts of JPAC to have recovered all this after thirty-four years in the acidic soil of a flooded crater in the jungles of Laos, and now to this team who were analyzing it all and putting the pieces of the puzzle together. My gratitude level was soaring.

I was given a grand tour of the entire lab after I had looked in all those little shoeboxes and asked questions that arose with each item that caught my attention. I took lots of photographs and they took pictures of me in that F-4E ejection seat. They graciously made copies of their work completed thus far to take back and share with my sons. I was walking on cloud nine when Barney and I left for lunch. Did I ever need food to ground me from the exhilaration of the morning!

We went by the Casualty Office on the way back to the VOQ so Barney could get Barbara Lewis' phone number for me. It seemed that both her husband and Gregg Hartness were to be buried on the same day, which just happened to be National POW/MIA Day, September 14th (also my son Scott's birthday). I got back to my room about 2:00 that afternoon and sat down to journal about the amazing experience at Brooks.

I looked at all the pictures, read all the initial reports from the items on which they had completed analysis. How I would treasure that wonderful photo of me with the entire team! One of that team who had served on the maintenance crew for the F-4s gave me a laminated poster of all the different kinds of aircraft that had been lost during our sixteen-year involvement in Southeast Asia. I chuckled again to myself about his response to my comment that the F-4 was the pilot's dream—"and the nightmare for maintenance," he added.

Suddenly I felt totally exhausted. My mind, my body simply could not take in anything else. Coming down at last from this emotional high, my eyes refused to stay open. I lay down to the sound of jets overhead and went sound asleep. Some two hours later I woke up, astounded that I could sleep like that during the day. I have never been one to nap. Usually I have to be sick to sleep during the day. I certainly wasn't sick. But my body reacted to all that adrenaline by having to finally just check out for a while. I lay there slowly coming back, visions of the morning floating through my mind. Maybe a nice walk, some fresh air would revive me, I thought. But first, I wanted a cup of tea. How glad I was that I made the trip down to San Antonio.

When I got back to Dallas, I shared the packet with my sons and with Brenda with great excitement. But that high would soon be dampened by the length of time it was taking for the Life Science Lab to complete their analysis and issue a final report. What about the osseous remains that were excavated from several of those trips into Laos? What happened to them? They weren't shown to me when I was there at Brooks. I emailed Barney with that question. After contacting JPAC he wrote back that the bone fragments were too small for DNA testing. They were still in Hawaii.

My first response was, *here we go again*. How can there be concrete identification without DNA testing? We know they were both in the plane when it crashed and it was definitely not a survivable incident. Did they get DNA from Hartness' dental remains? Are those bone fragments smaller than a tooth? We're never going to get a positive identification, I thought. But that's okay. I have more now than I ever thought I would have, knowing he died instantly the night of January 3rd, 1971. He didn't have to endure torture at the hand of the enemy. I feel really grateful for that assurance. It was enough.

I imagined that eventually we would have a group burial with the remains recovered, like my cousin from WW II. I grew up with S.L.'s army portrait hanging in the hall of our Pleasant Grove house. He was a bombardier in a B17 shot down over Brunswick, Germany on April 8th, 1944. Only the tail gunner escaped that aircraft. The nine others were listed as MIA. Their remains were buried together in 1950 at the Jefferson Barracks National Cemetery in St. Louis, Missouri. Chuck and Jim would remain together too, either in Texas or Arlington. For now, I had to wait and trust that the timing would be perfect when the closure that comes with a burial manifests.

I called Barbara to tell her how happy I was that her husband had also been positively identified. For her it had been forty years. Col. Lewis' B-57 disappeared in the jungles of Laos in 1965. She told me that she too had been told originally that his bone fragments were too small for DNA testing. They were recovered in 2004. But then they came up with some new device, some new technology that made it possible after all. So there was always hope. He had been buried in their hometown of Marshall in mid-August. Now the military was flying her and her family to D.C. for the Arlington service on the 16th for a group burial with his navigator. I also learned that she'd never had a memorial of any kind for her husband either when he had been presumed dead. I wondered now if Paula had had a memorial service in 1980.

The *Dallas Morning News* did lengthy articles on Gregg's service and Paula's journey as well. Murphy Martin's comments stood out for me from the front page article about her trip to Paris with three other MIA wives to ask the North Vietnamese diplomats there if they were wives or widows.[35] "The four of them—because they were the first wives to meet with the North Vietnamese—they became a kind of symbol. I think it's a legacy that should not be cast aside for the people who are losing loved ones in Iraq or wherever the military is today. Hopefully it is not lost on them what these wives went through to organize others."[36]

Mr. Martin was a former Dallas TV anchor who accompanied Paula and the others on that famous trip and who worked with Ross Perot and United We Stand. He was right. These women and others like them paved the way for the return of our POWs then—as well as the accounting for them now—and for making sure our country leaves no man behind in the future.

I really wanted more conversation with Paula, only this time in person. I was long overdue for a visit with my dear friend Nancy in Seattle. I thought maybe she could drive me to La Conner to meet with Paula and her new husband. I had no idea what I wanted to know from her beyond what I'd already asked or read. But for some reason I needed that contact with her now. It was a quick trip, but well worth it.

Somehow my contact with Paula rejuvenated me, as did the book I was reading during the trip, *Dance of the Dissident Daughter: A Woman's Journey from the Christian Tradition to the Sacred Feminine.* I had loved *The Secret Life of Bees* and wanted to know about Sue Monk Kidd's spiritual journey that had produced that tale. I figured I would relate on many levels as my journey had paralleled her same progression.

Vietnam had moved me to that place of the dissident daughter. It was when I began to question my government as a truthful authority. That transferred to the church as my involvement there grew as well. I really identified with her description of a revelation that came to her as she sat in church one November morning.

"The ultimate authority of my life is not the Bible; it is not confined between the covers of a book. It is not something written by men and frozen in time. It is not from a source outside myself. My ultimate authority is the divine voice in my own soul! Period. I waited. Lightning did not strike."[37]

That had been my exact reaction when I railed at God back in 1973—I waited to be struck by lightning. That was the expectation for questioning ultimate authority.

My desire to write about my own MIA odyssey grew stronger as a result of reading about her journey. She wrote, "Writing my book was an act of breaching. Women have whale instincts—to send out our vibrations, our stories, so that no one gets lost."[38] What a great metaphor. The restlessness, the open-endedness of the excavation process had helped me tap into feelings I buried back in the mid '70s when I shifted my focus to getting a college education. My studies had opened worlds of understanding for me psychologically. I wanted to share the lessons it had taken me years to glean from my MIA years.

By the end of September, I had ordered her new novel, *The Mermaid Chair,* from the library. This one too was a page-turner. I devoured it in three weeks' time. I was stopped in my tracks when I read, "I felt that the centerpiece of my history had been dug up and exposed as a complete and utter fiction.... It left a gaping place I couldn't quite step over."

Those words stood out on the page the way that ad for an abortion counselor had back in 1981, as if that was all that was written on the page. And I knew. That's it—that's the root of all that restlessness during the years Chuck's crash site was being excavated. The centerpiece of my history, my identity as an MIA wife was being dug up and exposed as a complete and utter fiction. I am who I am today based upon that defining event of my life—being an MIA wife, living always in the question.

I have lived not as a wife, not as a widow—always somewhere in between. I was so sure that Chuck had survived the crash, largely based on my belief that he had come to me in that dream to tell me he was alive. I also believed I would know if he were dead, I would feel it. These new revelations that Chuck had died that night raised the question of trust in myself, in my own intuition, in all the very beliefs that had kept *me* alive during those awful years. A fiction. Did that mean my whole life was a lie?

I spent the next couple of weeks reflecting, questioning myself. It was a terribly unsettling time. I replayed in my head all the times I had thought I knew Chuck would never return, only to have someone suggest otherwise or some new piece of information surface to open up the question again. How was I to know which voice to trust anymore? I remembered what my astrologer friend, Linda, had said about October being intense when Saturn went over my mid-heaven. Intense didn't begin to adequately describe those feelings. This inner turmoil stirred by the thought of having lived a lie lay beneath the surface, sent me all too often into a very critical, judgmental inner dialogue.

Gradually I came to see that the beliefs I had held over the years were a necessary fiction that had operated somewhat like myth. They had given me hope, allowed me to continue to function until I could find another meaning that would sustain me. Fiction does not necessarily equate with lie; myth expresses a deep truth, not factual information. It was quite an unpleasant process feeling all the judgments that arose from questioning the validity of my life because it was based on a fictitious assumption. But contentment did finally become the order of the day and I continued to wait for the closure I expected to follow the Life Science Lab's completed report.

The many hours I spend with Dave had stirred my reflections upon the past thirty-six years in very positive ways, helping me see the ebb and flow through a new organizational lens. The person I am today has indeed evolved by virtue of events that stemmed from Chuck's becoming MIA and my processing of them as I reacted and/or responded to my realities.

The retelling of my story to him during August helped me become clearer on what I wanted for this long overdue homecoming. Dave left that afternoon saying he'd call back to arrange a time to come do some photographs and video the next week.

In early September I received an email from my friend Michael Clarke, an MIA son who had done the study on prolonged ambiguous grief that I had participated in back in 1999. He lived in Hawaii and wanted to go to the lab with me when I go for Chuck's remains.

Dave Tarrant called shortly afterward. The DMN wanted to send him to Hawaii to cover that part of my journey as well. He too wanted to be with me when I saw the remains. The article he was writing would not be printed until after the service.

I was not sure how I felt about either of these requests and needed some time to consider the pros and cons for me. I was most hesitant about both. I felt that the presence of either of these men could interfere with my being able to just be with my own feelings. I knew Dave would be able to maintain the "fly on the wall" posture, but Michael had a far more personal investment. My primary concern was being able to be totally present to myself during my reunion with Chuck, and I didn't want either of their agendas to color that moment.

When I met with Joy then, she affirmed that this journey was about me and I should not feel any guilt about keeping it that way and trusting my own intuition about what I needed now. She told me I would be having lots more feelings as the time grew nearer. It had been twenty-two years before her husband had been found. She too *knew, yet didn't, sort of* before he was declared dead. He was buried in a group grave, no DNA identification, but they found the lighter she had given him at the crash site.

I felt so very blessed that it was she who would officiate for Chuck's service. We did indeed share a sacred bond. As young women we had become Air Force wives, madly in love with men who had a passion to fly. Her calling to become a minister had occurred in early 1991 before his remains returned home. And she was ordained in 2000. It was no accident that our paths had crossed a few months earlier.

Dave emailed me a new proposal that his editor had suggested since I was hesitant about him being at the lab with me. How about I meet with him after my trip to the lab? I felt comfortable with that and told him so. I decided to tell Michael that I very much wanted to see him when I was in Hawaii. Could we have dinner together that day I had off before going to the lab? I really felt I needed to be alone when I get Chuck's remains. I knew I had made the right choice in honoring my own feelings, even at the risk of hurting his. Brenda had told me that she didn't feel like talking to anyone as she held Jim's remains at the lab. I was pretty certain I wouldn't either.

Speaking with so many old friends over the next couple of weeks was very rewarding. I asked each to please consider sending me a written favorite memory of Chuck that I could share with his sons and grandchildren. During that time I also heard from people I did not know, but who had known Chuck. The news stories were really paying off.

Through one of them, I finally got in touch with Bill Berry, the guy we had double dated with on our very first date. I learned then that it had been a birthday celebration for him that night. I had finally reached both of Chuck's best friends in high school. It was looking like our entire wedding party would be at the service.

Lynn, who was my oldest military wife and best friend through our first two pregnancies and duty stations, shared with me that she too had felt she would never see Chuck again after we had met up again in Massachusetts in '69 at the Edaville Railroad. Until we had connected again via the telephone, she had not known of my fear, or that I too had felt that way as I watched him walk away from us toward his plane that August morning of 1970.

She would not be able to come to the service, but would definitely send her fondest memories. She and her husband at that time had divorced and she had married a Navy man. They had been in Nichols, New York for years now. Wendy who had painted Chuck's portrait back in the early '70s was also unable to attend, but her portrait of Chuck would stand behind the altar during the service.

Much to my delight, Dave Tarrant wanted to do an obituary for Chuck before we left for Hawaii. That would save me a lot of money. I would just have to take out a small obituary notice just prior to the service itself.

He set up another visit to my apartment with his photographer, Gerry, so we could get pictures for his article. He asked to take me to the airport the morning of my flight since he wasn't leaving until that evening. He wanted Gerry to come along that morning to document my departure for his big article. Everything was falling into place beautifully for me. I would truly be able to relax and just be present when I was at Hickam AFB to reunite with Chuck at long last.

Dave and I kept in touch via email as I finalized all the details of the funeral. He met with me again on September 19th with Gerry, and videographer, Ron, to get pictures for the story, which apparently would have videos online to accompany the newspaper's written article. I continued to be amazed at the time the DMN was devoting to this story.

Gerry photographed me laying out the 70+ photographs across my bed that I was working with for the video to run at the funeral, showing Chuck's life visually through the years. Ron asked me what Chuck was like as he observed this process. "He was a devoted family man, romantic husband, handsome, fun loving, brilliant, confident, lived his bliss, never worried, well-liked by everyone...," I began.

I'm sure he clearly got the message that Chuck was remarkably special. It made me think about how I was going to eulogize him at the service itself, what memories or stories I wanted to share to add to the portrait his uncle, his military friends and Joy would paint. I'd been too busy with all the details of organizing the "perfect" celebration of Chuck's brief but incredible life, I'd not really stopped to consider my part of his farewell service.

In nine days I would be flying to Hawaii to escort him home. I still needed to get some favorite stories from the boys to give to Joy. Dave wanted to meet with them Sunday evening, which hopefully would spark their memories of their dad and what they would want people to know about him.

I had three full months to prepare for Chuck's service and needed every minute of that time. I spent July just taking in the reality of an actual positive DNA identification. Everything went public then in August and my attention became focused on the media. However, thanks to the amazing coverage, everything fell into place by September as old friends came forward as well as new ones to help me pull together what was shaping up into a true grand finale homecoming.

BOOK IV

ALOHA

"I am Penelope, the one who wears a web on her face. I weave the tapestry of the life of my warrior husband by day, and unweave it by night. My message to you is this: the wait was long enough. The tapestry of your lives interwoven, rich enough."

Spoken to me by Linda Finnel on February 2nd, 1989
during a ritual seeking closure

CHAPTER 22

OFF TO HAWAII

Wednesday, 26 September 2007 0508 hours

I woke to someone knocking on my door, a wakeup call, courtesy of the hotel. As I stirred my mind went immediately to—get that carry-on from the storeroom downstairs, the one with the handle... Realizing it was only a dream, I roll over to see the clock—it's almost five. The alarm will be going off soon. Time to start the teakettle and get a move on it. Today's the big day.

I am flying to Hawaii this morning to escort my husband's remains home—remains that lay in the jungles of Laos for thirty years before being excavated from his crash site and brought to Hawaii; remains that have rested at JPAC (Joint POW/MIA Accounting Command), Hickam Air Force Base for the past six years until DNA technology had advanced enough to make a positive identification from a long bone fragment just three months ago. Now THAT feels like a dream.

What's more, the Dallas Morning News is sending their reporter, Dave Tarrant who is writing a feature story on me, to Hawaii as well, and he's the one taking me to the airport this morning. Unbelievable as it still feels, I know it is real—this day I never imagined would actually come to pass.

I allowed myself the luxury of my first cup of tea by candlelight with my journal before hitting the shower and finishing my packing. I'd prepared a checklist, just like pilots do before their flights, to make sure I haven't forgotten anything essential for the trip or to unplug the fountains and shut down the computer, lock the patio doors, turn up the thermostat. Being thoroughly prepared, however, didn't prevent those travel jitters. Those would disappear only when I was on my way to the airport and it was too late to change anything.

Gerry, Dave's photographer, arrived early. He would follow us to the airport. It felt very strange to have my life so documented, but how else could I get the word out to all those concerned folks who wore Chuck's bracelet during the Vietnam War? I still had hundreds of letters from bracelet wearers all over the country. Sharing my journey now to Hawaii felt appropriate. Gerry asked me how I was getting back from the airport upon my return.

"I'll probably take a shuttle," I told him.

"I can pick you up," he offered.

"Are you sure? The flight arrives at like 6:00 in the morning," I said.

The early hour was no problem, he assured me. Since he could not go with us, he wanted to record my return with Chuck in hand. I now had one less thing to worry about.

Dave rang the buzzer right on schedule and we were off. Locking my apartment door and leaving behind all the tasks that remained on my "to do" list, each step I took toward the elevator divested me of any fear that I had forgotten something.

Ready or not, here I come.

Dave filled me in on the details of his travel. He didn't leave until later that afternoon. Tomorrow he wanted me to meet their contracted photographer to get some beach shots before we went to the lab on Friday. It was still a stretch for me, this realization that the *Dallas Morning News* was willing to go to these lengths for a feature story about this incredible reunion. They dropped me off with plenty of time to spare. I looked forward to two hours alone with my thoughts about the journey ahead.

Check-in was quick, no problems. Security would be just as easy as I had familiarized myself fully with all the current regulations. I passed through the metal detector and walked on to retrieve my shoes when the woman scanning the carry-ons with x-ray announced loudly, "You have liquid in your bag!"

"I do not," I retorted a bit indignantly.

I had carefully put all my contact and facial products in the required quart zip-lock baggie as instructed. But sure enough—there was the small bottle of water I had brought for the car ride to DFW. I had totally spaced on that. She also found a tiny bottle of hand lotion in the small zipper pocket of my purse that I had overlooked for the allowed container.

Apparently she decided I was merely a ditz and not a terrorist who required a strip search at that point and she let me go on to my gate, without the confiscated items of course. Embarrassed, I walked on toward the gate putting that little encounter behind me, admiring my red socks through the straps of my Birkenstocks.

I sat down and finished a note to some old military friends about the memorial service and put it in a mail drop close to my gate. I couldn't remember when Tim's flight was to arrive, the mortuary officer from Randolph AFB who would accompany me to Hawaii. It was really nice to have some alone time to just sit and do nothing. The past few weeks had been extremely busy planning all the details for the celebration of Chuck's life. My goal was that afterward his grandchildren would feel like they knew that mysterious man in the portrait on the wall and that his sons would feel like I had done their father proud.

A lovely couple sat across from me. He was a writer going to Hawaii to check out a writer's retreat place on the Big Island. They asked if I was going on vacation. No, I told them, and I relayed my story. We exchanged email addresses. Both were eager to support me writing about this experience.

The boarding time was announced and no Tim. What if something has happened and he doesn't make this flight, I wondered? He was the one who had all the hotel reservations and the car rental once we landed in Oahu. I inquired at the check-in counter and was informed that he had just landed from San Antonio and would make the connection so I could go ahead and board the flight. What a relief! He knew where I was seated on the plane so I trusted that he would find me.

And find me he did, before we actually began to taxi. I had pulled out my neck pillow and my journal, stowed my carry-on under the seat in front of me and buckled up, when I noticed this man coming down the aisle looking at me, eyebrows raised in a question. I could read on his lips—*Sallie?*

From my window seat I acknowledged his silent query with my own—*Tim?* He stopped then, introduced himself and politely asked the man in the aisle seat if he would be willing to change places with him after our flight took off. He was amenable, so we were able get acquainted during the long flight over and discuss the agenda for our stay. At some point during our chitchat, I commented that Chuck's service back in Dallas was not a funeral, but rather a memorial service. Tim's immediate and curt response was, "Oh but I beg to differ with you. It is a funeral. It is final."

And he went on to talk about the military part of that individual service, suggesting perhaps "Air Force Hymn" for the flag-folding portion and perhaps "Air Force Song" for the processional.

"Good idea! The music selection has been the hardest part of the service for me," I confessed. Feeling a little taken aback by that funeral declaration, I opted to nap for a little while. I didn't want to think about the details of the service any more. I let myself fall into a nostalgic reverie about my other visit to Hawaii thirty years before.

Throughout the '70s mother, my three sons and I enjoyed planning a two-week summer vacation. Those out of the ordinary excursions were always special times to explore new places and rejuvenate from the stressful year before. Before Chuck left for Thailand in August of 1970, we all went to Galveston. SeaArama and the warm water of the Gulf were ample entertainment for active boys of three, five and eight.

In the summer of 1977 I requested that status review, knowing Chuck would be presumed dead. By the next summer I was feeling the need for a really special vacation to mark our now-accepted future without him. Hawaii seemed the perfect place. I had so looked forward to celebrating our 10th wedding anniversary in Hawaii for his R&R half way through his Southeast Asia tour. My unfulfilled dream would be shared with the whole family, compliments of his government insurance policy. It had been a spectacular vacation.

This trip would be less than three days, a solitary reunion and return anticipated with as much fervor as that Royal Orchid travel package so long ago.

Aside from the cramped space, the flight was pleasant enough—a far cry though from that first one on the massive two story 747 jumbo jet where we could get up and walk around during those 8 1/2 hours. Flying was definitely more fun in the '70s! Seeing the blue and green hues of the Pacific Ocean as we approached Honolulu re-energized my confined lethargy. I could not wait to get my bare feet in the sand at the hotel.

By the time we got our bags and the rental car, we found ourselves driving in five o'clock traffic to the Hilton Hawaiian Village. Of course the congestion was nothing like Dallas traffic, and the tropical breeze through the opened windows felt marvelous. I was still amazed that the Air Force had booked our stay at the very same complex we had stayed back in '78.

I had forgotten that the entire front desk lobby for the Village was all open air—a few pillars here and there delineating seating areas with lush gardens and fountains, framing gorgeous views right through to the ocean. Were there six different towers back then too? I could not believe my luck as the desk clerk handed me my key card for The Rainbow Tower—the very one I had stayed in so many years before. What were the odds? My 27th floor room faced Honolulu rather than Diamond Head but as Tim so aptly stated, "There are no bad views here." My balcony looked over a small boat harbor with the ocean just beyond. And the breeze was cool and refreshing—no need for the air conditioner at all. My patio door would remain open throughout my stay and the thermostat off. I unpacked, settled into this charming space, and called Michael to let him know I had arrived and to schedule some visiting time with him that night or the next.

Still a couple hours from the end of his work day, Michael suggested I take a walk on the beach and then decide what I wanted to do about meeting him for dinner that evening. I couldn't get downstairs fast enough! There were still a few families out, but the beach felt pretty private as I strolled toward Diamond Head, the sun to my back.

I was mesmerized by the incoming tide, letting it wash away all thought processes, content merely to soak in the sand and surf, be lulled by the rhythm and sound of each little wave across my toes. Heaven. Pure heaven. Nothing could be more relaxing. I walked until the beach disappeared for a stretch at one of the continuous hotels along this strip of Waikiki before turning back into the setting sun.

I watched it sink lower and lower, reveled in the color that painted the sky—an ombre of brilliant flaming oranges with a strip of deep blue in between layers of clouds—the contrast was striking. Why hadn't I brought my camera? No matter—the glory was etched in my memory forever. As the Rainbow Tower came closer into my view, so the sounds of music got louder and louder. Suddenly I realized that all I wanted right now was some quiet alone down-time. I couldn't meet with Michael. In fact, I just wanted to get some food and take it up to my room to eat. I discovered take-out across the street from the lobby and ordered a personal size Maui Zaui pizza. I found a small bottle of red wine to carry back while the pizza was cooking. Dining on my private balcony patio, I reflected on this very long day. It was 2 or 3 a.m. Dallas time by then and I was still awake. Amazing.

My sleep was choppy—it seemed I woke up every hour. But I got up at my usual 5:30 wake-up time. The room was spacious: a nice coffee bar which worked well for my tea preparation, a lovely little table and chair by the patio door for my altar, a perfect spot to journal. The red hibiscus floral bedspreads added a cheery note of color amongst all the blonde furniture.

The hibiscus is Hawaii's state flower, though with the plethora of orchids everywhere, you would think they were. This was my free day. I told Tim when he was making arrangements for me to come that I did not want a whirlwind trip like Brenda, Chuck's pilot's wife, had made. She flew in one evening, went to Hickam the next morning to pick up Jim's remains, and flew back that evening. I wanted a down day before going to JPAC.

He was able to arrange that, because he needed to get the group remains ready to be escorted home. I felt a little disappointed that I would not be able to see them too; the picture of them in the report would have to suffice. It was a worthwhile sacrifice for me to have this day to myself—half of it anyway. I was to connect in the afternoon with Dave and the photographer, and then with Michael for dinner.

As I journaled about the events of the day before, I reflected more on what Tim said about Chuck's service being a funeral. Maybe that's why the church didn't work out and I had to look at funeral home possibilities. I'm not at all sure I understood the distinction Tim made, but it felt somehow important.

I drew a meditation card—Higher Consciousness. "You have

been asking for Divine Guidance and your higher self has answered your prayers. Your Spiritual Path has helped you hear this voice," it read.

Oh my! I remembered hearing this voice in the night that told me to put my POW/MIA bracelet into the urn with Chuck. I wondered what I should do with the bracelet now. It had rested on an altar at home for years. I wore it only when I felt moved to do so—like on this trip to Hawaii to escort him home. I would feel into that idea as I explored the Village later. Perhaps it was a message from my Higher Consciousness.

It was getting daylight out now. I took my second cup of tea with me down to the beach. It was a little cloudy this morning. I found some interesting rocks and a gull feather as I moved in and out of the gentle waves along the shore. I brought my camera this time to record the beauty of the morning. How lovely and quiet it was now. Only a few other early birds were up and out at this hour. I walked east again toward Diamond Head, hoping to catch a glimpse of the sun peeking through.

What would it be like to live here and begin every day like this? I wondered. I could be so content just "hanging loose," letting all cares just roll back into the ocean with each wave that washed over my feet, feeling at one with this incredible paradise. When the sun finally broke fully though the clouds, I turned back toward the hotel.

The grounds of the Village are magnificent—orchids everywhere, ponds with ducks, swans, flamingos, ibis and koi—there's even a penguin island, along with colorful parrots and macaws—and lovely bronze Menehune sculptures throughout. Menehunes are magical little people of Hawaiian folklore, not unlike the leprechauns of Ireland. I still had two little Menehune figures from my first trip here that sit on my kitchen cabinets at home.

A wedding chapel stood in the center of this tropical paradise for couples from all around the world to come and say their vows. Only a failing battery in my camera moved me to go back up to my room. Depositing my tea mug and camera, I was ready to check out the shopping until my appointment with Dave and the photographer. Much to my delight, I found a black coral bracelet and earrings from Maui. I had bought myself a black coral and pearl ring on my first trip here.

Afternoon came all too quickly. I dropped my purchases off in my room, slipped into my bathing suit and shorts and headed back to the lobby to find Dave. We had a few minutes to catch up before the photographer arrived. When Marco did arrive and surveyed the situation, I got the impression that he thought walking the beach seemed too contrived for some reason. I wasn't sure just what he was looking for in the way of photographs for the story. Finally I told him that I was off for another stroll along the beach and he was welcome to come or not.

I found the water so very calming and wanted to soak in as much as I could in my short stay. It was what I would be doing whether the photographer was there or not. And off I went. He and Dave followed me and he did take photographs as we talked. It still felt strange to have this trip so documented—but it was an awesome reunion I was about to face—I didn't mind sharing my joy with the rest of the world. As long as I could have my privacy when I needed it.

After an hour or so, we were all getting thirsty and decided to come back to the bar where we could sit down and talk. My friend Michael joined us by happy hour time. It was great seeing him again. I remember that afternoon I first met Michael at the Cedar Tavern in New York back in the spring of 2000 to discuss his doctoral study. We talked non-stop for over four hours.

I saw him again in Washington, D.C. at a National League of Families meeting the following year. He had changed very little during the past six years. And he still hadn't published his study. Dave and Marco continued to visit a while longer and questioned Michael about his story. Before Marco left to meet his wife for dinner, he asked me if I planned to walk the beach tomorrow morning before going to JPAC.

"No, I am meeting Tim for breakfast at 7:00—we have to be there by 9:00," I replied.

"Will you be journaling then?" he asked. He had obviously talked to Dave about my routine, and Dave told him I begin every morning with a cup of tea and my journal, writing by candlelight.

"Of course. I will need that ritual even more tomorrow I imagine."

"Can I come and photograph you then?" he asked.

"At 5:00 a.m.? In my pajamas?"

I felt a little flustered at his request, not at all sure how I felt about that idea. He assured me that he would not be intrusive and would respect my quiet time. My hesitation subsided and I thought, what the heck? He wanted candid shots, nothing too staged.

"Okay—but don't come until 5:15—give me time to have a few sips of tea first."

And away he went. Dave decided to leave as well. He needed to prepare before tomorrow too.

Michael and I decided to walk the beach a little as we reminisced and watched the sunset before finding a restaurant to eat. I felt sad that Michael had yet to get any resolution about his dad. His case would be more difficult because the plane crashed into a river. He wanted to come with me to Hickam. He'd have the opportunity to speak with Johnie Webb about his dad's case. I told him no.

I was afraid of short-circuiting my own process if he were there, putting my own feelings aside to take care of his needs. That had been a pattern for me in the past. My commitment was to myself now, to feel whatever came up for me as I viewed Chuck's remains. Tomorrow was my time. Being a psychologist, he was most understanding and supportive, but I thought he was still a little disappointed.

I retired to my room feeling really blessed to have connected with Michael that afternoon. It was amazing the bond you felt with other MIA families—even though we hadn't been in touch as we sought to carve out a life apart from our common experience.

CHAPTER 23

HOLDING CHUCK'S REMAINS

Sipping my tea, writing by candlelight—

Friday, 28 September 0510 hours

... didn't feel I'd had too much to drink yesterday but I sure did not sleep well... my stomach was upset–was in the bathroom at 1:30... my mind kept thinking about Chuck and going to the lab—and the photographer. Almost wish I'd not agreed to this. Really don't think I want a photo of me closing the urn.

Dave and Marco arrived right on schedule. I let them in—total silence—and I came back to my journal.

I am feeling fluttery sort of—hard to describe—but it's like my heart is fluttering—Oh Chuck—I don't know what to expect today—but I sure know I want you to speak to me—I want so badly to feel your touch. To feel a sweet kiss—I remember Diane telling me about her dream of Clive and feeling him so present— I do so pray for that kind of experience—I loved you so much... Michael said he'd change things—have his dad come home— that I'd be the same person—but I just don't know—Please know and feel that my love for you is not less because I don't want to change any experiences that brought me here...I think you would understand because I know when you were in the light you didn't want to come back—but it didn't mean you didn't love us. Being in the magnificence of God's presence is truly sublime—I know that place–I saw the peace and contentment on your face when you came to me in my dreams that night; I felt your love. I am wanting so to just be in the moment, without expectations, open to whatever I feel when I hold what's left of you in my hand. This all seems so surreal.

When I was alone again, I thought that it wasn't too bad, that they were pretty unobtrusive, and I was hardly aware of their presence. I sure wished I could walk the beach again with my second cup of tea. I could use the grounding. Better draw a meditation card, I thought, and get myself ready to meet Tim for breakfast.

I drew the card for Family Harmony, which read, "Your relationship with family members is healing. Every person in your life is affected by your beliefs and expectation. You are beginning to feel a great healing occurring in your family relationships...I am grateful for all my family." Amen to that! Some people had expressed concern that I was on this trip alone, without any family. Yet that's the way I wanted it. This was *my* time with Chuck. The boys could have theirs later.

I took one last look at my altar before I blew out the candle. I was still in awe of having been drawn to it moments before I was to leave Dallas. My bag was already closed when I saw it on the altars there and felt it needed to go with me. It was one of the very special rainbow cone candles I had from the Solas Bhride Centre in Kildare Ireland; it was lit from the eternal flame maintained there by the Brigidine Sisters.

Also on the alter was a little Yoda figure that had traveled with me all over the world since the '70s, a Christmas present from one of my sons, all of whom were *Star Wars* fans. The wise Jedi was always my favorite character from those mythic sagas of our time.

The miniature Ganesha was a more recent addition to my traveling talismans, the Hindu remover of obstacles in elephant form—my lifelong totem animal. The feather, coral and rock were all gathered at the beach the day before. My Brigit's cross necklace I wore most of the time rested on Chuck's photo. I was wearing the sweetheart navigator wings this trip. Maybe I'd wear both today.

Blessed be.

Tim was waiting at a table outside when I got downstairs. What a lovely place to enjoy our breakfast. I could never tire of the ocean breeze or the sight and sound of the water in such proximity. Paradise indeed. How wonderful it would have been to have shared this setting with Chuck back in '71. Our sons surely enjoyed it in '78.

Tim informed me that we would need to check out before leaving for Hickam. Our appointment there was at 9:00 a.m., so we didn't have a lot of time to pack up. They would have a complimentary hospitality suite where we could change clothes after we returned from the base and then freshen up again before we needed to leave for the airport later that afternoon.

The drive to Hickam was pleasant, not too long. Nothing looked very familiar to me outside the Hilton Hawaiian Village. Tim and I talked of course, but my mind was pretty occupied with anticipation of what it would be like at the lab. Tim pointed out buildings on the base that still had the bullet holes from the Pearl Harbor attack. What a historical place.

My mother was almost sixteen weeks pregnant with me when that happened. I am sure I felt the impact on a cellular level—the shock, the fear, the anger, and the uncertainty that she probably felt. It never occurred to me to ask her where she was when she heard the news, or what went through her mind at that time when we were here together almost thirty years ago. How many questions have gone unasked of my parents? Now that was something I would change if I could—I'd have asked more questions of Mother and Daddy, more questions of Chuck.

We arrived at the Joint POW/MIA Accounting Command (JPAC) building on time and parked out front. We approached the door simultaneously with an officer dressed in camouflage fatigues. Tim appeared a little flustered and there was a moment of awkwardness as the two men met. I was introduced to this other gentleman and he opened the door for me. Inside the welcoming committee was present in the foyer with warm greetings as we entered. Johnie Webb motioned me toward a conference room down the hall, but I needed the ladies room first.

When I re-joined him in the conference room, I saw Dave and Marco to my right, sitting quietly in chairs by the wall, while I was seated on the left side of this beautiful mahogany oval table. Tim sat to my left, Johnie to my right at the head of the table. There was a packet before me in a blue folder and a refreshing glass of ice water.

As I thumbed through the packet I noticed a page with a photograph of the man we'd met coming in. It was none other than General Flowers, the JPAC commander, who had held the door for me. I showed that to Tim with a grin and nod that told him, now I know what your stammering was about.

Johnie asked if I had any specific questions before he showed me their newest film about the JPAC mission. I asked if I could get a copy of the photograph of the crash site that was in the beautifully bound final search and recovery report I had received. I wanted a large print for the altar at Chuck's funeral. He assured me he could get it to me on a CD before I left.

While I was well aware of the details of their field operations, I don't think I realized that all osseous remains coming back from a crash site were received in a flag-draped coffin, with full military honors. The ceremony, the respect shown was very moving. I felt incredible gratitude for the work of this dedicated Command. From the looks on Dave and Marco's faces, I think they were totally amazed at the depth of the efforts of our government to gain the fullest possible accounting of our missing.

I did ask Johnie about the penny found at the crash site—what would become of it? He told me he had heard stories that some aviators flew with a "lucky penny" in their boots. But there was no information about this particular coin.

"Since we don't know who the penny belonged to it will probably go on display along with other items stored in a glass case along the main hallway of the center from various excavations," he told me.

Then we toured the lab. Johnie pointed out the large Operation Homecoming commemorative cedar board that covered the wall of the entryway with the names of those that they had accounted for over the years. Their photographer took my picture with Johnie in front of it. They had to add another board down the next hallway for additional names like Chuck's.

One of the forensic personnel then took over and described the work that transpired there in the identification process. At one point we passed a cold storage area for preservation when they had a body to work with. I immediately thought about a case I had read about recently of a WW II plane being found with the crew inside, frozen for years in the mountains. Sure enough, the body bag I saw was the second from that crash. To witness the various aspects of the work done in the lab was indeed an honor.

As we came to the end of the tour, there stood before me a door that had paper covering the glass panes at the top. Behind that door Chuck's remains laid waiting for me. At last I entered that sacred space with only the mortuary officer and deputy commander. They wanted to make sure I was okay emotionally before leaving me alone to say my goodbyes.

Alone at last, I was struck with how small the bone fragments actually were. What I held in the palm of my hand were the end pieces, each about the size of my thumbnail, to what probably was a tibia, the center of which had been cut out for the sampling. Sitting there, literally holding within my left hand all that was left of Chuck's physical body, I felt an overwhelming sense of joy and peace.

There were no tears of grief. Having shed plenty of those over the past three months, now there were only tears of love and gratitude. No words filled this space now. I had filled pages in my journal with words to Chuck over the past eighty-five days. It was enough to just be filled with this awesome silent communion with my beloved, very like in my dream so long ago when Chuck spoke so clearly to me through his eyes, not through words.

Finally, satisfied that we had sufficiently expressed to one another all we needed to at this time, I invited the others in to witness the ceremonial placement of his remains in the elegantly plain 7" wooden square box bearing the USAF Seal and nameplate with details.

Marco and Dave remained silent observers as did Johnie. Tim and I prepared the urn to receive Chuck. I expressed my amazement at the minuteness of this bone fragment and the lack of any burn marks. Johnie explained that bones exposed to too much heat yield no clues as the heat destroys DNA.

"Clearly these have not been exposed to a lot of heat," he said.

"And that was because they were blown away from the fire?"

"Yes."

"It doesn't seem much bigger than a tooth," I noted.

"No, it isn't," he affirmed.

I placed those two little pieces on the bottom of the small photograph I had brought with me from my altar that morning to demonstrate their size. "It's just awesome," I whispered as the tears began to flow. Johnie gave me a comforting hug.

"I'm crying, but I'm happy," I assured him.

"I'm happy, too. I know it's been a really long, long difficult journey."

"I just never, ever thought we'd get anything back. I was not holding out hopes. I'm truly blessed to get this...Thank you! Thank you. Thank you!"

"Well, thank you for all your sacrifice," he replied.

You know I didn't exactly volunteer for this part. The only voluntary part was falling in love with a military man," I told him with a chuckle, the tears dissipating now.[39]

Turning now to Tim and the task of placing those remains in the urn, I removed the copper POW/MIA bracelet I wore for years engraved simply, *Capt. Charles Stratton, 1-3-71* and placed it inside with him too. It felt perfect that it rest there with him now. After we were finished and had sealed that precious box, Tim had another surprise for me.

I was presented with a flag. Just seeing young Master Sgt. Shawn Francis' face, on the verge of tears, as he spoke to me, stirred them up for me again as well. The respect and genuine caring everyone showed for this sacred work that they do for their fellow servicemen was heartwarming.

I left Hickam AFB filled with both pride and gratitude, eager to get in another beach walk to begin to integrate the powerful experiences of the morning. The emotional grief I had thought might surface was more like the elation I felt in San Antonio the first time I saw the physical artifacts. Those moments alone with Chuck were deeply felt, emotional for sure, but again, a definite high—no downer in any way. All the tears were ones of joy, not sadness. Those had apparently already been shed along the way. I wanted to stay with those feelings as I felt the sand beneath my feet and the warm water bathing them. I wanted to be alone for a while.

As I made my way back to the hospitality suite to change again after my beach walk, I ran into Dave. He wasn't leaving Hawaii until tomorrow. Part of me wished for another day as well, but I still had much to do back home. Having the down day Thursday was gift enough for this trip. We visited a while before connecting again with Tim. He wanted the full two hours at the airport before our departure and we needed to return the car before checking in, so it was aloha to Dave and the Hawaiian Hilton. Ready or not, Honolulu International, here we come.

Chuck's urn fit perfectly in the Laurel Burch canvas tote I had brought for it. No one would ever guess what was inside that wine-colored felt bag carefully placed in that tote. Though we had all the necessary paperwork to transport remains, Tim suggested we just place it on the conveyor belt with our other carry-ons at the airport entrance with no further explanation regarding the contents. During our waiting time after our arrival and check-in, I went to a floral shop while Tim shopped for something to take back to his wife and sons.

I really wished I had ordered a lei, symbol for aloha, to drape over Chuck's urn now. Any chance one would stay looking pretty for another week, I wondered? No, the woman told me, three to four days maybe, but not a week. How about a nice silk lei, she suggested. No, that wouldn't be the same. I wanted fresh flowers or none at all, but thanked her anyway.

We stopped at Starbucks, thinking we had more time to kill. As I started to eat my brownie, Tim suddenly realized we needed to be at the gate—now! It was 5:30 already and boarding began at 5:05. We took off, almost running, Frappuccino and brownie in hand. We were among the very last passengers to board our flight.

After placing Chuck in the overhead and sitting down to buckle up, we looked at each other and burst out laughing. I am sure his laughter was more about comic relief/release than anything else. I imagine he was questioning all the way to the gate how he was ever going to explain to his superiors that we had missed our flight. I was amused at how we both had so totally entered such a timeless state after we had gone through security into the airport, relaxed now that our mission for the day was completed.

I noticed that all the flight attendants were wearing leis and seemed in quite the festive mood. After we were airborne, the captain came on and announced that drinks were on him that afternoon. This was his final flight before mandatory retirement at age sixty. He had been an Air Force pilot before joining the airlines, he told us.

How incredibly fitting that he would be sharing his very last American flight with Chuck's. I wanted him to know what a very special passenger he was transporting home that day. So I wrote him a note telling him what a memorable celebratory flight we were sharing. I asked the flight attendant if she would see that the captain got the note.

Shortly afterward, that attendant came back to me and told me she had given the note to the captain's wife, who read it first and wanted to thank me, assuring me her husband would be happy knowing that he had been the one to fly Chuck back to Texas. The captain, also wearing a lei, greeted me by name as I exited the plane and thanked me again for my note. The following Christmas I would receive a card and lovely letter from his wife, along with a treasured photograph of the entire crew who flew that airliner that day.

I continued to marvel at how very perfect the entire trip had been from beginning to end. Gerry was there at the baggage claim to greet me and bring me home. He took photographs of Chuck's urn in its special shelf space where it would stay, its new place at home with me now.

CHAPTER 24

CELEBRATION OF LIFE

Tired as I was from the long flight and the intense emotion of the whole Hawaii experience, I did call the florist to order a lei for the altar. With eleven days now until the funeral, surely, by some miracle, they could get one here in time. It was the only aspect of all my three months of planning that I had failed to make happen, mostly because of the cost. Now I didn't care about the money. Having that lei felt absolutely necessary to me now. I was told they would try, but probably not.

By Monday afternoon they called me back to affirm their inability to obtain a lei in time for the service. I was sorely disappointed, though not surprised, and continued handling all the last minute details before Stephen's arrival Friday night. He wanted to go to the State Fair while he was here, something he missed about Texas now that he lived so far away. It felt very fitting to me to visit the Hall of State where Chuck had proposed to me.

When we finally arrived there in the early afternoon on Saturday, we went immediately to the MIA Wall. There we discovered a beautiful wreath in honor of Chuck and Jim, thanks to my veteran friend Gabe with whom I had chatted over the years there during my trips to the fair.

Sunday we spent time with all the family at Charles' and found out he needed hernia surgery as soon as possible after his dad's funeral. Stephen took his brothers and nephew shopping for shirts to wear to the funeral. Dawn mentioned that afternoon that Brandon wanted to bring balloons for his Grandpa Chuck for the service and asked if I was okay with that. Absolutely! I thought it was great that the grandkids wanted to participate in the celebration of his life.

Monday morning, Stephen was ironing his and his brother's shirts while I was gathering all the items to be placed on the altar. Everything seemed to be taking longer than I had anticipated and I was getting more nervous by the second. I still had to prepare my remarks for the service. I didn't trust myself to speak without some notes. Thank God Stephen was there to help keep me on track when I became too anxious.

As I was frantically trying to hurry so we could leave my apartment early enough to miss the late afternoon traffic on the way to the funeral home, there was a knock at the door. Stephen answered it and called to me to come and see what FedEx had just delivered. He was holding a very long box that he laid on the dining room table. I opened it and immediately burst into tears. It was filled with Hawaiian leis!

Stephen had known they were coming, but wanted me to be surprised. His boss was from Hawaii and had called his family there when he learned the details of the service. They had made a special lei for me that must have been made of six hundred orchids all tightly woven; a cigar lei for Chuck,; six single-strand orchid leis for all the girls in the family (Chuck's sister, niece and granddaughters); and six kukui nut leis for all the guys (the sons, nephew and grandsons).

There was also an open-ended lei of greenery for the altar. I could not believe it. My heartfelt wish for one lei for the altar had miraculously manifested tenfold plus. We spritzed them all with water and put them in the refrigerator, my spirits soaring with gratitude for this amazing gift.

9 October, 2007 0448 hours

Goddess, still my heart and mind this morning.

So began my brief journal entry. The big day had finally arrived and I still felt unprepared. Three months of preparation and planning to make sure everything would be perfect, yet I had been up all night trying to finish my remarks for the service. I was a nervous wreck, so much so that I actually felt nauseated. Stephen kept assuring me all would be fine. "You'll know what to say when the time comes," he reiterated.

Maybe I needed to carry that feather he had given me back in 1991 before the sermon at the Unitarian Church honoring women who had chosen abortion. I still felt like Dumbo, unaware that I could fly. I felt very happy with the altar and the particular representatives who'd come to eulogize Chuck; with having a former MIA wife actually officiate; and the way my every wish had been granted for welcoming Chuck home at last. How could I not feel ready now?

Normally when a widow prepares for her husband's funeral, she's still in the numb stage of grief. I was not so blessed that morning. My feelings were heightened to the max. I suppose that's the downside of having enough time to plan this event—the good news/bad news of the situation.

We arrived at Laurel Oaks at 9:13 a.m. to add some finishing touches to the altar. My brother Olin was there to greet us, a welcome presence for sure! Much to my surprise, Jonathan had already placed a lei of orchids on the altar. How was he able to obtain one when the florist told me they could not?

After adding the greenery and the urn with the cigar lei draped across it, we stood back to survey our finished creation before people began arriving, I was more than pleased. Chuck's portrait, painted by my dear friend Wendy, rested on an easel at the left end of the altar table; a 16" x 20" framed poster of the crash site in Laos framed the other end, now draped with the greenery lei.

In the center, we'd placed a beautiful bouquet of fall flowers interspersed with red roses beside Chuck's urn, along with all the other memorabilia depicting his career which we fanned out to either side. The flag that had been presented to me in Hawaii stood beneath Chuck's portrait, his black tailor-made party flight suit lay across the end of the table, with some greenery and an orchid lei and a POW/MIA bracelet pointing toward the urn.

In front of the urn itself was a photograph of Charles Jr. holding Elliana, our first great-granddaughter, and another POW/MIA bracelet. The various graduation programs and Air Force base books spread out toward the right end of the table. The velvet-backed frame with his medals and his gung-ho aviation cadet photograph rested against the easel on the right end of the table, along with a small picture of Jim Ayres, his pilot, propped up against it with a single orchid flower and more bracelets.

People began coming in early and the hugging and greeting began. I just hoped they all signed the guest book because there was no way I was going to remember everyone later. Some of these folks I had not seen in years. Many dated back to our high school classmates, friends from those years at Pleasant Mound and the Cub Scouts back in the early '70s.

The turnout for Chuck's homecoming was absolutely amazing, including representatives from all the Dallas television stations, though I was unaware of their presence until after the service. Like Dave had been in Hawaii, they stayed on the periphery and observed from a distance. At least half a dozen people gave me their POW/MIA bracelets as they greeted me.

Everyone was seated promptly at 11:00 for Rev. Joy Cox to open the ceremony with a prayer. I knew I had chosen well the minute I heard her words. Then the life video tribute began to play, and what a fabulous slide presentation Jonathan had created. It was perfectly synced with Izzy Kamakawiwo's version of *Over the Rainbow/It's a Wonderful World,* and the images of Chuck from crawling infant to handsome Air Force Captain at Korat AFB in December 1970 captured his life recorded in Jean's and my favorite photographs.

His uncle, Don Hall, began the shared memories giving us a glimpse of Chuck's essence via tales of their adventures together as young boys on the farm. The laughter and joy began with the image of the two of them running across the pasture where they had "no business being" to escape one huge territorial Brahma bull. "They must be to cattle what pit bulls are to dogs," he explained to all the non-native Texans in the chapel. Don spoke of how very proud he was of Chuck and his career in the military, that "in my book, Lt. Col. Charles Wayne Stratton has always been quite a hero." Don's remarks were every bit as eloquent as that letter he had written me back in 1971.

Dick Strine picked up on the humorous side of Chuck as an aviation cadet and had us roaring with the story of him snapping a hook 'em horns salute to a captain from Oklahoma as they made their way back to the barracks one day. His proud Texas gesture earned them both a severe reprimand and became a way for Chuck to tease Dick from across the classroom when things got too serious. It was such a timely anecdote considering the annual Texas/OU rival game had just been played the Saturday before.

Ron Banks added stories about their induction experience together on April Fool's Day, and their later radio intercept officer (RIO) game practices while driving to Connally AFB for classes. They both had come into the Air Force wanting to be pilots and planned to apply as soon as there were openings, so being a navigator and then radar intercept officer were means to an end at first. Ron mentioned Chuck's health problems that prevented him from ever doing so and that he had continued as a RIO in the 1-0-Wonder prior to Vietnam.

Ellen Kennedy, with her sister, Suzanne by her side for support, told her amazing story about wearing Chuck's POW/MIA bracelet as a teenager, as did all her sisters. She had wondered in 1975 when the war ended how she would ever know if "my guy" had ever returned. She kept the bracelet and just this past June had gone to see the traveling replica of the Vietnam Wall at the Pflugerville Cemetery with her family. As she searched the registry for Capt. Stratton's name, she was told that if he were MIA there would be a cross by his name, and was then directed to the panel where his name was etched.

As she rejoined her family that day, her mother was speaking with a woman who had little baskets of doves. She was offering them to visitors there to be released in honor of their loved one on that wall. She handed one to Ellen. Already feeling very connected to the people there that hot afternoon who had lost loved ones, she felt honored and overwhelmed, "and the connection became even stronger with Charles Stratton." She and Suzanne went back to the panel that bore Chuck's name and they waited until they were alone. "Then we said a prayer for him, that he would be at peace and come home someday...for his family, that they would be strong and hold on to his memory." When they opened the basket, fluttering and anxious to get out, the dove flew up into the air, "brilliantly white and free, up and over the wall between two flags among the row of American flags."

Two month later, almost to the day, she and her husband were at the breakfast table and she saw the metro article in the *Austin Statesman* about two MIA Air Force officers being identified. Could it possibly be "my guy"? As she read further she discovered the name was the same, including that W initial that was a mystery to her—but the rank was Lt. Col., not Captain. Funeral arrangements were pending, the article stated. "I want to go," she thought.

It took five calls to various Air Force personnel before she finally spoke with Tim Nicholson in Mortuary at Randolph AFB. He assured her it was "her guy," that his promotion had been posthumous, and services would be in October. He would pass along her number to his wife who could share those details. She wanted to present me with her bracelet and tell me about the dove.

Ellen had no idea about the synchronicity of her prayer for Chuck and the releasing of that dove. The final Search and Recovery Report was dated June 5th. It was no coincidence that she put on her bracelet that had been put away for so many years and gone to see that traveling Wall. Nor was it any accident that these were the people who agreed to share their memories of Chuck during the service. Their stories really did seem to follow a natural progression of his life and they had painted a great picture of this man we had all known in different ways over the years.

Buble's song "Home" played and brought forth my sons' tears, which they'd successfully held in until then. By the time I got up to add my portrait of Chuck as a husband and father, I felt as though everyone might be feeling a bit overwhelmed because I certainly was. I began with how we met and our whirlwind courtship of three months.

When he proposed to me he asked for me to wait for him until he graduated from Cadets. "And so began a pattern in our relationship. Separation and distance would always be a part of our life together." His career kept him in squadrons where crews were gone for days at a time. At McClellan his missions were 16-18 hours long.

He went to Florida TDY for over a month during the Cuban Missile Crisis. Then in the fighter squadrons, he flew and pulled alert duty for three days at a time, longer sometimes if they could not get back due to weather. When he went to Squadron Officer School in the summer of 1965, I stayed in Dallas with the boys and flew in to visit him a couple of weekends. And of course, during the war we spent almost seven years talking about "when he comes home."

We wrote to each other daily when he was in Harlingen and later in Thailand—those letters often ending with "more than yesterday, less than tomorrow, I love you."[40] Our identical Christmas gifts to one another while he was still an aviation cadet were bracelets with that inscription. Mine read "mtyltt, I love you, Chuck," addressing him by name as in a greeting; his read "mtyltt, I love you. Chuck" meaning his signature as in the end of his letters. We had a good laugh as we saw our gifts with the *exact* same inscription.

Besides his good looks and intelligence, I loved Chuck's confidence. He was a man who clearly knew who he was and what he wanted out of life and he went for it with gusto. He gave his best, to both his work and to his family. The boys had shared some of their fondest memories of their dad with Rev. Joy and she included them all in her celebration of his life. She read every word so beautifully and shared pertinent one-on-one commentary to each which I found so very endearing.

She gave an excellent summation. "Charles Stratton was many things during his lifetime—a husband, a father, a friend, a patriot. But most of all, I believe he was a man of faith. It became apparent to me as those who so loved him…with their stories…their memories… shaped in my mind a man who knew what life was all about. He understood who he really was and to whom he belonged. His was a spiritual path, unique and ever expanding. It was from deep within him that he designed and shaped and lived his life. He knew that it was God who loved him without condition, who guided him and watched over him and was right there with him during that last flight…to lead him safely home." Though we never shared a life within the church together, or really talked about religion, I know what she said was true.

"Chuck is home. His journey is complete. And as he passed through the valley of the shadow of death, he found it to be just that—a mere shadow. Chuck did not weep for what he had lost…rather he rejoiced in what his spirit found. And you are all here this morning to release what was and make room in your heart for what shall be. Your relationship with Chuck is reborn. Your memories will live on in your hearts forever. He is spirit as God created him to be, that spirit reaches out to embrace you in this very moment, in your sorrow and your joy…." Her words were so very comforting, and rang so true.

She read my favorite scripture, one that I relied so heavily upon during the '70s, Romans 8:28: "And we know that all things work together for good to those who love God, to those who are called according to his purpose." Then she concluded her remarks with the poem "High Flight," a favorite among fliers. The military presentation of the flag gave everyone a moment to just be silent and absorb the amazing stories shared during the service that had given me all I had imagined and then some.

My family went into the room Jonathan had arranged for lunch and ate and visited while I did interviews with the press. My daughter-in-law later expressed anger toward the media presence, primarily over her concern that it hampered Scott from letting go of his grief. I, on the other hand, was grateful for their presence and their manners. They truly stayed in the background and were not at all intrusive. I had wanted Dallas to be able to welcome home their hero and share in our joy. They had certainly been there with us during those MIA years.

I had time for only a brief bite to eat. Mostly I wanted something to drink before we all boarded the limo for the National Cemetery. There was room for all my sons and grandchildren, so I had my private time with them during the half-hour drive. The grandkids thought riding there in the limousine was great fun and pretended to drink champagne from some of the bar glasses they discovered. They were also texting their friends about the experience. Haley described it as feeling like "the royal family!" I thoroughly enjoyed their delight and us all being together.

As we lined up for the procession of cars to the designated shelter for the service, I met up with Brenda and her family. From the crowd there I was very grateful that the cemetery had finally listened to our request to be the only and last service of the day. We could see a huge circle of flags surrounding the shelter where we were going. The Patriot Guard was there in numbers, as was the press. As we got out of the limo at the shelter, I saw the man who had made it his mission to be at returning soldier's funerals with his Liberty Bell. I had met him at the Dallas Veteran's Day parade with Brenda a year or so ago.

Because of the numbers still filing in behind us and having to walk longer distances to get to the shelter, we had to stay standing outside waiting for the flyover which would normally have taken place afterward, but the planes were airborne and scheduled to be there at a specific time. There could be no delay where they were concerned.

As we waited in the very warm afternoon sun, the fireman with the bagpipes, dressed in all his regalia, played and marched toward the shelter, the hearse with the casket following behind. We were all sweating from the heat of the sun by then. I really felt for all those in uniforms. I know my sons were happy they had on cotton shirts with no jackets.

And as usual, tears flowed as those jets flew over finally and the Missing Man peeled off from the formation, signaling time to ceremoniously remove the flag-draped casket from the hearse to begin the processional into the shelter. Tim seated the boys and me to the right, and Brenda, Lacy and Jim's sister to the left. Our families then gathered in behind us. Most of the crowd was still in the sun outside the shelter that was not large enough to house everyone.

The service itself was relatively short, very traditional, led by a military chaplain. Given the long service for Chuck, it was probably just as well. Still, part of me wished I had asked Rev. Joy to officiate for the group service, feeling it would have been less rote, a little more personal.

We were then asked to stand and look to our right for the traditional Three-Volley Salute about to take place above a ten-foot stone wall that curved in a semi-circle around the shelter. I was very happy to see that there were two women in that Honor Guard, both standing on the right end of the seven. Taps was then played, always a moving, tearful moment.

We were seated again for the folding of the flag. It was very impressive with the complete Honor Guard standing on either side of the casket. There had been only two who had unfolded the flag I'd brought back from Hawaii, and ceremoniously refolded it to present to me to conclude Chuck's individual service. Flag cases with medals were then presented to both Brenda and me to conclude the military ceremony.

Brenda and I hugged one another and cried. Then we had the pleasure of ringing the Liberty Bell together after all the military presentations. In that moment when we released that rope, I literally felt that resounding bell tone reverberate in my body such that I actually felt lighter, truly free at last.

The grandchildren went looking for the shell casings after the service was completed while guests mingled and visited. There were friends and family for Col. Ayres as well as many who had been at Chuck's service that morning. I saw some friends who had not been able to attend his individual service.

Dawn came to me after a bit, calling my attention to the wall where the gun salute had taken place. All the grandkids and their little friends were up on that ridge with their helium-filled treasures yelling "Happy Birthday Grandpa Chuck" as they released Welcome Home, Happy Birthday, and patriotic red, white and blue balloons.

I do believe that was *the* highlight of the entire service for me, watching them release their tributes in unison to the grandfather hero whom they had never known. Haley, our oldest granddaughter wrote in her memory donation, "I couldn't turn my eyes away until the balloon vanished from sight. I wonder if Grandpa Chuck did the same thing?" I just bet he did, with tremendous love and pride filling his heart.

EPILOGUE

Then you must go off again, carrying a broad-bladed oar,
Until you come to men living who know nothing of the sea...
Then you must fix your oar in the earth
And offer sacrifice to the Lord Poseidon,
Then return to your home and offer
Perfect sacrifice to the immortal gods
Who hold high heaven, to each in turn.

~The Odyssey[41]

Dave Tarrant's three-part story, "Losing Chuck, Finding Sallie," finally printed on December 2nd, 3rd and 4th, 2007. As had been the case when the DMN news story hit the press, I was out of town. I had flown up to New York to visit with Stephen and re-connect with my dear friend Lynn who had not been able to attend Chuck's memorial. Dave had driven me to the airport and we talked about what he was going to include in his story that had evolved into a three-part series.

My biggest concern was that he wanted to include the traumatic conversation that erupted with Jean on the way to San Antonio. I shuddered at the thought of her very Baptist family also reading that I did not accept the tenet that Jesus died for our sins. Dave felt it was a pivotal moment, very important to his piece, so I agreed to trust his judgment and gave him the okay to use it.

Dave sent me the DMN link so Stephen and I could read what

he'd written. We were amazed that it appeared on the front page and that the online version included additional videos and photographs. I could hardly believe he was given so much space for this story. It was amazing and so beautifully written. Dave received a nomination for the Pulitzer and won the Texas Associated Press Managing Editors award for best feature series. The reception of his articles refueled my own desire to write a version that included more detail about the "Finding Sallie" part. Dave was most encouraging and suggested I start reading memoirs and maybe look for a writer's group for support.

I learned of The Writer's Garrett in this quest and signed up for my first workshop on April 5ᵗʰ. I came away with these questions: *What IS the narrative arc of my book? What is my intention? Who is my audience?* It was apparent I had a long way to go yet, but I was willing to learn and certainly wanted to write something others would find compelling enough to read. I just needed to start writing and halt the mere intellectual aspiration to do so that had been floating around in my mind since the late '70s.

I do believe the seed was first planted during my Religion as Story and Psychology of Women classes back at SMU. It was even a verbalized intention in 1995 when I went to live in Ireland for a year, but I wrote nothing but journal after journal of reflections. Then when I was given that first computer I actually typed many pages, none of which coalesced into any resemblance of a book.

It was through my connections with this group that I first learned of the Mayborn writing competition. By now I was motivated sufficiently to actually make a commitment to enter a chapter for the manuscript competition by their June deadline. And with that specific goal in mind, I actually managed to follow through with Chapter One and a short synopsis of how I was envisioning the memoir at that time. It was a big breakthrough for me and I received a lot of helpful suggestions on how to make my writing more narrative and less telling.

In September of 2010, my oldest son received a cancer diagnosis that shook my world again. My writing took a backseat as my priority became supporting him through months of chemo and radiation prior to surgery. So for a couple of years my work with the memoir received little time and energy. As Charles improved, so did my resolve to finish a manuscript.

I came across a daily Tarot card that seemed to speak to that "Priestly" dream I'd had back in June of 2007—The Hierophant. The reading linked this figure to Melchezidek, who initiated the Hebrew priestly tradition, the one who passes on the teachings. I suddenly saw that dream as a message from Chuck, that accepting ordination was about passing on my story, telling it in my own voice. Perhaps the crazy man who was following me in that dream that I needed to lose represented the voices of others as well as my own inner critic that hindered my efforts.

As I wrote, I waivered back and forth about where to start and what the title should be. When I mentioned to Dave that I could think of no better title than his for the series he wrote, he assured me I could use it if I wanted. I toyed with the title *Penelope's Shroud* because it captured the mythic root of my spiritual journey.

For Penelope completing that shroud meant breaking the tie that bound her to Odysseus. It would serve as a sign that she had completed her duty to him and his family, an action she was reluctant to finish because she believed he would come home as had been prophesied. I saw my dream of him back in 1973 as just such a prophecy.

The prolonged Missing in Action classification for our servicemen was unique to the Vietnam Conflict. Those captured were not treated as prisoners of war under the Geneva Convention provisions. Military custom was to presume a serviceman dead one year and a day after they'd become missing if there was no evidence to indicate he was still alive. That policy was suspended to avoid the risk of declaring a man dead who might still be alive in one of Hanoi's prisons. While all wars constellate Penelope in terms of the waiting wife, Vietnam exacerbated the challenge of weaving that final shroud for much longer.

The story of Penelope's weaving that shroud by day and unraveling it by night is told three times in *The Odyssey* and from three different perspectives. Such repetition I see as an indication of the significance of this archetypal pattern. The first to relate the story in this Greek epic is one of the suitors to justify their behavior to Odysseus' son, Telemachos. His version insists that Penelope is to blame for their consumption of the estate because she refuses to choose another husband from amongst them. Furthermore, he declares that she is acquiring a great reputation for herself by resisting them.

Penelope herself provides the second telling of the shroud story to the sympathetic beggar who had shown up at her house and tells her, "Lady, no mortal man on the endless earth could have cause to find fault with you; your fame goes up into the wide heaven, as of some king."[42] She tells him her reputation would be greater and more splendid if Odysseus were to come back to her and take care of her life. But instead she grieves and longs for him as her suitors, having discovered her wiles, force her to finish the shroud and choose a new husband as she had said she would when she first asked them to wait. She is unaware at the time that this stranger is her beloved husband returned to claim his household.

A dead suitor in Hades repeats the third telling of Penelope's shroud after Agamemnon questions the kind of calamity that consumed so many young men at the same time. His interpretation of her deceptive ploy was that her intention all along was to destroy them rather than choose marriage to any of them, so the shroud she finished was for them. He goes on to say that at the same time she displayed this great piece of weaving, "an evil spirit, coming from somewhere, brought back Odysseus,"[43] and it could be seen that the gods were helping him as he chased them through the house in his fury. So the intervention of the gods and an image of the finished shroud that "shone like the sun or moon"[44] add a new dimension to this shroud–weaving tale taken now into the depths of the underworld.

In retrospect, I see where I have completed three shrouds over the past thirty-six years. The first was in 1977 when I chose to have Chuck presumed dead so I could create a new future for myself without him. The motivation then was not based on a feeling that he was really dead, but more about the realization that the woman he had left behind was dead, radically changed in his absence. So, truth be told, it was a shroud for that MIA wife he left behind.

The second was in 1989 as I had become aware that the PFOD (presumptive finding of death) was but a legal detail that had not really severed the deeper ties to our marriage. I saw how my heart was still married to Chuck. No wonder I had trouble totally committing to another man, even though I felt I was "in love" again. So ritually, I endeavored to complete Chuck's shroud. Bringing back his remains made possible the final completion of that weaving.

The dilemma of an MIA wife is like the weaving and unraveling of Penelope's shroud in Homer's *The Odyssey*, always dwelling in a betwixt and between space, struggling to find some degree of certainty that will allow her to finish that shroud. Indeed, it is *the* challenge for anyone who has lost a loved one into the realm of limbo, including the woman who has had an abortion and never processed her feelings about that decision and its significance with regards to potential guilt, regret, or her own religious values.

What does it take to complete that kind of uncertainty, to be able to fully embrace the hand you've been dealt and find peace where there are no answers, even possibly to identify the gifts offered through the experience?

I am sure there are as many answers to that question as there are those who have lived in some form of limbo. For me, it was Chuck's appearance in my dream that initially gave me hope and allowed me to survive that unknown, followed closely by my Athenian activism with the POW/MIA issue out in the larger world. Athena provided me insights through art and literature during my years of returning to college that helped me to better understand my journey. And she has guided me in the weaving of the tapestry chronicled here.

Only two books that I know of have been written from the perspective of the MIA wife from the Vietnam Era.[45] While both are very personal narratives, their primary focus seems more on their activism in searching for their husbands. To date, I know of no one who has written about finally getting to bring the remains of an MIA back to the states. My intention for this memoir focuses more on my spiritual evolution initiated by the experience of being an MIA wife, the ultimate gift of all that pain and heartache.

My very personal experience in 1973 of God's loving embrace after I had cursed Him allowed me to move forward and bolstered my courage to respond to the call to go back to school. My penchant for study took over where that activism had left off and my exposure to art, literature, and other world religions became my coping mechanism. It was my introduction to mythic consciousness and the importance of my own dream world that really brought meaning into my search for myself. The myth of Persephone's abduction into the underworld had a profound effect on me as well. While it did not provide answers per se, it gave meaning to my experience in a way that opened me to the mystery, and afforded me a trust that I was not just going crazy.

Looking back over my process during these thirty-six years as I prepared for Chuck's homecoming and farewell, I realized more and more my affinity with Odysseus and his many adventures during his attempt to return to Ithaca and Penelope. Treated as a dream, all the characters of *The Odyssey* are aspects of myself as well. Poseidon was the protagonist in this epic. He thwarted Odysseus's return out of revenge for his son, blinded by Odysseus and then taunted hubristically.

Poseidon, Lord of the Seas, is the most primitive god in the Greek pantheon and was commonly called the Earth-Shaker. Jean Shinoda Bolen refers to him as Zeus' shadow, ruling the realm of emotion and instinct, the undersea realm of repressed feelings. "Anyone who has found herself unexpectedly overwhelmed by waves of intense feelings that well up from the depths, or has had her body tremble and shake with grief or rage or revenge, has had a firsthand experience of Poseidon."[46] My cool-thinking, father's daughter Athena was quite adept at repressing her feelings. Bolen writes that through Poseidon, a realm of great depth and beauty can be known.[47]

Poseidon shook my world to the core that January morning, then exploded from my depths in rage at the Sky Father of my upbringing in 1973, creating space for the beauty still all around me. Odysseus must make amends to Poseidon. After taking revenge on the suitors and restoring his household, he must leave home again and travel to a land that knows not the sea and plant his oar as a tribute to Poseidon, one that will no doubt spark questions about this god of the watery depths.

I see this memoir as my oar, a way to pay homage to every experience, person, god and goddess, guardian and guide it took to bring both Chuck and me back home again. It's been a spiritual journey I never imagined nor would have volunteered to take, but one for which I am sincerely grateful.

SELECT
PHOTOGRAPHS

Sallie Hodges, WW Samuell High School Graduate, 1960

Chuck writing to me from his room at
Aviation Cadets, 1960

Cutting our Wedding Cake, February 18, 1961

On a long Navigation Mission from McClellan AFB, 1961-2

Chuck after Operation Golddigger during the Cuban Missile Crisis. He 'd grown a mustache there and they called him "baby snooks." He had to dye it to make it show up. I thought he looked quite handsome with it. Sacramento, November 1962

Squadron New Year's Eve Party, Griffiss AFB, 1962-3

6-Our first family Christmas card from McClellan AFB, 1963

THE STRATTONS
CHUCK SALLIE BUTCH & SCOTTY

Our home in Rome NY, 1964

Christmas card from our home in Rome, New York, 1965

Best wishes
from our family
to yours

Chuck, Butch, Scotty, Sallie
and Ginger 1966

Christmas card. Base housing, Rome, New York,
Griffiss AFB. I was pregnant with Stephen then. 1966

Daddy's home and swarmed by (left to right) Stephen, Charles Jr.,
Ginger, and Scott. Oxnard AFB, 1968

Moonbeam McSwine and Hillbilly Chuck
Squadron Party at Oxnard AFB ,1968

Thanksgiving, Base Housing
Otis AFB, Cape Cod, 1968

Eadeville Railroad in South Carver, Ma. with Lynn and all our kids,
before shipping off to Tucson, 1969

Chuck's "bad ass" (so dubbed by Charles Jr.) photo from Otis AFB, 1969

Korat AFB, Thailand, in his squadron party suit, 1970

Christmas card from Dallas, 1970

Dallas Morning News front page photo, (left to right) Charles Jr., Sallie
holding Stephen, and Scott on tricycle with GI Joe, March, 1971

One of many Dallas area billboards, 1972

Our photograph for the Pleasant Mound United Methodist Church Directory, 1973 and of course we added our very own signatures

My *Looking Younger* makeover image, by Robert Jones. I posed August, 2007 after the first interview with Dave and Salcedo.

Altar for Chuck's funeral bordered by his portrait painted by Wendy
and his crash site in Laos. His box urn in the center. His Korat party
suit rests beneath the flag, with a lei, a bracelet on a plaque, Chuck's
various manuals, and a photo of Jim Ayres, his pilot, and a snapshot
of his new great granddaughter, Elliana Star, at Laurel Oaks Funeral
Home Chapel, October 9, 2007

The Fort Worth firemen volunteered to play the bagpipes. They were
standing with the Patriot Guard as the casket was prepared to be
removed from the hearse.

The Honor Guard taking Chuck's and Jim's casket under the awning surrounded by Patriot Guard at the DFW National Cemetery.

Dave Tarrant and me at the Group Burial Funeral at DFW National Cemetery waiting for the missing man flyover before going under the awning. October 9, 2007. Photo taken by Stephen Stratton.

Left to right, Charles, his sons Dustin and Scott at Chuck's and Jim's
tombstone at DFW National Cemetery, 2007

Stephen at his dad's tombstone, Christmas, 2008

Chuck's boots beneath his name of the panel,
taken by Stephen Stratton

Etching of Chuck's name on the Wall

The Air Force Song—Wild Blue Yonder

Off we go into the wild blue yonder,
Climbing him, into the sun,
Here they come zooming to meet our thunder,
At 'em boys, Give'er the gun! (Giver'er the gun now!)
Down we dive, spouting our flame from under,
Off with one heckuva roar!
We live in fame, or go down in flame,
Hey! Nothing'll stop the U.S. Air Force!

(Chuck took this picture from another F-4)

NOTES

[1] *Penelope's Story: The Shroud Weaver's Tale* by Jo Ann Rosenfeld, p. 207.

[2] *The Daily Press*, Escanaba, Michigan, November 20, 2010, "Memorials Have Deep Meaning" by Richard Clark.

[3] *Boundaries* by Maya Lin, p. 4:10-4:11.

[4] *Gods in Everyman* by Jean Shinoda Bolen, pp. 72-3.

[5] *The Last Innocent Year: America in 1964—The Beginning of the 'Sixties'* by Jon Margolis.

[6] *Force and Space Digest*, June 1970.

[7] *Dallas Morning News*, May 15, 1971, p. 4, "Thunderbirds Fly on Teamwork."

[8] Ibid, May 27, 1971, p. 5, "Group Has Ceremony on Behalf of Prisoners."

[9] Ibid, June 16, 1971, "Rogers Rejects POW 'Ransom.'"

[10] Ibid, June 20, 1971, "Missing POW Fathers Missed Greatly Today" by Doug Domeier.

[11] *Dallas Times Herald*, July 4, 1971, p. 44A

[12] *Dallas Morning News*, September 22, 1971, p. 8, "Sterrett Signs Appeal for POWs."

[13] *Air Force Times*, 13 October 1971, p. 20, "POW Kin Take No-Politics Stand" by Ruth Chandler.

[14] *Dallas Morning News*, October 3, 1971, p. 4, by Doug Domeier.

[15] Ibid, October 16, 1970, p. 9, "POW Booth at Fair Reported Successful."

[16] Ibid, November 28, 1971, p. 12, "4th Party's Stand-In Slogan: Vote for Dr. Spock, Baby."

[17] Ibid, December 12, 1971, p. 3, "POW Plea Available For Cards."

[18] Ibid, December 18, 1971, p. 1.

[19] Ibid, March 25, 1972, p. 16, "Ex-POW Urges Prisoner Solution" by Doug Domeier.

[20] *The Odyssey* by Homer, Book XIX, ll. 136-144, Lattimore translation.

[21] Ibid, January 30, 1973, p. 1, "The Wait Goes On Still No Word of Prisoners in Laos."

[22] Ibid, February 22, 1973, p. 1, "Laos List Unbelievable, Three POW Wives Say."

[23] Ibid, January 29, 1974, p. 12, "MIAs Forgotten, Families Charge."

[24] Ibid, September 11, 1974, p. 1C, by Jane Ulrich.

[25] Ibid, December 19,1974, p. 43, "State MIA Leader Hits Panel Finding" by Doug Domeier

[26] Ibid, December 25, 1974, p. 1C, "MIA Family Waits, Watches, Hopes at Christmas" by Laura Allen.

27 *Story and Verse for Children*, selected and edited by Miriam Blanton Huber.

28 *My Life So Far* by Jane Fonda, pp. 469-70.

29 I didn't read Jane's autobiography until 2005 after my friend loaned me her copy of *My Life So Far*. It affirmed my thoughts about her being used by the Vietnamese. I found amazing parallels with our journey's through the same time period. I didn't know that the movie, *Coming Home*, was her idea based on her relationship to paraplegic Ron Kovic, a Vietnam vet she met at an anti-war rally in 1972.

30 *The Mermaid Chair* by Sue Monk Kidd, p. 29.

31 *Dallas Morning News*, p. 1A, "Aiming at a 'Target of Opportunity'—After First Blow, U.S. Plans Massive Salvos to Intimidate Iraqi Troops" by Richard Whittle.

32 Ibid.

33 *Dallas Morning News*, April 10, 2003, p. 1A, "Pleased U.S. Officials Say Iraqis on Way to Freedom—Hussein's Fate, POWs, Weapons Search Among Unfinished Business" by David Jackson.

34 Ibid, May 26, 2003, p. 6B, "Mobile Memorial Taps Emotion—Traveling Exhibit in Allen Honors Those Lost in Vietnam" by Lesley Tellez.

35 Ibid, September 11, 2005, Metro Section, p. 1, "Wives or War Widows? N. Texans Led Charge" by Paul Meyer.

36 Ibid.

37 *The Dance of the Dissident Daughter* by Sue Monk Kidd, p. 76.

38 Ibid, p. 2.

39 The dialogue came from Dave Tarrant's articles later. I could not have told you what I said in those precious moments. I was glad Dave was there to witness it all.

40 It was not until writing this memoir that I discovered those lyrics were from a 1957 single by doo wop group The Dream Kings.

41 *The Odyssey* by Homer, Book XI, ll.119, 129, Lombardo translation.

42 Ibid, XIX. 107-08.

43 Ibid, XX.149.

44 Ibid, XXIV.148.

45 *Is Anybody Listening? A True Story About the POW/MIAs in the Vietnam War* by Barbara Birchim, with Sue Clark, published in 2005; and *The Search for Canasta 404, Love, Loss and the POW/MIA Movement* by MIA wife Maureen Dunn and Melissa B. Robinson, a reporter for the Associated Press, published in 2006.

46 *Gods in Everyman* by Jean Shinoda Bolen, p. 73.

47 Ibid, p.78

Made in the USA
Coppell, TX
03 November 2022

85723109R00174